W9-DIF-952

ECONOMICS
AT THE WHEEL
The Costs of Cars and Drivers

ECONOMICS
AT THE WHEEL
The Costs of Cars and Drivers

Richard C. Porter

Department of Economics
The University of Michigan
Ann Arbor, Michigan

ACADEMIC PRESS

San Diego   London   Boston   New York   Sydney   Tokyo   Toronto

Cover photo: © 1999 PhotoDisc, Inc.

This book is printed on acid-free paper. ∞

Copyright © 1999 by ACADEMIC PRESS

All Rights Reserved.
No part of this publication may be reproduced or transmitted in any form or by any
means, electronic or mechanical, including photocopy, recording, or any information
storage and retrieval system, without permission in writing from the publisher.

Requests for permission to make copies of any part of the work should be mailed to:
Permissions Department, Harcourt Brace & Company, 6277 Sea Harbor Drive,
Orlando, Florida, 32887-6777.

Academic Press
a division of Harcourt Brace & Company
525 B Street, Suite 1900, San Diego, California 92101-4495, USA
http://www.apnet.com

Academic Press
24-28 Oval Road, London NW1 7DX, UK
http://www.hbuk.co.uk/ap/

Library of Congress Catalog Card Number: 98-88417

International Standard Book Number: 0-12-562360-7 (hb)
International Standard Book Number: 0-12-562361-5 (pb)

PRINTED IN THE UNITED STATES OF AMERICA
99 00 01 02 03 04 MM 9 8 7 6 5 4 3 2 1

Contents

Preface

The freedom that the automobile
has given the average American
is a good thing,
even though it may take him a long time
to learn how to use it.

Elmer Davis
America as Americans See It

Students have often asked me why I hate cars so much. I tell them, and I think truthfully, that I don't hate cars. They have given the industrialized world a degree of mobility that could not have even been dreamed of in the 19th century—when few European peasants ever got more than 20 miles from their birthplaces during their entire lifetimes.

I am as addicted to automobiles as anyone else. I rarely manage to give them entirely up for more than a week at a time. Sometimes, I must admit, I binge drive, all the way to Chicago and back. But I try to use cars in moderation. And that is the message of this book—that we use automobiles to excess and that we would all be better off if we could restrain our rate of consumption. I am not going to claim that people are irrational in their overuse of the car—indeed, you will soon see how rational it is to drive a lot. But "secondhand driving"—like "secondhand smoking"—imposes many costs that could and should be reduced.

But the book has another, equally important, goal—to get students who have had a little economics into the habit of using that economics when they think about social problems, policies, and solutions. The "economics" part of the title is just as important to me as the "cars and drivers" part. I think of the car as a "vehicle" for teaching students to think economically.

I chose the car as that vehicle partly because I live in Michigan, where cars are especially important in many ways. The money that pays our salaries and tuitions often comes from somewhere in the automobile industry. While talking about automobiles, I can also think economically about other things of interest to students. For some, it is sex, alcohol, speed, or parking; for others, it is death, air pollution, global warming, or oil spills.

This book arose from lecture notes. The classes have never been so large that I have been unable to ask students questions and get answers. I have tried to preserve that style here. Thus, there are many questions without answers. Don't just skip over them. They give you a chance to do some thinking on your own rather than just memorizing my (and others') thinking. Most of them are flagged with a "Q." To these, the answers—or rather, my thoughts about the questions—are given in the back of the book, just before the References. Sometimes there is a single, clear, right answer, but more often than not various sensible responses are possible. So don't just look for "the" answer. But do remember to look for an *economic* answer. For example, when asked why the rich buy more child-restraint car seats but use them less than the poor, answering "because the rich think they care about their children but really they don't" misses the point—it might be the right answer, but it is not an *economic* answer.

The book is also filled with little boxes of side material. If you are in a hurry, you can skip them without loss of continuity, but it will be a shame if you do. Most are intended to be provocative or amusing; each one not only offers a little information about the auto periphery but also challenges you to think through the implications of some problem or policy.

The prose is frequently interrupted by citations. It bothers many readers, I know, and I apologize. But I want to encourage you to track down at least a few of these references when you disagree with what I am saying or want to know more about the subject. Some of these references are heavily mathematical or statistical, but you still may be able to browse and learn from them. The full citations are all in the reference section at the end of the book.

I mentioned that this book arose from lectures in a semester course called The Economics of the Automobile. The only prerequisite for the course has been Economics 101 (Introductory Microeconomics). I have been co-teaching this auto course for several years with two colleagues, Paul Courant and Jim Levinsohn. Paul looks at how the car has affected the size, shape, and structure of America's cities and regions; Jim looks at the productive process, industrial structure, and international trade of automobiles. None of those things are in this book (except for a few things I could not resist stealing from their lectures). I thank them for providing synergy for the course.

I also thank past students of the course—for asking the right questions and giving the right answers, reassuring me that the lectures were on the right track—and for asking the wrong questions and giving the wrong answers, telling me where the material needed to be made clearer.

Too many people have helped me learn about cars and drivers to list all their names. But some have been particularly helpful, and I want to thank them individually: Amy Ando, Chris Augustyniak, Joshua Baylson, Ted Bergstrom, Jean Berkley, Peter deBoor, Joan Crary, Jim DeMocker, Carolyn Fischer, John German, Laura Gottsman, John Hall, Winthrop Harrington, James Hedlund, Chuck Kahane, Greg Keoleian, Daniel Khazzoom, Jim Makris, Virginia McConnell, Geneva Moores, Stan Nicholson, Evan Osborne, Ray Perry, Paul Portney (personally and also for offering the facilities of Resources for the Future as a base when I was working in Washington), Chris Proulx, Barry Rosenberg, Steve Salant, Kathryn Sargeant, William Schroeer, Hilary Sigman, Jim Simons, Phil Tepley,

Gail Thomas, Klaas Van't Veld, Thomas Walton, Clifford White, Shelley White, Marina Whitman, David Wiley, Mark Wolcott, and Don Zinger.

Despite all this help, errors will persist. When you find them, I will appreciate it if you call them to my attention (rporter@umich.edu). Also welcome are comments, quarrels, ideas, anecdotes, etc. I always like a good eco-chat by e-mail. I am sometimes away from e-mail for a month or two, so the response may be delayed, but you will always get a response eventually.

Ann Arbor, Washington, DC, and Bridgetown

ALL DOLLAR FIGURES ARE IN 1995 PRICES

Throughout, U.S. dollar figures have been converted to 1995 prices, using the U.S. GDP deflator. For example, if a source says the value of something was $100 in 1982, that $100 figure is multiplied by 129.1 (the GDP deflator for 1995, with 1987 = 100) and then divided by 83.8 (the GDP deflator for 1982); the 1995 value is therefore $154.06, and is probably rounded off to $154, or even to $150. Foreign currency data are converted into U.S. dollars at the then-existing foreign exchange rate between that currency and the U.S. dollar, and then converted (as above) into 1995 prices.

Please forgive my laziness. Although it is no longer 1995, there has been so little inflation in the last few years that it doesn't seem worth the time to pull the dollars up to date.

Glossary

BAC	blood alcohol concentration
B/C	benefit–cost analysis
CAC	command and control
CAFE	Corporate Average Fuel Economy
CO	carbon monoxide
CO_2	carbon dioxide
EPA	Environmental Protection Agency
HCs	hydrocarbons
i	the interest (discount) rate
MLDA	minimum legal drinking age
MPG	miles per gallon
MPH	miles per hour
NHTSA	National Highway Traffic Safety Administration
NO_x	nitrogen oxides
p	the probability per mile or per potentially fatal crash of killing oneself or of being killed in a highway accident (the context indicates which)
P_g	the price per gallon of gasoline
PM	particulate matter (formerly known as TSPs—total suspended particulates)
P_t	the price of time (i.e., the driver's driving wage rate)
Q_g	the quantity of gasoline purchased per year
Q_m	the number of miles driven per year
Q_t	the amount of time spent driving per year
SO_x	sulfur oxides
V_L	the dollar value put on one's life by one's self or by society (the context indicates which)
VMT	vehicle-miles traveled
WTP	willingness-to-pay

CHAPTER 1

Introduction

"The only amusement for a youth came to be
going out in a car with a girl,
or going out in a car to look for a girl,
or going out with a girl to look for a car.
Since you can't drive all the time,
they had to invent the pop and hot dog stand,
and since you can't stand and eat all evening,
they had to build a dance hall beside the pop stand.
You can't dance forever, so . . . ."

Stephen Leacock
Good-Bye, Motor Car

Barely 1 century ago, the Duryea Motor Wagon Company of Springfield (Massachusetts) rolled 13 cars out of its construction barn—and sold them. The idea of mounting an engine on wheels had been around for a long time, and cars had even been produced before 1896, but until then only one car at a time. The mass-produced car was an instant success. In 1905, the first car theft was reported. In 1911, painted center lines on roads began to appear. By 1913, more automobiles than horse buggies were being manufactured. By 1914, "stop" signs and traffic lights had begun to sprout.

In 1908, Henry Ford introduced the moving assembly line and was turning out thousands of Model T vehicles per year. That turned the automobile from a rich man's toy into a middle-income-family necessity. The change was rapid. For someone earning a wage equal to that of a Ford assembly-line worker, the Model T cost 7 months' wages in 1908. By 1916 it cost less than 3 months' wages and Model T sales had passed a half-million per year; by 1920, half the cars in the world were Model T Fords (Rae, 1965).

SPREAD OF THE AUTO

During the 1920s, the car continued to flourish. By 1929, there was one registered vehicle for every five Americans—a ratio not surpassed until the 1950s. By 1935, parking meters pushed up out of the sidewalks.

1

Road construction also boomed in the 1920s. The Federal Highway Act of 1921 began the process of federal subsidies to state highway departments, and the states themselves began levying gasoline taxes to finance their share of intercity road costs. By 1929, the average gasoline tax had risen to 30 cents per gallon (remember, dollar figures are throughout inflated to 1995 prices). Thirty cents is not much different from today's gasoline tax rate, although the average American family was much poorer then. The first transcontinental auto trip took 63 days; by the end of the 1920s, it took 1/10th that time. It seemed that everybody drove, even Bonnie and Clyde—Mr. Barrow wrote Mr. Ford, "I have drove Fords exclusively when I could get away with one."

Slowed by economic depression in the 1930s and World War II in the 1940s, automobile growth did not recommence until the 1950s when middle-income families began moving from the cities to rapidly expanding suburbs that were badly or not at all served by mass transit facilities. The automobile made suburbia possible, and the suburbs made the automobile essential.

Until the 1950s, long-distance auto travel was either done on city street extensions, which meant traveling through the center of every village on the route, or done on state-financed toll roads. The National System of Interstate and Defense Highways Act of 1956 ended this, providing for a 40,000-mile network of toll-free superhighways—"the Interstates"—built almost entirely at federal expense. As a result, the car could compete with other forms of transportation for intercity, as well as intracity, travel.

Today, there are half a billion cars on the world's roads, roughly two-fifths of them in the United States. They have given us mobility, which not only makes us better off as consumers but allows us to achieve economies of scale in production and retailing. This mobility, however, has come at heavy cost. In this book, we will explore many aspects of that cost.

We will also look at U.S. government policies to limit the costs that autos impose upon us. In one sense, these policies have been successful. Our cars get more miles per gallon (MPG) than they used to; new cars produce many fewer air-polluting emissions than their predecessors did; and highway deaths per vehicle-mile traveled (VMT) have come down steadily since the 1960s.

In another sense, we have failed. The cost of U.S. policies has been high—as you will soon see. And we use as many gallons of gasoline today as we ever did, the air over many of our cities is still unacceptably polluted, the total number of highway deaths per year in the United States has fallen little in the last half-century, and traffic congestion is becoming an ever worse problem in our cities.

In introductory microeconomics courses, you learn not only how markets function but also that "markets work" in the sense that they produce the right amount of product at the lowest cost and allocate that product to the people with the highest willingness-to-pay for it. You also learn that some markets do not work.

EXTERNALITIES

The "market" for automobile driving does not work. It is perhaps our best example of "market failure"—or should I say our worst example? Why does this market fail? Externalities. When someone's actions impose costs on other people, these costs are called external costs. If that word is foreign to you, read the appendix to this chapter carefully. Indeed, the concept of externalities is so critical to understanding this book that I highly recommend to every reader at least a quick run through that appendix.

Almost all our automobile problems arise from the car's generation of external costs.[1] When we get into our cars, we are prepared to pay the private costs of driving. But we ignore the external costs which, when added to the private costs, make the social cost of driving extremely high. Optimally, we would only drive each mile if our personal benefit exceeded the marginal *social* cost; in fact, we drive whenever our personal benefit exceeds the marginal *private* cost. As a result, we drive too much—way too much.

Governmental bodies in the United States are not unaware of the automobile's externalities. There are policies aimed at almost all of them, that is, aimed at reducing the external costs of driving. Unfortunately, as we will see, most of the policies selected are not cost-effective. Most *do* reduce the external costs, at least somewhat, but whatever success they achieve is gained at a cost that is much higher than necessary. We will search for policies that are cost-effective—cost-effective in the sense that, whatever externality reduction they achieve, they achieve it at the lowest possible cost.

There is no single solution to all of our auto problems, but there is one that comes close: steadily raise gasoline taxes by a few (real) cents per year for several years. By the time gasoline taxes go up by another $1 per gallon—still much less than the gasoline taxes already instituted long ago in almost all other industrialized countries—we as a nation will have stopped taking frivolous driving trips, where the private benefit to the driver falls far short of the social cost. In the process of driving much less, we will use much less gasoline, create much less air pollution, kill far fewer people on highways, and. . . . But that is what the rest of the book is all about.

The advantage of gasoline taxation is that it gets the government out of the business of telling people what kinds of cars to drive. Some people will react to higher gas taxes by driving fewer cars, others fewer miles per car, and still others more fuel-efficient cars. By leaving the decision to individuals, people will react by driving less, but in a way that is the least costly to their own welfare. Gas taxation is a cost-effective way of reducing our driving because people have an incentive to react in cost-effective ways. Throughout this book, we will be looking at the ways higher gasoline taxation can help solve our car troubles.

Gasoline taxation does not solve all our auto problems, by any means. Automotive air pollution, for example, is caused (mostly) by exhaust emissions. Higher gas taxes help here, by reducing gasoline consumption, but gasoline taxes by themselves do not affect emissions per gallon. Gasoline taxes do not solve the problems of drunk driving, speeding, congestion, oil spills, etc. Again, we will come to these in the chapters ahead. In short, we will also be looking for market-oriented ways other than higher gasoline taxation to help solve our automobile problems.

Since the purpose of this book is to get readers to think economically about these issues, little attention is paid to the question of why the U.S. government persistently utilizes policies that are so obviously not cost-effective. It is not that we officially ignore the problems caused by automobiles—there are plenty of policies that are intended to correct automotive externalities. If you are politically minded, you may enjoy thinking, as you are reading the coming chapters, why our federal and state governments have so regularly adopted a direct command-and-control (CAC) approach instead of a more cost-effective indirect market-oriented approach.

I will venture my two guesses here, and you can test them, along with your own hypotheses, as you go along through the book: (1) government policymakers believe that everything about automobile demand and use is price-inelastic, so that market-oriented solutions would achieve too little and too slowly[2] and (2) government policymakers fear that the magnitude of the costs of automobile policies would shock and dismay citizens/voters, so that policies that hide the costs are preferred even if they greatly raise the costs they hide.

ENDNOTES

[1]In theory, externalities work both ways, as benefits as well as costs. If you plant flowers at your curbside, and your neighbors enjoy them, you have provided an external benefit. Alas, as you might guess, external costs are much more common than external benefits, especially as concerns cars.

[2]The term "price elasticity" will appear regularly in the chapters ahead. A little review follows. The term refers to the extent to which consumption of a product changes when its price changes. If a given percentage change in price has a big effect on consumption, the demand is said to be price-elastic; if it has a small effect on consumption, price-inelastic. More precisely, the price elasticity of demand is defined as the percentage change in the quantity demanded divided by the percentage change in the price. Technically the price elasticity is a negative number—the quantity demanded goes down when price goes up, and vice versa—but we conventionally omit the minus sign. Price-elastic means this number is bigger than one; price-inelastic means it is smaller than one.

Appendix: External Costs and Policy

"Your right to swing your fist ends where my nose begins."

American Proverb

In perfect competition in equilibrium, price equals marginal cost (MC) in the short run, and price equals the minimum possible long-run average cost (LRAC) in the long run. Thus, all those potential consumers whose willingness-to-pay (WTP) for a good exceeds the lowest possible opportunity cost of producing the good get to consume it. As a corollary, no resources are wasted producing goods for people whose WTP is less than the opportunity cost of production. As you well know if you took the usual introductory microeconomics course, these are the great virtues of the perfectly competitive equilibrium, that it channels scarce resources into their most valued uses.

But all this is premised on the assumption that all valuable resources bear prices that reflect their scarcity. When people, either producers or consumers, are able to use a scarce output or input without having to pay for it, all the optimality attributes of competitive equilibrium break down.

Consider a consumer who consumes just two things: food and a neighboring river to dispose of his or her garbage. The consumer pays a price for the food, but in an unregulated environment, the consumer pays nothing for the use of the river. If the countryside abounded in rivers, so that people were not inconvenienced by the presence of the garbage, there would be no problem.[1A] Rivers would be a "free good" if they were so abundant that river pollution caused no inconvenience to any human being. And the proper price of free goods is indeed zero.

If, however, rivers are scarce, downstream producers and consumers *will* be inconvenienced by our hypothetical consumer's method of garbage disposal. Commercial and recreational fishing will be damaged, swimming will be less pleasant and healthful, drinking water will need to be treated, etc. In short, the use of the river for waste disposal burdens society even though it does not cost anything to the person who does the disposing. There are social costs even though there are no private costs. This excess of social cost over private cost is the external cost.

The private cost is the scarcity signal that this consumer receives and responds to; if the private cost of the river is less than the social cost, the consumer will overuse the river. In general, where there are external costs attached to the production or consumption of something, too much of it will be produced or consumed. In this example, one can say either that too much river garbage is being produced or that too much river quality is being consumed.

DEALING WITH EXTERNAL COSTS

There are several ways of correcting this misuse of resources:

1. Downstream residents could band together and negotiate with this consumer, offering a payment in return for reduced waste dumping. This solution was suggested and analyzed by Ronald Coase and is called Coasian negotiation (Coase, 1960). It has the advantage of yielding economically efficient outcomes because people will continue negotiating as long as there are ways to make one of them better off without making the other worse off. And, if you don't like the idea of the blameless downstream residents having to pay the antisocial upstream resident to reduce his or her pollution, you can make river pollution illegal unless the polluter has permission from all the downstream residents; then the upstream polluter will have to negotiate with the downstream residents and pay them for the right to continue polluting. But the Coasian solution has a big disadvantage: the downstream residents must be sufficiently few and sufficiently organized that they can band together and negotiate. For most automobile-related externalities, the number of people affected is too great for a negotiation to take place at reasonable cost.

2. The government could pass a law banning or restricting certain practices that generate external costs. This is the usual approach in contemporary society, once an external cost is recognized as a serious misallocation problem. It is called the "command-and-control" (CAC) approach. It overcomes the problems of negotiation among large numbers of affected parties. But there is no reason for thinking that the politically-legally-bureaucratically-adversarially determined CAC allocation is efficient. To see this possible inefficiency, think of two factories (ABC Corp.

BOX 1A.1 A Hypothetical Coasian Negotiation
Consider a neighborhood of only two neighbors. Neighbor Alpha wakes up a lot at night and likes then to take a short, restful car trip, but nondriving Neighbor Beta gets headaches and insomnia from the noise made by Alpha's car entering and leaving the driveway. Suppose the money value to each of them of Alpha's car trips is the following:

	Marginal willingness-to-pay (WTP)	
Number of trips per night	of Alpha to make trips ($)	of Beta to avoid trips ($)
First	8	1
Second	6	3
Third	4	5
Fourth	2	7

Neighbor Alpha starts off making four car trips per night—no more because a fifth trip (we assume) makes Alpha no better off. Alpha's WTP for the fourth trip is only $2, while Beta's WTP to avoid its noise is $7. Neighbor Beta can negotiate with Alpha, agreeing to pay something between $2 and $7 each night in return for Alpha's cutting the trips down to three per night. Indeed, for a further payment between $4 and $5, Beta can get Alpha to cut the number of trips down to two—but no further because the Alpha's WTP for the second trip ($6) exceeds Beta's WTP to avoid it ($3).

Suppose there were a law forbidding the use of driveways during the night without the neighbor's permission. Alpha's WTP for the first trip is $8, while Beta's WTP to avoid it is only $1. For a payment somewhere between $1 and $8 per night, Alpha can get Beta to give permission for one trip per night. For a further payment between $3 and $6, Beta will give permission for a second trip each night. Negotiation for a third trip fails.

Notice three things here. One, the same outcome emerges from the negotiation, regardless of whether Alpha has the right to unlimited nighttime driving or Beta has the right to nighttime silence. Two, the negotiation always exhausts the ways that *both* of them can be made better off (which in economic jargon is called a Pareto Optimum). Three, the silliness of the example shows the difficulty of finding one-on-one pollution problems where automobiles are concerned.

---

and XYZ Inc.) alongside each other on a river. Each disposes of the same waste in the same quantities into the river. ABC Corp. has a cheap alternative waste disposal process, but XYZ Inc. has only a very costly alternative. For the sake of "fairness," CAC would probably order each to reduce its pollution by the same amount, say by half. But the same result, a 50% reduction in total pollution, could be achieved more cheaply by somehow arranging to have ABC Corp. cease polluting altogether while XYZ Inc. continues to pollute as before.

3. The government could estimate the external cost being caused per unit of river-waste-disposal and tax all river dwellers that amount per unit of river-waste-disposal. This solution was first suggested by Arthur Pigou and is called a Pigovian tax (Pigou, 1920). It has the great virtue of "internalizing the externality." Consumers and producers now face a new private cost, the pollution tax, and they reduce their pollution in response to it. Though the producers and consumers may not recognize it, if the marginal tax exactly equals the marginal external damage, they are effectively responding to the external cost of the pollution as if it were a private cost.[2A] There are disadvantages: (1) the Pigovian tax may levy what is politically seen as an unfair or inequitable tax burden on some people; (2) the Pigovian tax must be levied precisely on the variable that is causing the external cost, not on some roughly correlated or administratively convenient other variable; and (3) the government must be confident that it has correctly measured the damage done by the externality, for an incorrect Pigovian tax will lead to an inefficient level of pollution.[3A]

4. The government could issue to all current polluters a number of "rights" or "permits" to pollute, presumably fewer rights in total than the previously excessive levels of pollution. Firms and people that could reduce their pollution cheaply would presumably sell their rights to firms and people that could reduce pollution only at great cost. This is called a system of marketable permits. It is efficient in the sense that the government achieves its desired reduction in pollution at least cost—agents will trade permits as long as cost reduction is possible.[4A] Possibly costly Coasian negotiations are not needed; possibly inefficient CAC allocations of the permits are corrected by the subsequent trades; and possibly objectionable income redistribution of Pigovian taxation can be avoided.

BOX 1A.2 Airline Taxes for Air Traffic Control

Air traffic control is a major cost of all large airports. Since each additional commercial flight requires a marginal expansion in such control, it is appropriate to tax flights for causing these extra resource costs. Currently, Congress is debating whether the charge should be largely a tax per flight or a tax per miles flown. The former favors large airlines that fly longer flights; the latter favors small commuter and discount airlines that fly shorter flights. The issue is usually seen as strictly political.

Economics sees it differently. Which tax is appropriate depends upon what aspect of flying imposes costs on traffic control. If takeoffs and landings impose the burden, then the correct Pigovian tax is so much per flight. If time and distance in the air impose the burden, then the correct tax is so much per hour (or per mile) in the air.

Suppose the burden were entirely caused by takeoffs and landings. What would you think of a proposed tax that was so much *per passenger* (Q1A.1)?

5. If the pollution is industrial, the industry could be nationalized and run in a socially profitable, though possibly privately unprofitable, manner. For ideological reasons, this is not much done in the United States. Having the government own all automobiles and allocate their use is an especially far-fetched thought for the United States.

Clearly, at least clearly to most economists, the fourth approach of "marketable permits" is the preferred approach, especially when the polluters are business firms, who are accustomed to buying and selling from other firms. When the generators of externalities are persons, as with most automotive externalities, a system of permits and their accompanying markets may be difficult to organize. Then the clearly best approach (again clearly to most economists) is the Pigovian tax—possibly accompanied by a change in other taxes to minimize adverse income redistribution.

FURTHER COMPLEXITIES AND CONFUSIONS

There are some final confusions about external costs and Pigovian taxes that we should clear up before going any further:

1. *Real* external costs exist only if one consumer or producer directly imposes unpaid *real* costs on another consumer or producer. Imposing unpaid *monetary* costs on another is *not* an externality. For example, when I vote for higher drivers license fees, I am making many other people worse off, but only indirectly. I should not be taxed for my vote. When I switch my breakfast drink from apple juice to orange juice, I am lowering the demand and hence the price of apples and raising the demand and hence the price of oranges. I am making all apple consumers a bit better off and all orange consumers a bit worse off. But these too are indirect monetary costs. My vote in the marketplace is also not a real externality.

2. It is sometimes thought that, because many of the external costs generated by drivers impact other drivers, these reciprocal externalities somehow balance off and obviate the need for Pigovian taxes. Not so. When you and I each dump our garbage into the other's backyard, we are each generating an external cost, and a Pigovian tax to reduce this activity is called for. A tax on each unit of such dumped garbage would make each of us aware of the external cost of our activity and induce each of us to reduce (or cease) it. Externalities exist independently of the identity of the victim. The fact that the victim also sins does not lessen the severity of the sin.

3. It is sometimes claimed that the total taxes paid by cars and drivers far exceed the external costs they impose on society and that therefore no further Pigovian tax is warranted. Not so. Again, the purpose of a Pigovian tax is to reduce the antisocial externality-generating activity, and such taxes must be levied on the margin of such activity. Levying taxes on something else does not affect the cost

of generating externalities and hence does not affect the amount of them generated. Suppose, for example, that we knew (somehow) that each car in the United States generated each year exactly $100 in social costs that the driver did not pay; and we then levied an annual $100 tax on every car. Some people might give up their cars, but those who kept them would have no incentive to alter their driving behavior. Cars would "cover" their full costs, but the external damages generated by each car would go undiminished.[5A] There is a difference between an *external cost* and an *implicit subsidy*. An external cost is a damage imposed directly on another person; an implicit subsidy is a cost that is paid by someone else. External costs call for Pigovian taxes; implicit subsidies, unless intended by government policy, call for user fees. We shall see that cars and drivers both impose many external costs and receive many implicit subsidies.

4. A deadweight loss is an unfortunate by-product of excise taxation.[6A] This is sometimes thought to be a reason for avoiding such taxation as a means of correcting externalities. It isn't a good reason. If the correct Pigovian tax is applied to alleviate an external cost, there is also a gain in reduced external costs, and this gain will always outweigh the deadweight loss of the tax.

BOX 1A.3 Who Causes the Externality?

When Driver A runs over Pedestrian B, Driver A imposes an external cost on Pedestrian B. The Pigovian tax response is to (somehow) tax drivers for killing pedestrians.

If, however, the pedestrian had not been in precisely that dangerous location at that dangerous moment, no accident would have occurred. Can we not argue that the victim is as much to blame as the driver? Should not the dead pedestrians (or, more realistically, the estates of the dead pedestrians) also be taxed? The answer is *no.* Think about why we should not tax the victim—and don't just say it would not be "fair" (Q1A.2).

How about subsidizing drivers who do not hit pedestrians, say, by giving drivers an income tax refund of so many cents per mile for accident-free travel? Aside from administrative cost and implications for the size of government budget deficits, can you think of another flaw to this approach (Q1A.3)?

BOX 1A.4 Abandoned Automobiles and Externalities

Suppose an auto that is abandoned in a public place costs the rest of society $100 in eyesore, towing, and disposal costs (over and above any salvage value of the parts or materials).[7A] A $100 deposit paid by the purchaser of every new car and refunded to the owner when and if the car was ultimately disposed of properly would provide a correct Pigovian response to this externality (Lee *et al.*, 1992). The payment of the deposit is essentially a tax on what external cost? The redemption of the deposit is essentially a subsidy on what external benefit (Q1A.4)?

ENDNOTES

[1A]You might be thinking that maybe the fish in the river would be inconvenienced. But remember the anthropocentricity of (most) economics—the value of everything depends upon how much currently living human beings are willing to pay (WTP) for it.

[2A]Look back to Box 1A.1. If the government correctly estimates that the optimal number of Alpha's car trips per night is two and that the external damage of an additional trip (the third) is $5, then it could (in theory) levy the correct Pigovian tax of $5 per (driveway at night) car trip and thereby induce Alpha to give up the third and fourth trips—since Alpha's WTP for these is not large enough to cover the tax.

[3A]Instead of taxing pollution, the government could subsidize the abatement of pollution—such abatement after all is an external benefit, the exact opposite of an external cost. This is almost the same thing as taxing the pollution since rational maximizing firms and people must now recognize that each unit of pollution means the loss of a unit of subsidy, so the subsidy creates an opportunity cost of polluting just like the tax. But there is one important asymmetry: the tax makes firms and people worse off and causes exit, while the subsidy makes firms and people better off and causes entry. Abatement subsidies could end up increasing pollution if the newly entered firms or newly immigrated people add more pollution than the old established firms and residents subtract (Porter, 1974).

[4A]Look back at Box 1A.1. Suppose the government issued marketable car trip permits, one per night per citizen. Alpha would want to buy more; Beta would want to sell. A price between $3 and $6 would induce Beta to sell to Alpha. If the permit price rose above $8, Alpha would also sell the permit and cease nighttime driving.

[5A]To satisfy your curiosity, one detailed study concluded that motor vehicle users actually pay about three-fourths of their full social costs (OTA, 1994; Sperling, 1995). Full social costs in that study, and in most others like it, count not only external costs but also potentially private costs of the auto that are subsidized by some government budget. The problem with these estimates is that there is seemingly no limit to the costs that can be attributed, albeit very indirectly, to automobiles; if you stretch these attributions far enough, you can end up with cars paying less than 10% of their "full" costs (Miller and Moffet, 1993).

[6A]Recall what deadweight loss means. When a product is taxed, and the quantity produced and consumed declines, both consumers and producers of the product are made worse off. On the other hand, the government collects tax revenue. The deadweight loss is measured by the excess of the amount of consumer and producer losses over the amount of tax revenue.

[7A]This, by the way, is no longer true—junked autos are now worth towing in for the scrap value. We will talk about this in Chapter 16.

The Economics of Driving

CHAPTER 2

The Cost of Driving

"Which of you, intending to build a tower,
sitteth not down first, and counteth the cost,
whether he have sufficient to finish it?
Lest haply, after he hath laid the foundation,
and is not able to finish it,
all that behold it begin to mock him. . . ."

Saint Luke

Gospel

Making a careful list of the costs of driving cars is a good way to see the reasons why Americans drive so much and why automobile driving represents a market failure. We break down these costs into various categories:

1. *Variable* Costs versus *Fixed* Costs. Variable costs are those that vary closely with the miles driven, while fixed costs are the costs of owning, registering, and insuring the car. Fixed costs depend little or not at all on the amount of use the car gets.
2. *Explicit* Costs versus *Implicit* Costs. Explicit costs are cash costs, while implicit, or imputed, costs are those that are paid for in other ways. The other ways may involve lost time, inconvenience, or risk to life and limb.
3. *Private* Costs versus *External* Costs. Private costs are those paid for by the driver, while external costs are those foisted onto other people without their permission. External costs are the excess of social costs over private costs.

Although it may seem to be a dull way to start—and I have to admit it probably is—it is important that we get these various costs conceptually clear from the start. Much of what follows in later chapters will only make sense if we thoroughly understand these various aspects of driving costs.

PRIVATE COSTS

We begin with the explicit, private, variable costs. These are the obvious costs, for such things as gasoline, oil, routine maintenance, periodic tire replacement, speeding tickets, and parking fees. They are explicit because the car doesn't move until you come up with the cash or plastic to pay for them; they are private because you and nobody else pays for them; and they are variable because they depend closely (almost proportionately) on how many miles you drive.

Then there are the explicit, private, fixed costs. These are the costs of a drivers license, auto registration, and auto insurance. They are fixed because you pay them out as a lump sum—so much per year. These costs are completely, or pretty much, independent of how much you drive.

Less obvious, but no less important, are the implicit, private, variable costs of driving. Whenever you drive a car, you use up your own time and you endanger your own life and limbs. The inclusion of one's own time as a cost may seem curious — after all, the major reason why people drive is to save time, not to expend it. But the time you save by not walking or taking the bus goes onto the benefit side of the driving decision, just as does the added enjoyment you get out of life by getting somewhere else quickly. The time you spend in the car getting there goes on the cost side of the driving decision.

It may also seem curious that we include risk to the driver's own life and limbs as a cost. Very few people, before getting into their car, ask themselves, is this trip worth the risk of injuring myself or even losing my life? But the fact that the question is not usually asked does not make it irrelevant. Roughly 1 out of every 10,000 registered U.S. drivers will die behind the wheel this year, and, while the probability is low, the cost is immense. Implicit costs are much easier to forget or ignore than explicit costs, but they are still there.

Finally, among the privately paid costs, there are the implicit, private, fixed costs—depreciation and interest. Like insurance, depreciation depends to some extent on how much the car is driven, but a car's age is the major factor in its depreciation. Classified ads for used cars always tell first the model year of the car,

---

BOX 2.1 To Drive or to Fly?
To get home for Christmas vacation, you have a choice between flying and driving your car. The flight costs $300 and takes 2 hours; driving costs you $100 (in explicit, private, variable costs) and takes 12 hours. If you can't make up your mind which to do, it indicates that you value your time at how much per hour (Q2.1)? (Actually, your implicit wage is somewhat less than $20 per hour because we are here ignoring the differential risk of an accident on the two travel modes—death rates per mile are much lower on airplanes than in cars.[1])

and only later in the fine print how many miles it has been driven. In short, for cars, resale value is much more a function of age than use.

Interest costs are implicit, of course, only if you pay cash for the car. Then the relevant interest cost is the interest that you could have earned by putting that money in your next best investment opportunity. For those who take out an auto loan to finance their car purchase, the interest becomes an explicit (though still private and fixed) cost.

EXTERNAL COSTS

This takes care of all the major private costs, explicit and implicit, and variable and fixed. There remain the external costs—costs that drivers impose on society but do not pay themselves. Since these external costs are the main stuff of much of the rest of this book, we can be brief here.

Decisions to drive are decisions to make America still more dependent on foreign oil supplies. But drivers do not get charged for the additional military

---

BOX 2.2 Used Cars and "Lemons"

A particular used car is either worth more or worth less than the going used-car price for that make and model. The owner knows whether his or her car happens to be a "peach" or a "lemon," and owners are less likely to sell off their peaches than their lemons. As a result, a used-car buyer runs a high risk of getting a lemon. Because potential buyers have good reason to fear that any used car they buy will later reveal hidden defects, they will not buy unless the price is low enough to offset this higher probability of it being a lemon (Akerlof, 1970). That is why used car prices always seem too low to sellers, at least when they are selling a peach, and always seem too high to buyers, because they fear they are getting a lemon.

When sellers know more about the quality of their product than buyers, it is called asymmetric information, and the market distortion that results is called adverse selection.[2] The high rate of price depreciation of cars is only partly due to their wearing out or going out of style; it is also due to the problem of adverse selection in the used-car market. For example, according to the *Kelley Blue Book* (www.kbb.com), if you bought a 1998 Chevy Cavalier for the suggested retail price of $12,310, drove it home, and then sold it, you would have gotten only $10,190 for it—the first mile or the first day knocks 17% off the value.

It is not just private owners who sell off their lemons in the used-car market. All states now have laws requiring auto dealers to repurchase new vehicles that prove to have irreparable defects. But 12 states (including Michigan) permit the dealers to resell those cars without any indication that they have previously been repurchased as "lemons" (Adelson, 1996).

BOX 2.3 Keeping the Old Car versus Buying a New Car

Suppose, to take an extreme case, that you have a very old set of wheels; it runs well enough for your basic needs but has zero resale value. The cost of operating this bucket of bolts consists mostly of the private variable costs, both explicit and implicit. If you were to bury the heap (assume costlessly) and buy a new car, the cost of operating the new car would consist not only of these variable costs but also of much larger fixed costs. Why? Three reasons. One, you (if you are a typical consumer) will want to take out collision insurance.[3] Two, you must count the depreciation (loss of resale value, some 20% per year).[4] Three, you must count the interest cost on the purchase price (an explicit cost if you borrow and an implicit cost if you empty your savings account).

Why would you ever buy a new car in these circumstances? Two reasons. One, the jalopy will have ever increasing maintenance, breakdown, and repair costs, so the variable cost of operating it will be higher than the variable costs of the new car, and they will be getting ever higher as the Tin Lizzie gets older. These higher variable costs will eventually offset the fixed costs of the new car. Two, you (and your friends, dates, and relatives) will presumably get more pleasure and reliability out of driving the new car than the clunker, and that will also speed up the replacement decision.

So you replace the rattletrap when its average variable private cost per mile begins to exceed the following: the average variable private cost per mile of the new car plus the average fixed cost per mile of the new car minus your willingness-to-pay per mile for having a new (versus the old) car. Would you be more likely to replace the old boat if you drove a lot or drove only a little? If you planned to trade the new car in after 1 year or planned to keep it for a long time (Q2.2)?

---

strength that the United States believes it has to maintain in order to ensure our uninterrupted deliveries of this oil, largely from the tempestuous Middle East. Cars emit air and water pollutants, which harm life and well-being in many American cities. Drivers are not charged for this harm to others. We are becoming increasingly concerned with global warming, which could lead in a few centuries to catastrophic changes for life on this planet. Cars contribute to this, too, in unpaid-for ways.

Automobile drivers not only endanger themselves on the highway, they endanger others—roughly half the deaths each year on American highways are of passengers, cyclists, and pedestrians. Like deaths due to "secondhand" smoke, deaths due to "secondhand" driving are the ultimate externalities.

Driving causes congestion and requires the devotion of valuable land and capital for heavily subsidized roads and parking spaces. Cars also cause water pollution, noise, litter, police costs, and court costs. And when the car's life is over, the carcass needs to be disposed of somewhere, somehow, and by somebody.

To summarize this chapter to here, these major driving costs are listed in Table 2.1.

TABLE 2.1   The Costs of Operating Automobiles

Private costs		External costs[5]
Variable, explicit	Fixed, explicit	
		Military
Gas and oil	Auto registration	Air pollution
Maintenance	Insurance	Global warming
Tires	Drivers license	Others' lives
Tickets		Congestion
		Land and roads
		"Free" parking
Variable, implicit	Fixed, implicit	Water pollution
		Noise
Own time	Depreciation	Highway litter
Own life	Interest	Police costs
		Court costs
		Auto disposal

MAGNITUDE OF THE PRIVATE COSTS

How big are the private costs of operating an automobile? Some are readily estimated. Table 2.2 displays some of the costs of operating a "typical" car, driven
10,000 miles per year and replaced every 5 years. (Remember that all dollar values
throughout this book have been converted into 1995 prices.) The total annual
variable costs (not counting time and risk) are about $1000 (about 10 cents per
mile), while the total annual fixed costs are about $4700 (nearly 50 cents per mile).
Fixed costs are nearly five times as much as variable costs, and most of the fixed
costs are implicit costs for people who pay cash for the car.

Which costs are relevant to a driver's decision depends upon the decision being
made. If you are contemplating the purchase of a car, and comparing it to an alternative of doing without a car and using taxi, bus, bicycle, or feet, then the relevant
cost is the total private cost—fixed and variable, explicit and implicit. But once
you have bought your car, and you are contemplating whether to drive on a particular trip, then the relevant cost is the private, variable cost, explicit and implicit.

What do we learn from all this cost thinking? First, that the marginal cost of
driving an additional mile, once you own a car, is quite low. This goes a long way
to explaining why Americans drive their cars so much. And second, that the cost
of owning a car is quite high. The private fixed cost is nearly $5000 a year, a sum
that will take a family on a handsome Caribbean vacation for a week. Americans
clearly value their automobility highly. Of course, the marginal car in a multicar

TABLE 2.2   Variable and Fixed Private Costs
(in Dollars) of Operating Automobiles

Variable, private costs	
Gasoline and oil	0.063 per mile
Routine maintenance	0.025 per mile
Tires	0.009 per mile
Fixed, private costs	
Insurance	760 per year
License and registration	190 per year
Depreciation	3010 per year
Interest	730 per year

Source: Bureau, 1995.

family is usually not new and is usually not turned over every 5 years, so the fixed cost of many cars is much lower than $5000 a year, but it is still not cheap.

It is time to examine more closely the private, variable costs of driving since these are the costs that matter when a car owner must make a decision over whether or not to drive a marginal mile. Since the most important of these costs are gasoline, time, and risk to one's own life, we will focus on these. The total variable private cost (TVPC) of driving per year can be written in equation form as

$$\text{TVPC} = P_g Q_g + P_t Q_t + p Q_m V_L, \qquad [2.1]$$

where the right-hand-side variables are defined as follows:

P_g, the price per gallon of gasoline
Q_g, the quantity of gasoline purchased per year
P_t, the price of time (i.e., the opportunity cost of driving time)
Q_t, the amount of time spent driving per year
p, the probability per mile of killing oneself or being killed while driving
Q_m, the number of miles driven per year
V_L, the dollar value the driver puts on his/her own life

Three of these variables—P_t, p, and V_L—need further explanation.

• P_t. If a driver could choose the allocation of time among work, driving, and other leisure activities, then a marginal hour of driving or leisure would cost, in an opportunity cost sense, the driver's hourly wage. The price of driving time (P_t) would then be the wage rate. But research has shown that most people value their driving time at much less than their wage rate. Therefore, P_t means some fraction of the person's wage rate, typically about one-third.

• p. The probability that a driver dies on the highway is affected, of course, not only by the driver's own abilities but also by highway crowding, highway qual-

---

BOX 2.4 To Buy or to Lease?

Much malarkey needs to be sliced through here. What really happens when you lease a car, say for 3 years, is that you buy the car now and sell it back to the lessor 3 years from now.[6] But there are two important differences between the lease and the buy–sell process. One, the lessor finances the car, and hence the interest rate you pay is the rate that the lessor offers, and that may be a lower interest rate than you can get on your own. But it may be higher—if, for example, you are carrying a big balance in a low-interest-rate savings account. Two, the lessor is guaranteeing the repurchase price 3 years from now, and that guarantee may be worth something to you, especially if you don't want to keep the car longer than that.[7] For most consumers, it does not make much difference. But beware—Dilbert advises marketing specialists to "offer lease options to people who are bad at math" (Adams, 1996).

High-income people do more leasing (relative to buying) than low-income people (Guha and Waldman, 1997). Why (Q2.3)? And the lessors of cars write careful maintenance requirements into the lease contract. Why (Q2.4)?

---

ity, the quality of medical support facilities, the state of medical trauma technology, etc. We will later painstakingly examine this probability and its determinants.

- V_L. What do we mean by "the dollar value the driver puts on his/her own life"? We will explore this concept in great detail later, when we talk about highway safety and highway death (in the appendix to Chapter 7). Only a brief idea of it is needed here. Whenever you cross a street, you run some tiny risk of being run over by a car. If we valued our lives infinitely, we would never cross streets, since the benefit of getting to the other side is always finite. The fact that we take risks with our lives for finite benefit indicates that we place finite value on our lives. How large a value is a question best left for later. Generally, we will explore values of V_L between $1 million and $5 million whenever this variable becomes relevant.

Going from the total variable private cost (TVPC) of driving per year to the average variable private cost (AVPC) per mile is straightforward. We divide Equation [2.1] by the number of miles driven per year (Q_m);

$$\text{AVPC} = \frac{P_g Q_g + P_t Q_t + p Q_m V_L}{Q_m}, \qquad [2.2]$$

or, simplifying,

$$\text{AVPC} = \frac{P_g}{\text{MPG}} + \frac{P_t}{\text{MPH}} + p V_L, \qquad [2.3]$$

where MPG is average miles per gallon (Q_m/Q_g) and MPH is average miles per hour (Q_m/Q_t). There is no reason for thinking that the average variable private cost of driving is very different from the marginal variable private cost of driving, so we may consider AVPC in Equation [2.3] as the privately paid "price" of driving an extra mile.

How important are each of the three terms in Equation [2.3]? Each of the six variables in the equation will differ for different drivers driving different cars, on different roads, for different purposes, and in different parts of the United States. But we can choose a rough national average value of each: P_g is currently about $1.20, MPG is about 20, P_t is about $4.00 (roughly one-third of the current average U.S. hourly wage income), say MPH is about 10 in urban areas and 40 in rural areas, p is about 0.00000001 (i.e., 20,000 driver deaths in 2 trillion miles of car driving), and estimates of V_L run around $3 million. For these numbers, the annual average variable private cost of driving a mile (Equation [2.3]) becomes

$$\text{AVPC} = \$0.06 + \begin{array}{c} \$0.40 \text{ (urban)} \\ \text{or} \\ \$0.10 \text{ (rural)} \end{array} + \$0.03. \qquad [2.4]$$

The gasoline cost term should be roughly doubled to allow for all the other variable private cash costs (oil, tires, etc.), and we should roughly double the risk-to-life cost term to allow for serious accidents that injure but do not kill drivers. This yields the following:

$$\text{AVPC} = \$0.12 + \begin{array}{c} \$0.40 \text{ (urban)} \\ \text{or} \\ \$0.10 \text{ (rural)} \end{array} + \$0.06. \qquad [2.5]$$

BOX 2.5 Valujet

Valujet flew its first plane in October 1993 and, until recently, had grown to some 200 flights a day, with some 100 passengers per flight, at an average of $200 less per ticket than the "standard" airlines. How did they sell so cheap? Computerized, no-ticket, no-agent reservations; nonunion labor (with low pay but high profit-related bonuses); old planes; and subcontracted training, maintenance, and repairs (*The Economist*, 1996a).

The 11 May 1996 crash of Valujet Flight 592 in the Everglades, which cost some 100 lives, was their first crash (and was probably caused by a misunderstanding between the airline and one of its subcontractors). Valujet was grounded for safety reasons after this crash. It was permitted to reopen 4 months later, but it was not immediately "swamped" with reservations (Brannigan, 1997).

Many people are willing to take a riskier, cheaper Valujet flight rather than a safer, costlier Northwest flight (between the same cities, at the same time, etc.). What does this willingness say about the value they place on their own lives (Q2.5)? Would you fly Valujet (or Air Tran, as it is now called)? If not, then would you travel by Northwest or by car (or not at all)? (We look more closely at the "value" of life in the appendix to Chapter 7.)

BOX 2.6 Driving Differences by Gender

Among the many changes in driving variables that we will be discussing, we should not overlook the dramatic gender change on the highways during the past few decades (Downs, 1995; Pisarski, 1992; Rossetti and Eversole, 1993). Between 1969 and 1990, the number of female licensed drivers increased by 84%, while the number of licensed males increased by only 38%. And the average woman driver traveled 76% more miles per annum, while the average man drove only 46% more miles per annum.

These numbers seem to suggest that women are behaving differently from men in their driving. Wrong. They are behaving more and more like men. A smaller percentage of women used to get drivers licenses than men; now the percentage is almost identical. A smaller percentage of women used to work than men, and hence fewer women drove to work; now this gap has also closed.

Time is an important ingredient in driving cost, even in rural areas on high-speed roads. The cash outlay is less than half the average variable private cost. For these rough average figures, the marginal private cost of driving is some 28–58 cents per mile.

Take a final look at each of the six variables in Equation [2.3]. Other things being unchanged, driving is made *less* expensive by:

lower real gasoline prices (P_g)
lower real wage rates (P_t)
lower real valuations of one's own life (V_L)
more fuel-efficient autos (MPG)
higher maximum speed limits (MPH)
safer automobiles and/or safer driving (lower p)

Note that these six forces are not independent of each other. For example, as cars become safer (i.e., p is reduced), the "price" of miles falls and more miles are driven, which at least partially offsets the reduction in highway deaths caused by the reduction in p. Similarly, as cars become more fuel-efficient (i.e., MPG is raised), the "price" of miles falls and more miles are driven, which at least partially offsets the reduction in gasoline use caused by the increased MPG. Higher MPG is partly achieved by making smaller, lighter cars, which may reduce MPH and definitely raises p. Higher maximum speed limits (MPH) will reduce MPG and may raise p. We will be exploring these, and many other, interactions.

FINAL THOUGHTS

Drivers escape many of the social costs of their driving. They do so in two basic ways. One, there are external costs of driving. Each mile imposes costs on other people, some of whom are other drivers (e.g., congestion) and some of whom are innocent bystanders (e.g. pedestrians who are run down). And two, many of the costs of driving are subsidized by governments, from taxation that takes equally from people who drive a lot and people who drive little or not at all (e.g., highway construction), or are subsidized by businesses, through higher prices of goods and services charged equally to those who drive and those who don't (e.g., free parking to employees and customers). Most of this book consists of a close look at these externalities and implicit subsidies.

ENDNOTES

[1]You may be curious about the relative hazards of car and plane travel (per person per mile). In 1994 in the United States, there were 42,170 deaths due to motor vehicle accidents and 855 deaths due to aviation accidents (*Economist*, 1996d); on average, Americans suffer some 50 times as many deaths from cars as airplanes while traveling some 5 times as many miles in cars. Of course, the preponderance of airline death is at takeoff or landing, so miles traveled may not be the right comparison. According to one study, for sober, seat-belted, 40-year-old females driving big, heavy cars on rural Interstates, it is safer to drive on trips of less than 600 miles (Evans *et al.*, 1990). But the even safer way to travel is by bus!

[2]Occasionally, it works the other way round—for some products, buyers know better than the seller about the quality of the product. For example, when you buy auto insurance, you know better than the insurance company whether you are a competent driver or not. On this, wait for Chapter 10.

[3]Collision insurance is the part of your insurance policy that covers damages you do to your own car. Collision insurance is optional; what all states require is liability insurance, which covers the damage you do to others. We will talk again about collision insurance in Box 10.1.

[4]Note that this is not straight-line depreciation. Consider a car that costs $20,000 new, and forget inflation. Typically, its resale value will fall to $16,000 after 1 year (i.e., $16,000 equals 0.80 of $20,000), to $12,800 after 2 years (i.e. $12,800 equals 0.80 of $16,000), etc. After 5 years, the car is worth a bit under $7000; after 10 years, a bit over $2000.

[5]Not all the items in this list are external costs, though all represent a private price (P) that is below marginal social cost (MSC). With external costs, price equals marginal private cost (MPC), but MPC < MSC because some costs are imposed on other people. With such things as "free" parking and uncongested highways, MSC equals MPC—no costs are imposed on other people; but they are provided at less than their cost—that is, P is less than marginal and/or average private cost. These are called "implicit subsidies". We return to this distinction in Chapter 14.

[6]The lessor is the one whose property is put out to lease; the lessee is the one who receives the property for use.

[7]In the past, many auto manufacturers have cross-subsidized their leases from profits on new-car sales—perhaps because lease customers are more loyal or replace cars more often, both of which boost long-run profit (Henry, 1997). But these subsidies may now be ending, partly because the cost has proved unexpectedly high and partly because lease customers are increasingly being given the right to buy or re-lease the vehicle, which means the leasing companies may be beginning to face a "lemons" problem—that is, people will buy or re-lease the "good" leased cars and only return the "bad" ones (Kim, 1996; Child and Harris, 1996; Connelly, 1996, 1997; Wernle, 1998; Henry, 1998). Finally, there are tax implications. Most states charge a lease tax on the lease payments, but this lease tax is smaller than the sales tax if the car had been purchased.

The Demand for Driving

"More Americans own cars than pay income taxes."

Janet Elder

No Longer in Love, Not Ready to Walk

Most people drive cars in order to get somewhere, so the demand for automobiles and the demand for gasoline are really derived demands. What is really demanded is "driving"—which is a hard-to-define combination of quantity of miles and quality of miles. With a given number of cars, a family is better off with more gasoline since this permits more driving; with a given quantity of gasoline, a family is better off with more (or better) cars since different family members can then be going to different places at the same time, or different vehicles may be used for different purposes.

Thus, it is helpful to think of "driving" as an output produced by various inputs. Some of these inputs, such as cars, are like "capital" in the usual production function, inputs that are variable only in the long run; others of these inputs, such as gasoline, are like "labor," inputs that are variable in the short run as well.

SHORT-RUN DEMAND FOR DRIVING

For each car owner, then, the short-run demand curve for "driving" is a downward-sloped function of the marginal private cost of miles. This cost, as we saw in Chapter 2, consists mostly of gasoline, time, and risk. The costs of time and risk change slowly, so in the short run the major source of fluctuation in the marginal private cost of driving is the gasoline price.

Casual reflection suggests that the short-run price elasticity of demand for driving miles with respect to the gasoline price is very low. Gasoline accounts for less than half of the marginal private cost of driving (look back at Equation [2.5]). Thus, if the price elasticity of driving with respect to the marginal private cost of miles were, say, one, the short-run price elasticity of driving with respect to gasoline cost would be less than one-half—you can figure out why (Q3.1).

While we expect a low elasticity of demand for driving with respect to the price of gasoline, we should not expect it to be zero. Figure 3.1 shows that the price elasticity is indeed not zero. There the trend of the real retail gasoline price (including taxes) is shown with dark squares (and the left-hand y-axis), and the trend of vehicle-miles traveled (VMT) per car per year is shown with open circles (and the right-hand y-axis). Note that the two trends are almost mirror images of each other, like the reflection of a mountainous terrain in a lake.[1] From 1960 until the late 1980s, whenever the real retail price of gasoline went down, VMT per car went up, and vice versa. Notice particularly the years of dramatic price increases, 1973–1974 and 1979–1980, the years when the Organization of Petroleum Exporting Countries (OPEC) most sharply reduced world petroleum supplies. Prices rose suddenly in those years, and vehicle usage went down, significantly and immediately.

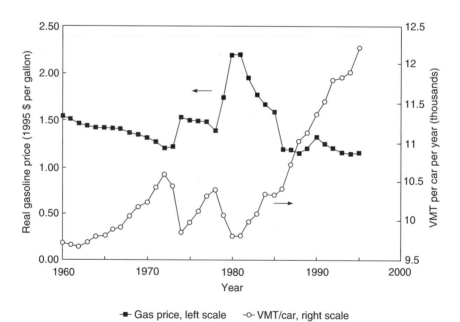

—■— Gas price, left scale   –o– VMT/car, right scale

FIGURE 3.1   Gasoline Price and Automobile Mileage

Econometric studies of the short-run price elasticity of gasoline demand with respect to gasoline price support this casual theorizing, finding estimates in the 0.1–0.5 range (Dahl, 1986, 1995; French, 1989; Dahl and Sterner, 1991; Goodwin, 1992; Walls *et al.*, 1993).[2] A 10% increase in gasoline price causes Americans to reduce their gasoline use by between 1% and 5%, and vice versa for a 10% decrease in gasoline price. In the short run, Americans alter their driving habits modestly in response to changed gasoline prices.

LONG-RUN DEMAND FOR DRIVING

The long run is more complicated. Total gasoline use is then affected not only by the miles traveled per vehicle but also by the number of vehicles and their average fuel efficiency. And all three of these variables can change in the long run. In the long run, demand for driving is a function not only of the price of gasoline but also of the price and quality of automobiles.

To simplify these complex relationships, let us look at the trends of U.S. motor vehicle ownership and new car prices over the past 30 years. Figure 3.2 shows these trends. It is tempting to attribute the rising per capita vehicle ownership to the declining real new car prices, but we must remember that real incomes have also been rising during this period, and the growth of vehicle ownership is probably due more to high income elasticity than to price elasticity.

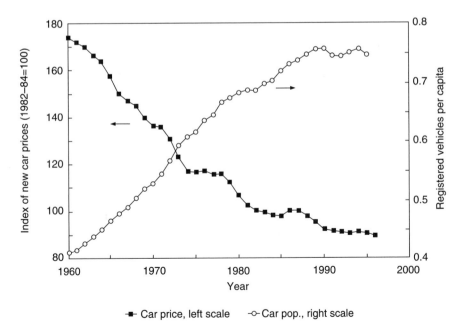

—■— Car price, left scale   —○— Car pop., right scale

FIGURE 3.2   New Car Price and Automobile Ownership

Were you not startled by the trend of new car prices in Figure 3.2? Did the real cost of new cars actually fall by nearly half over this period? No, certainly not. What this trend in Figure 3.2 is telling us is that the real cost of a *constant-quality* new car fell by nearly half—new inventions, improved quality, mandated safety and emissions equipment, and features that used to be optional but now have become standard equipment have all combined to greatly increase the real price of the average *actually purchased* new car.

To give concrete meaning to these thoughts, consider a basic low-priced sedan. The two-door, six-seat Hudson Pacemaker, for example, cost just under $2000 in 1950. If you could buy that same car today, and its price had risen at the same rate as the overall urban Consumer Price Index (CPI), it would now cost about $12,000. The rate of growth of productivity has been high in auto production throughout this century, however, and this means that the price of the 1950 sedan would have risen by 1995 to only a little over $6000.[3] A typical basic sedan today costs about $18,000. For that $18,000, you are getting about $6000 worth of 1950 car plus some $12,000 worth of "extras" that were not included in the 1950 car (Bennet, 1995).

What are these "extras"? Basically, they consist of three kinds of changes. First, there is much government-mandated equipment in new cars today. This is largely antipollution and safety equipment—soon to be examined closely—some of which consumers want and some of which consumers do not want but must buy. Second, there are many standard features of today's cars that either did not exist a half-century ago or were optional extras in 1950 cars—such as air conditioning, side mirrors, power steering, and automatic transmissions. And third, today's cars are more durable than 1950 cars, being built with stronger and more rustproof materials.

These "extras" tell us something about the trend in used car prices over the past few decades. While the real price of constant-quality new cars has been falling steadily, the real price of constant-quality used cars has been almost constant. As new car prices have risen, with the continual addition of often unwanted improvements, and old cars have become more durable, some car owners have been turning from purchasing new cars to buying or keeping a close substitute, used cars. It is *not* a coincidence that used car prices have been rising relative to new car prices and that the average age of the U.S. auto fleet has also been rising (Lavin, 1994).

Do not get the impression that people are clamoring for the modern equivalent of the 1950 Hudson Pacemaker. While rational, selfish people may not want to buy antipollution equipment, much of the safety equipment *is* wanted. Remember, the Yugos of a few years back were not hot sellers—especially after the wind blew one of them off the Mackinaw Bridge into Lake Michigan. If most people did not like the "extras" enough to be willing to pay for them, either they would not have been offered (at least as standard equipment) by rational carmakers or ownership of cars would not have risen over the past few decades from about two cars per five people to almost four cars per five people (Figure 3.2). People would have bought fewer cars and driven them more—that is, they would have substituted miles per vehicle for number of vehicles in their mileage production function.

Let's get back to the long-run price elasticity of gasoline demand. In the long run, if gasoline prices change, and stay changed, we expect that consumers will make basic adjustments in their consumption patterns. Higher gasoline prices, in the long run, could lead to the purchase of more fuel-efficient vehicles, changes in shopping or commuting arrangements, living nearer one's workplace, etc. In short, we expect the long-run price elasticity of demand for driving (or for gasoline) to be larger than the short-run price elasticity of demand. However, since Americans have never experienced sustained higher gasoline prices (see Figure 3.1), clear U.S. evidence about the long-run price elasticity of demand for gasoline is difficult to come by.

We do, however, get hints of high long-run price elasticity from the international differences in gasoline prices (among countries of comparable income per capita). Figure 3.3 shows the average vehicle fuel efficiency (MPG) and real retail gasoline prices across several industrialized countries in the late 1980s (Hinrichs, 1996). West Europeans have reacted to their high gasoline prices in three about equally important ways: (1) the average car is driven 22% fewer miles per year than in the United States; (2) Europeans own 30% fewer cars per person than do Americans; and (3) European cars average 41% more MPG than do American cars (OTA, 1994). You cannot just add these percentages up, but they do mean that Europeans consume 61% fewer gallons of gasoline per capita per year than do Americans.

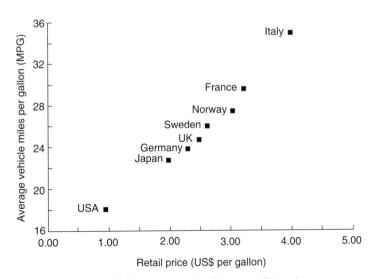

FIGURE 3.3   International Fuel Economy Comparisons

You are probably wondering why there is so much difference in the retail prices across countries. The answer is gasoline taxes. In Figure 3.4, for most of the major industrialized countries, two numbers are summed together—the pre-tax retail price and the tax levied on that price (so the sum of the two is the post-tax retail price) (Marcus, 1992).[4]From left to right, the countries are displayed according to the size of their retail gasoline prices; the main reason why retail prices differ is different rates of taxation.[5] Italy's gasoline tax rate is the highest of the countries shown, being over 300% of the pretax retail gasoline price—which means that the tax causes a quadrupling of the retail price. Gasoline taxes range on down to roughly 100% for Canada, Australia, and New Zealand—which means that the tax causes a mere doubling of the retail price in those countries. The United States is the anomaly to the right.

Unlike most other industrialized countries, the United States does not impose much tax on gasoline (and never has). Currently in the United States, the federal gasoline tax is $0.18 per gallon, and the state gasoline taxes range from $0.04 per gallon (Florida) to $0.36 per gallon (Connecticut).

Formal econometric estimates of long-run price elasticity of demand for gasoline find significant price responsiveness in the United States, in the 0.6–1.2 range. Given time to adjust, Americans appear capable of a lot of adjustment in their

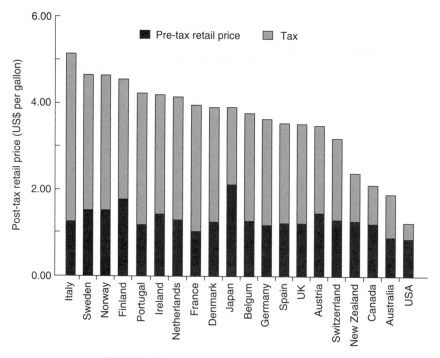

FIGURE 3.4   Gasoline Prices in Various Countries

BOX 3.1 Long-Run versus Short-Run Elasticities

For most products, like gasoline, we think the long-run price and income elasticities are greater than the short-run price and income elasticities.[6] (Recall why.) But the reverse seems to be true for automobiles for both price and income elasticities, as the table below shows (Hymans, 1971; Pindyck, 1979). Why (Q3.3)?

	Years after price or income change			
	1	2	5	20
Gasoline demand				
Price elasticity	−0.11	−0.22	−0.49	−1.17
Income elasticity	+0.07	+0.13	+0.32	+0.78
Automobile demand				
Price elasticity	−1.20	−0.93	−0.55	−0.40
Income elasticity	+3.00	+2.33	+1.38	+1.00

Note: The negative signs of the price elasticities are shown in the above table to make sure that they are clearly understood.

driving habits and driving machines in response to a fuel price increase (Baltagi and Griffin, 1984; Dahl and Sterner, 1991). This surprisingly high long-run price elasticity strongly suggests that conventional wisdom is wrong in thinking Americans are inalterably driven to driving—we are certainly not bonded to every last mile of it.

The long-run *income* elasticities of demand for gasoline and automobiles are around one, indicating that if U.S. real income per capita continues to rise at, say, 2% per year, U.S. per capita gasoline consumption and new automobile purchases will also continue to rise at a rate of 2% per year (Dahl and Sterner, 1991).

GASOLINE TAXATION

Why have we been concerning ourselves so much with demand elasticities for gasoline? Because, during future chapters, we shall keep noting that driving and gasoline consumption cause serious external costs. If real gasoline prices remain constant or fall and real incomes rise, these externality problems are going to get steadily worse. So we will be thinking about higher real gasoline prices as a means to curb this growth in driving. And that will get us thinking about higher gasoline taxation. How higher gasoline taxes affect the price and quantity of gasoline and the income distribution is very dependent on the price elasticity of demand for gasoline (see the appendix to this chapter).

Whenever gasoline taxes are considered, people begin to worry that the incidence of such taxes is largely on consumers rather than producers, and largely on poor consumers rather than rich consumers. Both of these worries need examination.

Estimates of the price elasticity of supply of gasoline are typically similar (though of course of opposite sign) to those of the price elasticity of demand, which means that gasoline consumers probably pay about half of any gasoline tax. The other half is paid by gasoline suppliers, probably mostly by the rent-collecting owners of petroleum reserves. And remember, a large fraction of U.S. oil is imported, so that much of this supply incidence may be on foreigners.

Although much of any gasoline tax falls on producers, what does fall on consumers hits the poor harder than the rich. Studies show that the incidence of a gasoline tax is regressive. Poorer consumers expend a higher percentage of their incomes on gasoline than do richer consumers.[7] But income is more erratic, from year to year, than expenditure, and expenditure may be a better indicator of the usual socioeconomic status of a family than its income. Gasoline (and motor oil) expenditure as a percentage of total expenditure is only 3.9% for the lowest decile families, rises steadily to 6.1% for the fourth decile, and then falls steadily to 3.4% for the top decile (Poterba, 1991). Thus, for the bottom half of the expenditure distribution, gasoline taxation is progressive; only in the top half of the expenditure distribution is it regressive.

However, this regressiveness in the upper half of the income distribution is not inevitable. Gasoline taxes could be set higher for the higher-octane fuels, which are mostly purchased by the better-off owners of large and powerful cars. The resulting gain in equity involves, of course, a sacrifice in efficiency since higher octanes usually do not generate greater external effects. A more appropriate way to address efficiency *and* equity when gasoline taxes are raised would be simultaneously to cut income taxes and to increase their progressivity.

Finally, one should note that gasoline taxes also affect families differentially, depending on where they live. In southern and western states, families of the same income level drive more and hence pay more in gasoline taxes (for any given gasoline tax rate). If gasoline taxes were being raised simply to provide government revenue, this would represent horizontal inequity.[8] But here we will be contem-

---

BOX 3.2 Gasoline Taxes and Income Distribution

It has been suggested that one way to raise gasoline taxes in order to reduce gasoline consumption without any regressive income redistribution would be the following: each gasoline purchaser would keep a receipt for each gasoline purchase, and the total gasoline taxes paid would be refunded at the end of the year as a credit on the person's income tax. How much do you think this would reduce gasoline consumption (Q3.4)?

BOX 3.3 **Mickey Mouse Policies for Gasoline Shortages**

In one of the periods of sudden gasoline shortages in the 1970s, the governors of California and New Jersey each had a brilliant idea for reducing gasoline consumption and shortening the queues at the gasoline pumps.[9] In one state, cars were not permitted to buy *more* than 5 gallons of gasoline at one time, and in the other state, cars were not permitted to buy *less* than 5 gallons at one time. In Pennsylvania, motorists had to buy *exactly* $5 worth of gasoline on each trip to the pump, no more, no less.

In several states, drivers of odd-numbered and even-numbered license plates alternated days on which they were permitted to buy gasoline. (In Paris and Mexico City, odds-and-evens have at times alternated days on which they were permitted to *drive*.) In many states, "gasless" Sundays were observed.

What's going on here? To some extent, all these policies are the hobbyhorses of noneconomists who grumble that "it's bad enough that gasoline is scarce without making it expensive as well." In fact, however, all these policies *do* make gasoline more expensive—it is just that drivers pay with time and inconvenience instead of money. Who benefits from policies that make buyers pay with time instead of money? Low-wage buyers (because their time is less valuable). But society as a whole loses; make sure you see why (Q3.5).

plating gasoline taxes as correctives for negative externalities, which is a different matter. If southerners and westerners drive more, and are thereby generating more external costs, the tax is an efficient way of discouraging some of those socially costly miles. On the other hand, where the population is small and spread out, external costs like air pollution and congestion are much lower, and hence the appropriate corrective taxes are lower.

ENDNOTES

[1]There is also an upward time trend running through the VMT per car data. American real income per capita was generally rising during this period, and driving definitely has a positive income elasticity of demand (see Box 3.1).

[2]"Econometric" studies are statistical studies of economic data. While these can get quite complicated, they basically are reliant on natural data, not on controlled "laboratory" experiments. Thus, an estimate of price elasticity would typically be generated by comparing: (1) different states or different countries with different gasoline prices and different gasoline consumption rates at a single time, noting how much less gasoline was consumed per capita in places where the prices were higher; or (2) a single state or country over a number of years, during which time the price and consumption of gasoline had varied, noting how much less gasoline was consumed per capita at times of higher prices.

[3]How does the Bureau of Labor Statistics (BLS) estimate the price today of a car that is no longer actually sold? It divides, on a year-by-year basis, any price increase into a pure price increase and a quality improvement cost. Consider a car that costs $10,000 in one year and $12,000 the next year.

But the newer model has a "gizmo" as a standard feature. If the gizmo is an entirely new feature, then its cost is estimated directly, say at $800, and that figure is subtracted from the $12,000 to estimate the cost of the old, gizmo-less car in the later year. The pure price increase is then considered to be the difference between $11,200 and $10,000, or 12%. If, however, the gizmo was available as an optional extra in the preceding year, say at a price of $700, then one can compare the $12,000 current price with the old price including the gizmo, $10,700, to find the pure price increase of $1300, or 12%. What if the gizmo is a piece of antipollution equipment that nobody wants but is mandated by the government? Is this quality improvement? Yes, says the BLS, arguing that we collectively find the equipment beneficial even if it is not privately demanded (Norwood, 1990).

[4]The data in Figure 3.4 are from 1991 but are converted into 1995 prices.

[5]Gasoline is nearly given away in some oil-rich developing countries—in Iran, for example, the price is 16 cents per gallon, in Ecuador 23 cents, and in Venezuela recently raised from only 11 cents to 30 cents (Gupta and Mahler, 1995; Schemo, 1996). Think about such pricing: is it smart to sell domestically at a low price what you can export at a high price? Who gains by such policy? Who loses (Q3.2)? By the way, in case you are curious why Japan's pre-tax retail price is so much higher than that of the other industrialized countries, it is not that Japan is an inefficient refiner of crude oil but rather that refiners there price as a cartel and gasoline is sold only at *very* full-service stations.

[6]Recall the definition of the term "income elasticity." It is the percentage change in the quantity demanded occasioned by a given percentage change in income. If a 10% increase in income causes a bigger than 10% increase in demand, the product's demand is income-elastic; if a 10% increase in income causes a smaller than 10% increase in demand, the product's demand is income-inelastic. There are also "inferior goods," with negative income elasticity, but for sure neither automobiles nor gasoline is in that category.

[7]Recall that a regressive tax is a tax that takes a larger percentage of a poor person's income than of a rich person's income.

[8]Recall that horizontal inequity occurs when two people, or families, with similar incomes are taxed differently for no compelling economic reason. Taxing apples and not oranges, for example, would mean that similar families would pay different taxes depending capriciously on whether they preferred apples or oranges.

[9]Why were there queues? Because, in the 1970s, whenever gasoline prices started to rise, the government used price controls to prevent the rise. Price controls create excess demand, and one way of rationing the scarce gasoline supplies is "first come, first served"—that is, queues.

Appendix: Who Really Pays a Gasoline Tax?

"To tax and to please,
no more than to love and be wise,
is not given to men."

Edmund Burke

Speech on American Taxation (1774)

The incidence of a tax—who really pays it—can be very different from the impact of that tax— who actually turns the tax revenue over to the government. The incidence of any tax depends upon the relative magnitudes of the price elasticities of demand and supply. Consider the very simple linear supply and demand functions

$$Q_s = (1 - E_s) + E_s P_s \qquad [3A.1]$$

$$Q_d = (1 + E_d) - E_d P_d, \qquad [3A.2]$$

where Q_s and Q_d are the quantities supplied and demanded, P_s and P_d are the prices received by suppliers and paid by demanders, and E_s and E_d are the price elasticities of supply and demand at the equilibrium price and quantity (i.e., $Q_s = Q_d = Q = 1$ and $P_s = P_d = 1$).[1A]

Now introduce a tax of t per unit. Regardless of whether the impact is on buyers or sellers, the effect is to drive a wedge between P_d and P_s, so that in the new supply–demand equilibrium, $P_d - P_s = t$. Again solving the previous two equations, we get

$$P_d = 1 + \frac{t E_s}{E_s + E_d} \qquad [3A.3]$$

$$P_s = 1 - \frac{tE_d}{E_s + E_d} \qquad\qquad [3A.4]$$

$$Q = Q_s = Q_d = 1 - \frac{tE_sE_d}{E_s + E_d} \qquad\qquad [3A.5]$$

The price that demanders pay has risen by a fraction of the tax (t), the fraction being the ratio of E_s to the sum of E_s and E_d. The price that suppliers receive has fallen by a fraction of the tax (t), the fraction being the ratio of E_d to the sum of E_s and E_d. The fraction of the tax paid by demanders divided by the fraction paid by the suppliers is therefore simply E_s/E_d. The higher E_s is, the greater is the incidence on demanders; the higher E_d is, the greater is the incidence on suppliers.

When an excise tax is imposed, the price paid by consumers goes up and consumers lose consumer surplus, and the price received by producers goes down and producers lose producer surplus.[2A] The government gains tax revenue. The extent to which the sum of the loss of consumer surplus and the loss of producer surplus exceeds the tax revenue is the deadweight loss (DWL) of the tax.

TAX ON IMPORTED OIL

Thus far, this appendix has been concerned with a tax on the production or consumption of gasoline in the United States—no distinction has been made between domestically produced oil and imported oil. We now look at a different sort of tax, a tariff on imported oil (with no tax at all on domestically produced oil). This examination will be briefer and without algebra.

When a U.S. tax is levied on imported oil, but not on domestic oil, the price that foreign oil producers actually get for their oil will be lower than what American oil producers get by the amount of the tariff. A U.S. oil tariff induces foreign oil producers to send less oil to the United States. This, in turn, reduces the total supply of oil here and puts upward pressure on the U.S. oil price. As the U.S. price rises, U.S. consumers use less petroleum and U.S. petroleum producers supply more oil. Comparing the before-and-after equilibria, the tariff induces the United States to consume less, import less, and produce more than before. Exactly how much more or less of each depends upon three price elasticities: of U.S. demand, of U.S. supply, and of foreign supply to the United States.

Thus, the incidence of the tariff is such that U.S. oil consumers and foreign suppliers of oil to the United States are made worse off, and U.S. oil producers and U.S. citizens as taxpayers are made better off (because the new tariff revenue lets the government either lower other taxes or spend more on programs that benefit its citizens). The four groups together must be worse off, but it is very possible that the three American groups together are made better off by the tariff. How could this be? The tariff is doing two things as far as the United States is concerned, one good and one bad. The bad effect is that we are taxing a segment of the oil market and hence creating deadweight loss for ourselves. The good effect is that we are exploiting our monopsonistic position as an oil importer.[3A] We cannot tell in general which effect will dominate. But the tariff definitely reduces our oil imports and hence our oil "vulnerability" (on which much more will be said in the next chapter).

How big should a U.S. tariff on oil be? There are literally hundreds of such estimates based on models of widely varying assumptions and sophistication. The suggested tariff also ranges widely, but the "ballpark estimate" is a tariff of $15 per barrel for vulnerability reasons and a tariff of $20 per barrel for monopsony reasons (OTA, 1994). These two tariffs together would mean a rise in U.S. gasoline prices of anywhere from $0.20 to $0.80, depending on the relevant price elasticities, but the gains in tariff revenues and rents of U.S. oil producers would more than offset the loss of consumer surplus.

Why does the United States not leap at this chance to extract welfare gains for Americans at the expense of foreigners, especially OPEC foreigners who have long tried to exploit us? Partly, the reasons are domestic: it is not easy to find a way to channel the tariff revenue to the oil consumers who lose from the tariff-induced price rise. Moreover, the tariff redistributes regional incomes to 9 states and away from the other 41 states (Elving, 1990). But the chief reason for rejecting an oil tariff is that foreigners may retaliate, either by disrupting their oil supplies to us or by levying new or higher tariffs on our exports to them.

ENDNOTES

[1A]The price elasticity of supply is positive, and that of demand negative, but remember we are ignoring the minus sign here for the price elasticity of demand. That is the reason for the minus sign in Equation [3A.2]. The curious intercepts in the supply and demand Equations, [3A.1] and [3A.2], were carefully chosen to simplify things by making these initial equilibrium values of P and Q equal to one.

[2A]Recall the definition of these two concepts of surplus. Consumer surplus is the excess of the maximum that consumers would be willing to pay for the product over the amount they actually pay for the product. Producer surplus is the excess of the amount producers actually receive for the product over the minimum that they would be willing to accept for the product.

[3A]Recall what monopsony means. It means that the buyer is not a price-taker but can affect the price by varying the amount demanded. A tariff restricts American oil import demand and pushes up the U.S. oil price, which hurts our consumers. But it also pushes down the price we have to pay to foreigners for imported oil, which benefits our citizens.

Energy and Air Pollution

CHAPTER 4

Fuel Efficiency

"I'd like to drive a tank."

Marcie Brogan

(who commutes 40 miles daily in a Hummer)

When the Organization of Petroleum Exporting Countries (OPEC) tripled the price of its crude oil in 1973 (from $12 to $36 per barrel in 1995 prices), it woke American policymakers up to the fact that the United States had gone from the world's largest exporter of petroleum to the world's largest importer since World War II. The price of gasoline, and other fossil fuels, quickly rose to reflect the new crude oil prices. Manufacturers, consumers, and drivers found ways to economize—energy consumption per unit of GNP fell by one-third in the United States over the next 20 years. But policymakers felt that market forces would fail to adequately reduce American energy consumption and began to mandate the increased fuel efficiency of American cars and light trucks.

We will look first at the question of what market failure prompted government intervention in gasoline demand, and then we will look at the form of that government involvement.

MARKET FAILURE IN GASOLINE

There are many possible reasons for suspecting market failure in a product like gasoline. Throughout the world, the exploration, refining, and selling of petroleum products has long been controlled by large firms in oligopolistic or monopolized national markets. The United States is a sufficiently large importer of oil that it could have monopsony power, which would mean that we could increase the welfare of our own citizens by reducing our imports.[1] Moreover, the consumption of petroleum products, especially in motor vehicles, generates many negative external costs, as we have outlined in Chapter 2 and will begin to examine closely in the next chapter. Where there are negative externalities, a free market will overproduce and overconsume.

Market failure may also emanate from the fact that fossil fuels are nonrenewable resources, which means that the optimal rate of exploitation is very sensitive to the interest (discount) rate and to knowledge about remaining reserves and future alternative power sources. Private firms might apply too high a discount rate, which would lead them to extract and exhaust the resource too rapidly. And it is possible to argue that governments might have better knowledge about reserves and alternatives and that this knowledge urges a different rate of utilization of those reserves than a private market would bring about.

But the U.S. government did not concern itself with reducing gasoline consumption until the mid-1970s, and all the preceding arguments existed long before then—except for one. When OPEC began to utilize its cartel power in 1973, it added a new element of monopoly to a market already fraught with monopolistic elements at the exploring, refining, and selling stages. Monopolies, however, do not necessarily extract nonrenewable resources too rapidly. On the contrary, facing a downward-sloped straight-line demand curve, a monopoly exploits its power by extracting the resource too slowly so that the current price is kept above competitive levels. A by-product of this too-high price is that the time over which the resource is utilized is stretched out, and the conversion to alternatively fueled vehicles would be made too late, not forced too early, from a social viewpoint.

There remains only one plausible reason for the sudden determination of the U.S. government in the 1970s to reduce American use of petroleum. The exercise of OPEC control over oil production—and the OPEC countries then owned nearly 90% of the world's known oil reserves—made it clear to American policymakers that the U.S. economy, powered by fossil fuels, was now hostage to foreign governments' decisions. We had become vulnerable—to use a phrase popular in the 1970s, we were "heavily dependent upon uncertain foreign oil sources."

This dependence added a perceived new external cost to gasoline consumption: the more oil we consumed, and hence the more oil we had to import, the more we as a society either had to endure risk of deprivation or had to devote additional resources to our, and our allies', military strength so that we could forcibly prevent such deprivation if it were threatened. Some see evidence of this in our spending an average of an additional $15 billion a year over the last decade or two on this account. Indeed, we spent over $50 billion in 1990 on "Operation Desert Storm" to free Kuwait from an invader that did in fact threaten our continued oil supplies (Hubbard, 1991; Greene and Leiby, 1993; Korb, 1996; Fuller and Lesser,

1997). If these costs had been "internalized" into gasoline prices over the past decade, it would have required an additional gasoline tax of something up to possibly $0.60 per gallon throughout the period.[2]

We have been spending more money in the Middle East because of our dependence on the oil there. Almost everybody agrees on that. What is at question is whether we *need* to spend more money in order to ensure our continued supply of oil. Most economic research says no, concluding that OPEC is at best a "clumsy cartel" (Adelman, 1980; Bohi and Toman, 1993; Griffin, 1985). It would be hard for any oil-exporting country, or group of countries, to stop oil imports into the United States without stopping their exports to countries that would happily redirect the oil to us. And if these countries ceased exporting oil altogether, with what would they pay for their imports?

Suppose, however, that OPEC did succeed in stopping oil shipments to the United States, even transshipments from other countries. The price of oil would rise dramatically in the United States. There would be huge profits available to OPEC members who defected from the oil sanction, either overtly leaving OPEC or covertly shipping oil anyway. The temptations to defect from a cartel are shown more formally in Box 4.2.

BOX 4.1   The Strategic Petroleum Reserve
In order to acquire a reserve that could be released when needed, thereby preventing a disruption in U.S. oil supplies and prices through OPEC import cutoffs, the U.S. federal government accumulated 600 million barrels of oil over 1977–1990 in underground salt domes in Texas and Louisiana.[3] The idea is clear. If OPEC were to shut off U.S. imports, the domestic U.S. price would rise dramatically; in the short run, the U.S. supply of oil and the U.S. demand for oil are each highly price-inelastic, and self-sufficiency might require near doubling of the U.S. price.[4] The strategic petroleum reserve (SPR) presumably reduces the risk of such a cutoff by making it less immediately profitable to OPEC.

In principle, such a SPR could even be profitable to the U.S. federal budget—after all, the goal is to buy oil when the price is low and stable, and then to sell it when it is high and rising. In fact, however, the United States has tended to acquire the SPR in times of high oil prices and not sell hardly at all.[5] Moreover, management, depreciation, and interest are costing something like $2 billion per year (Greene and Leiby, 1993; Blumstein and Komor, 1996). That's 2 cents per gallon of gasoline sold in the United States.

The other question that has been raised about the SPR is whether additions to the SPR make the *total* U.S. oil stockpile any larger. Government oil purchases raise current oil prices and reduce fears of future scarcity, thereby raising the cost and reducing the benefit of private stockpiling. One study estimated that, for every barrel of oil added to the SPR, one half barrel less is stockpiled privately in the United States (Smith, 1988).

BOX 4.2 OPEC and the "Prisoner's Dilemma"

With the formation of an active cartel, OPEC raised world oil prices from about $12 per barrel (in 1995 prices) to over $50 per barrel by the end of the decade. By 1986, however, the oil price was back down to $13. OPEC was unable to sustain its exercise of monopoly power. The cartel's failure reflected its inability to solve the "prisoner's dilemma." The dilemma is that, while earning monopoly profit requires member cooperation in the restriction of output, it is in each cartel member's own interest to cheat and produce a larger output than was mutually agreed on.

The "dilemma" can be illustrated as a two-person non-zero-sum game. Each player has to choose whether to cooperate and produce only an agreed share of the monopoly output or to cheat and produce more than that agreed share.

The payoff matrix is shown below. The two players are called A and B. The profit of each is shown in the cells, with A's profit given first, and B's second. For simplicity, the profit of each is taken to be, depending on the strategies chosen, either 1, 2, 3, or 4 (say, in billions of dollars).

Strategies for A	Strategies for B	
	Cooperate	Cheat
Cooperate	3,3	1,4
Cheat	4,1	2,2

Look at A's strategy choice. If B cooperates (by restricting B's output), A is better off cheating and producing excessively (4 > 3), and if B cheats, A is better off also cheating (2 > 1). No matter what B does, cheating is a dominant strategy for A. The same reasoning shows that cheating is a dominant strategy for B.[6]

In short, the dominant strategy for A and for B is to cheat regardless of what the other player does. As a result, however, each ends up with a profit of only 2 when a (monopoly) profit of 3 for each is available—if only the two cartel members could somehow agree to restrict their outputs to the joint-profit-maximizing level. Is there a way out of this "dilemma"?[7]

REDUCING THE USE OF GASOLINE

Whatever the actual motivation, American policymakers perceived a need after 1973 to restrict automobile and light truck consumption of gasoline. How? The Energy Policy and Conservation Act of 1975 imposed Corporate Average Fuel Economy (CAFE) standards on all auto and light truck manufacturers who sold vehicles in the United States.[8] The weighted average of miles per gallon (MPG) for each manufacturer's car sales was required to be at least 18 MPG by 1978 and 27.5 MPG by 1985.[9] Manufacturers that failed to meet this standard were to be fined $50 per vehicle sold for each gallon (of MPG rating) by which they failed.[10]

BOX 4.3 The "Gas Guzzler" Tax and the "Luxury" Tax

Beside CAFE, two taxes were introduced in the 1970s in an effort to reduce U.S. gasoline consumption, the "gas guzzler" tax and the automobile "luxury" tax.

The gas guzzler tax is an excise tax levied on new cars that fail to meet even moderate MPG standards. Currently, the tax begins at $1000 for cars that get 21.5–22.5 MPG and rises progressively to $7700 for cars that get less than 12.5 MPG.[11]

The luxury tax is an excise tax levied on new cars that sell at very high prices. Since high-priced cars are usually low-MPG cars, this also is, albeit indirectly, a tax on fuel inefficiency. As of 1998, the tax rate was 8% of the excess of the sales price over $36,000.[12]

Clearly, both of these taxes discourage the purchase of low-MPG cars (though not much). But do either discourage driving these cars once they are purchased (Q4.6)?

BOX 4.4 Gasoline Rationing

The U.S. government rejected the idea of gasoline rationing in the face of OPEC price increases, but it has not always rejected this idea. During World War II, though gasoline was not yet imported, the price elasticity of supply was low in the short run. In order to provide huge amounts of gasoline for military use without bidding up the price of gasoline, the government rationed civilian usage. Each motorist was given coupons that permitted the purchase of 5 gallons of gasoline per week (about two-thirds of the average prewar consumption at that time). These coupons, even if unused, could not be sold.

Why was the U.S. government unwilling to use the price mechanism to collect its wartime gasoline needs? Why was rationing used rather than "first come, first serve" queuing (Frech and Lee, 1987)? Why were the ration coupons passed out per licensed driver rather than per person? Why were the coupons nonmarketable? If we really want to reduce gasoline usage now, why do we not consider a return to gasoline rationing (Q4.7)?

One of the first questions CAFE raises is, why control the *average* fuel economy of a fleet of cars rather than the fuel economy of each car? Manufacturers like to provide a spectrum of cars, some large and powerful, and some small and fuel-efficient. With the average requirement, they could continue to do this. Indeed, the average requirement permitted car manufacturers to raise the MPG of their various models in a cost-effective way, equating the marginal cost of the CAFE-mandated higher MPG across their models. Big cars would have lower MPG because it is expensive to make them fuel-efficient; small cars would compensate for this by exceeding the CAFE standards because it is cheap to make them more fuel-efficient.

This much makes some sense. But it is hard to resist the next question. If the averaging of fuel-efficiency standards across each manufacturer's models permits them to achieve a more cost-effective increase in MPG, then would it not be even more cost-effective to permit such averaging on an *interfirm* as well as an *intrafirm* basis? This could have been achieved by permitting manufacturers to buy and sell CAFE excesses and CAFE shortages between firms.

HAS CAFE WORKED?

The real question, of course, is how effective have the CAFE standards been in re-ducing U.S. gasoline consumption? This is a big and difficult question. Actually, the answer involves three questions: (1) How have CAFE standards affected the fuel efficiency (MPG) of new cars? (2) How have the changes in new cars affected the composition and age of the overall car and light truck fleet? (3) To what ex-tent have changes in fuel efficiency been offset by increases in total vehicle-miles traveled (VMT)? We now look at each of these three questions in turn.

The fuel efficiency of new cars has improved a great deal since CAFE was intro-duced, with all major car producers and importers meeting all the CAFE deadlines on schedule (see Figure 4.1).[13] The introduction of lighter cars, greater horse-power-to-weight ratios, smaller engine sizes, front-wheel drive, and fuel injection meant that new U.S. automobiles nearly doubled their average MPG under CAFE standards. But how much of this improvement was due to the CAFE standards?

Most of this mileage improvement occurred in the late 1970s, during which pe-riod real retail gasoline prices were doubling (from around $1.10 in 1972 to around

---

BOX 4.5 Separate CAFE for Domestic and Imported Cars
When CAFE was introduced, there was union fear that U.S. auto manufacturers would respond by reducing the sale of domestic (low-MPG) vehicles and simply importing more of their foreign-produced high-MPG vehicles. To protect Ameri-can auto jobs, CAFE standards were placed separately on each of the domestic and imported fleets of auto companies that provided both kinds of cars.

In this era of international sourcing of parts, however, it is no easy task to define whether a car is imported or domestic. The law defined as domestic any car that has 75% or more of its parts produced in the United States (or Canada). Of course, this gave automakers one more degree of freedom for the CAFE game. By moving crit-ical parts production in and out of the United States, cars could be quickly reclassi-fied for CAFE purposes. Costly evasions ensued. For example, switching production of a few parts to Spain and Mexico let Ford reclassify its gas-guzzling Crown Victo-ria and Mercury Marquis as foreign and hence more easily meet its domestic CAFE standard. And General Motors at one time was even *flying* auto parts back and forth across the Atlantic.

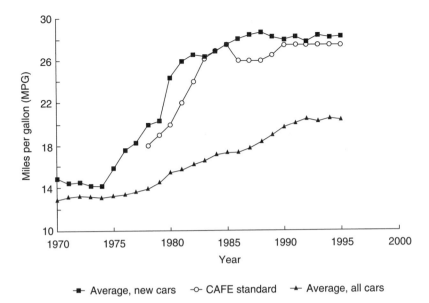

-■- Average, new cars   -○- CAFE standard   -▲- Average, all cars

FIGURE 4.1   Fuel Efficiency and CAFE Standards

$2.20 in 1981, in 1995 dollars). Only in the 1980s, when OPEC was no longer able to discipline itself to restrain output and real gasoline prices began to decline, did the major auto producers begin to have trouble meeting CAFE standards. At that time, CAFE standards stopped rising.[14] It is difficult not to conclude that CAFE standards for fuel efficiency rose when the market would have produced greater fuel efficiency in any case and that CAFE standards stopped rising when they began to require manufacturers to produce more fuel-efficient cars than consumers wanted to buy (Crandall et al., 1986; Leone and Parkinson, 1990).[15]

CAFE standards began to "bite" in the 1980s in the sense that if prices of vehicles were set to reflect costs of production, consumers would purchase so many of the lower-MPG vehicles that manufacturers would fail to meet the minimum fleet-average MPG standards. Manufacturers began to react to this dilemma with larger price markups for their lower-MPG vehicles and smaller price markups for their higher-MPG vehicles.[16]

As the bigger, lower-MPG vehicles that consumers wanted became relatively more expensive, consumers reacted in surprising ways. While many reluctantly either bought the now-cheaper higher-MPG vehicles that they did not really want or paid the higher prices for the lower-MPG vehicles that they did really want, others reacted either by buying vans, SUVs, and light trucks or by holding onto their old cars longer. Since trucks had less strict CAFE standards and since old cars had been built when there were less strict or no CAFE standards, these reactions meant that the average fuel efficiency of the overall auto fleet rose ever more slowly toward the CAFE standards on new cars (see Figure 4.1).

Look at the data. Light-truck sales in 1980 made up 18% of the total sales of passenger cars and light trucks (2.0 million out of 10.9 million); by 1993, light-truck sales had risen to 37% of the total (5.0 million out of 13.5 million). In November 1997, light-truck sales surpassed car sales in the United States for the first (peace) time in history (Bradsher, 1997g). During that same period, 1980-1993, the average age of registered cars rose from 6.6 years old to 8.3 years old; in 1980, 8% of the registered cars were retired from the active fleet, but in 1993 only 6% were retired (Bureau, 1995). Even though the fuel efficiency of new cars has doubled since 1975, the average fuel efficiency of all cars has risen by barely one-half and the average fuel efficiency all cars and small trucks together has risen by barely one-third.

While CAFE made new cars more expensive, it did not raise the marginal cost of driving miles (see again Equation [2.3]). To the contrary, as the MPG of new cars doubled, this in itself halved the gasoline component of driving costs per mile. How much "rebound" effect toward increased driving occurred as a result of these MPG improvements and the concomitant reduction in the price of driving? Estimates say about 10% (Greene, 1992).

Bottom line? Between 1980 and 1993, the total vehicle miles of car travel rose by 46%, more than offsetting the increase in fuel efficiency. Between the two forces, total U.S. consumption of gasoline went up by 15% over this period.

COULD CAFE WORK?

Is there a future for CAFE? After all, there is a limit to how many miles the average American driver wants to go in cars, so that ever higher MPG standards ought eventually to drive down total gasoline consumption. The issue here is at what cost? Both engineering estimates and evidence from abroad suggest that further

---

BOX 4.6 The Fuel Efficiency of U.S. Army Vehicles

While fears of gasoline shortage were forcing greater fuel efficiency onto civilian vehicles, what was happening to the fuel efficiency of military vehicles in the United States? The basic army vehicle used to be a Jeep (GP), which gets 17–20 MPG. In the last decade, the army has switched to the Humvee (HMMWV, also called a Hummer), which gets only 6–8 MPG if gasoline-powered (more if diesel). During World War II, the basic army tank, the Sherman, got 5 MPG (with "highway" driving). Today's tank, the M1 Abrams, gets less than 0.5 MPG (Major C. T. White, personal communication).

Am I trying to suggest that our military vehicles should also be required to get 20-odd MPG? Hardly. But the comparison does underline how cost-ineffective it is to arbitrarily force certain vehicles to achieve high MPG standards and not address at all the fuel efficiency of other vehicles—such as heavy trucks. (On this issue, see also Box 14.5.)

increases in the fuel efficiency of the American automobile will be very expensive unless cars are reduced in size a great deal, many safety and comfort features are removed, or cars are basically redesigned (OTA, 1991b; NRC, 1992). New U.S. cars now get almost as much MPG as European cars even though fuel prices are much higher in Europe than in the United States — this hints that further MPG rises would be expensive.

A numerical example illustrates the problem (Eads, 1995). Suppose a government policy raised automotive fuel efficiency from an average of 14.3 MPG to an average of 16.7 MPG. This would save 1 gallon of gasoline for every 100 miles driven. That kind of MPG improvement did not prove very costly. Suppose government policy later tries to increase fuel efficiency from an average of 50 to 100 MPG. That would prove very expensive, but it would also save only 1 gallon of gasoline for every 100 miles driven.

Basically, higher CAFE standards would force automakers to create and sell cars that are not wanted by American consumers; given the current price of gasoline, American car buyers are continually showing that they want vehicles that guzzle gas and generate horsepower.[17]

Gasoline consumption can be reduced by either increasing MPG or decreasing vehicle-miles traveled. Cost-effective policies to reduce gasoline consumption should push each of these two factors to the point where the marginal cost of saving another gallon of gasoline is the same for each factor. We have pushed higher MPG hard, and pushed lower miles not at all. At this point in America's MPG history, the welfare of drivers would be reduced much less by measures that induce Americans to drive fewer miles than by measures that force Americans to further increase the fuel efficiency of the vehicles they drive (Charles, 1991; NRC, 1992). The easiest way to reduce miles is through gasoline taxes.

Think how much more gasoline taxes could do than can CAFE. CAFE standards have no direct effect on the kind of cars that consumers demand or on the kind of gasoline-using options that consumers add—like air conditioning and four-wheel drive. CAFE regulations affect only MPG and have no direct effect on miles that new cars are driven—and the indirect effect is perverse since higher MPG reduces the marginal private variable cost of driving. CAFE has no direct effect on old cars, except to encourage people to keep their old gas guzzlers longer. And CAFE has a lesser effect on both the mileage and the cost of light trucks, so it induces people to switch toward these less fuel-efficient vehicles.

Higher gasoline taxes, on the other hand, provide incentives to use less gasoline, in old cars as well as new, and in light trucks as well as cars. In the short run, gasoline taxes induce people to drive fewer miles; in the long run, they also induce people to buy more fuel-efficient vehicles. A gasoline tax of something like $0.35 per gallon would have achieved the same fuel savings as CAFE; but, as study after study has shown, CAFE has cost Americans (in lost consumer and producer surplus) many times as much per gallon of gasoline saved (Leone and Parkinson, 1990; Kleit, 1990; Charles, 1991; Nivola and Crandall, 1995).

While gasoline taxes can reduce U.S. gasoline consumption, and at low social cost, a good question is whether such taxes can reduce the U.S. dependency on foreign oil. Middle East oil is much cheaper to produce than U.S. oil, so that if U.S. oil refiners were given a free choice where to purchase the reduced supplies that increased gasoline taxes would necessitate, the United States would continue to import huge quantities of oil. Only U.S. production would decline as U.S. oil demand declined.

The United States could prevent this outcome, say by levying sufficiently large import taxes (tariffs) on imported oil. While this might be in the U.S. interest, since it would reduce our oil imports, such a tariff would impose losses in consumer surplus for our own citizens—unless the United States were exercising newly discovered and significant monopsony power in the world oil market (Walls, 1990). Moreover, such a tariff would run counter to global efficiency.

Globally, in order to minimize the present value of the global resources used up to extract the planet's oil, we should extract the planet's low-cost oil first and extract its high-cost oil only later (or not at all if a new lower-cost fuel emerges in the interim).[18] United States and global interests may diverge here. Finally, an oil tariff would deflect our demand from foreign to domestic oil and would thereby deplete U.S. oil reserves more rapidly. Ironically, the reduced dependence today on foreign oil sources would mean greater dependence tomorrow.

FINAL THOUGHTS

This look back at CAFE teaches us an important lesson about policy tools. When the government tries to make people do something that they don't want to do—like save on gasoline—people will adjust their behavior in lots of hard-to-predict ways so as to continue doing what they want to do. So policy tools must directly attack the behavior that the government wants to change. Changing the MPG of new cars was not a direct enough attack on mileage and gasoline consumption. When the policy instrument (the cup) is far from the policy target (the lip), there is, as we are often told, many a slip. There was a lot of "slippage" between the CAFE policy "cup" and the gasoline-use target "lip."

There are also doubts, in my mind at least, whether we should even be trying to save gasoline in order to avoid foreign oil dependence. We are dependent on foreign coffee also, but we don't limit the number of cups each U.S. coffee-maker can serve each day. However, as we shall see in Chapter 6, worries about global warming are also worries about gasoline consumption. And these may be more serious concerns.

In any case, there are hints that CAFE's clunkiness may mean its end and that other means of reducing our gasoline consumption may be tried. The recent "Comprehensive National Energy Strategy" of the Department of Energy does not once mention CAFE (DOE, 1998). John Dingell, long a Congressional

---

BOX 4.7 The International Energy Agency
The United States was not the only country to panic in 1973 over OPEC's new-found ability to suddenly curtail world oil supplies. In 1974, the International Energy Agency (IEA) was created by 16 industrialized nations (5 more joined later). Its purpose was to ensure that if oil supplies were sharply reduced, each member country would suffer an equal percentage decrease in its domestic consumption. Those whose consumption was falling less would be obligated to sell oil to those whose consumption was falling more—presumably at the new higher world prices though that was never entirely clear (Salant, 1984; Horwich and Weiner, 1984).

Fortunately, no action was ever taken by the IEA, which continues to exist. Think about the mess that would have ensued if it had tried to enforce equal percentage cuts in oil consumption across its member countries (Q4.9).

---

spokesman for auto manufacturers and the auto union, has stated that nothing less than higher energy taxation will work. Even automakers are publicly recognizing it. As Chevrolet head John Middlebrook tersely put it, "With gasoline prices where they are in this country today, people are just not driven to buy fuel-efficient products" (WSJ, 1997a).

ENDNOTES

[1]If it sounds funny to you that we could increase our welfare by reducing our consumption, look again at the last part of the appendix to Chapter 3.

[2]Some estimate the security costs of oil to run as high as $3.00 per gallon (Broadman, 1986); but such estimates essentially attribute the entire U.S. defense budget to the protection of the U.S. gasoline supply. Others remind us that what we spend to correct an externality is not a good measure of the damage done to us by that externality (Bohi and Toman, 1993). Still others maintain that, no matter what happens in the Middle East, oil will continue to flow to the United States and Europe and hence that there is no externality on this account (Fuller and Lesser, 1997).

[3]This is a little over 1 month's consumption—or 2 months' imports—for the United States.

[4]Those who like an algebraic challenge can prove that if the U.S. short-run oil demand curve has a price elasticity of exactly (minus) ½, the U.S. short-run oil supply curve has a price elasticity of exactly (plus) ½, and the United States currently imports exactly half of its total oil consumption, a total cutoff of imports would double the U.S. price (Q4.1).

[5]By the way, U.S. law requires that half the oil purchased for the SPR must be carried in (high-cost) U.S.-flag tankers, a policy intended to reduce the dependence of United States on foreign oil tankers. What does this requirement do to the delivered price at which SPR oil is purchased? Incidentally, this use of U.S. tankers ends up costing much more than would direct construction and/or operating subsidies for the same number of U.S. tankers supported (Tarpgaard, 1986). Can you figure out why (Q4.2)?

[6]This is called a Nash equilibrium, a pair of strategies from which neither player wants to change unilaterally. You can work it out more formally if you want. Let Player A choose to cooperate a random

fraction, a, of the time, and let Player B choose to cooperate a random fraction, b, of the time. The expected profit of Player A is

$$\text{Exp. Profit A} = 3ab + a(1\text{-}b) + 4(1\text{-}a)b + 2(1-a)(1-b).$$

Think about what value of a Player A should choose (Q4.3).

[7]Here is a hint: suppose they play this "game" over and over again. Is there then a way for each to "teach" the other not to cheat? Recall tit for tat (Q4.4). For more on the "prisoner's dilemma" and the analysis of many other non-zero-sum games, see Dixit and Nalebuff (1991).

[8]Speed limits on Interstates were also lowered, from 65 to 55 MPH. This increased fuel efficiency, which peaks at even slower speeds than 55 MPH, and it raised the price of driving (see Equation [2.3]). It is estimated to have reduced gasoline consumption by about 5% (Lesser and Weber, 1989). We return to speed limits in Chapter 13.

[9]You may find the following arithmetic puzzle interesting. If the CAFE standard were 25 MPG, and a manufacturer sold two cars, one with 20 MPG and the other with 30 MPG, would the manufacturer have met the CAFE standard? Curiously, the answer is no. Work it out, using the assumption, which the government makes, that both cars are driven the same number of miles (Q4.5).

[10]The year refers to the *model* year, not the calendar year. CAFE standards were also set on light trucks, somewhat later and somewhat lower. Today, while car standards are 27.5 MPG, those for light trucks remain at 20.7 MPG.

[11]The gas guzzler tax applies to less than 2% of all car sales, so it is of little practical importance. It is also conceptually incorrect, for it taxes automakers differently even if they achieve the same fleet-average MPG if some firms mix in some gas guzzlers and other firms do not. Much discussed recently is a proposal to convert this tax into a system of "feebates" (i.e., fees and rebates), whereby low-MPG cars are taxed and high-MPG cars are subsidized. The advantage, beyond the fact that it would affect the decisions of all car buyers, is that it could be designed to be revenue-neutral—with tax revenues exactly balanced by subsidy expenditures—and hence politically more palatable.

[12]The luxury tax was 10% until September 1996 and is currently scheduled to be phased down by one percentage point per year.

[13]Sometimes the CAFE requirements were met legally but not in fact. For example, in January 1998, General Motors realized that it was not going to meet the standards for the 1998 model year, so it simply called some of its bigger vehicles "1999 models," postponing the problem until the next year (Miller, 1998). What will happen next year (who said politicians were short-sighted)? But it is not really that short-sighted—as of 1 January 1999, the Department of Transportation permits them to bring out year 2000 models.

[14]In the mid-1980s, the CAFE standards were temporarily relaxed lest GM and Ford suffer heavy tax burdens for failure to meet the current CAFE standard.

[15]Of course, producers of heavy luxury cars were constrained early (Greene, 1990); some—such as BMW, Jaguar, and Mercedes-Benz—simply stopped trying to meet CAFE standards and paid the fines. Rolls-Royce is exempt because it produces fewer than 10,000 cars per year. None of the American "Big Three" carmakers has ever suffered CAFE fines, but, because they produce a mix of big and small cars, it has been more costly for the American manufacturers to meet the CAFE standards than it has been for the Japanese, which means that CAFE inadvertently gave a competitive advantage to the Japanese manufacturers.

[16]Some people have suggested that CAFE thereby permitted GM and Ford, America's major big-car builders, to more fully exploit their duopoly power in the low-MPG vehicle market (Nivola and Crandall, 1995). To refresh yourself on why two firms cannot always agree on a joint profit-maximizing price, recall that U.S. antitrust laws forbid explicit collusion and that, even with an agreed price, each firm would be tempted to cheat by cutting its price below the agreed level and stealing high-profit sales from the other firm (see Box 4.2).

[17]The average horsepower of new domestic cars is now back above 140 for the first time since the early 1970s (Child, 1995).

[18]Recall what is meant by present value. One dollar today, banked in a deposit account earning an interest rate of i per year, will be worth $\$(1+i)$ next year. Reasoning in the reverse direction, one dollar next year is worth less than one dollar today; indeed, it is worth $(1/[1+i])$, or $(1+i)^{-1}$, dollars today. In general, one dollar T years from now is worth $(1+i)^{-T}$ dollars today. The present value of all oil extraction costs is a sum: this year's extraction cost plus next year's extraction cost times $(1+i)^{-1}$ plus the following year's extraction cost times $(1+i)^{-2}$, etc. Show that the present value of extraction costs is minimized by extracting cheaper oil sources first. A hint: consider just two barrels of oil, one with a higher cost than the other, and extract one barrel this year and one next year (Q4.8). It is just another version of the old farm adage, pick the low-hanging fruit first.

CHAPTER 5

Air Pollution

*"The health of nations
is more important
than the wealth of nations."*

Will Durant
What Is Civilization?

Air pollution, particularly in cities, has been increasingly viewed as a serious health problem in the United States, and those who generate these external costs have been increasingly regulated over the past half-century. Automobiles, or more generally transportation—called "mobile-source" emitters—contribute significantly to three of the major elements of urban air pollution: carbon monoxide (CO), nitrogen oxides (NO_x), and hydrocarbons (HCs, also called volatile organic compounds, VOCs). (See Table 5.1.)

Carbon monoxide irritates the respiratory tract and causes coronary damage; nitrogen oxides and hydrocarbons contribute to the formation of smog (ozone), which in turn can cause discomfort in healthy persons and serious complications for people with respiratory illness. High concentrations of particulate matter are associated with elevated rates of death and hospitalization for pulmonary diseases (EPA, 1996a; EPA, 1996b).[1] As long as polluters do not pay the costs of this air pollution, they will generate too much of it.

IMPROVING AIR QUALITY

The question has long been not whether or not to reduce air pollution, but by how much and by what means. Since the extent of the reduced discomfort and

TABLE 5.1   U.S. Air Pollution Emissions from Man-Made Sources

Source	Millions of short tons per year				
	CO	NO_x	Hcs	SO_x	PM
Transportation	77	11	9	1	1
Fuel combustion	5	12	1	18	1
Industrial processes	7	1	11	2	1
Other	11	0	3	0	0
Total	98	24	23	22	4

Note: SO_x are sulfur oxides and PM is particulate matter. The data are for 1994. Zero means less than 0.5 million tons; totals may not add due to rounding.
Source: EPA, 1995a.

illness is not clear—and the measurement of peoples' willingness-to-pay (WTP) for reduced discomfort and illness is uncertain—it is not easy to know how much the pollution should be reduced. But it has always been clear that reducing automotive air pollution had to be part of the overall strategy.

The approach of the federal government has been to define threshold concentrations of the major air pollutants, with the thresholds being levels above which serious health problems are encountered. These thresholds are generally exceeded in large cities, where autos, factories, and electricity generators are concentrated. And the damage done by any given level of air pollution, whatever it is and whatever it costs, is clearly higher in places where population densities are higher.

Different policy approaches have been taken for mobile-source and stationary-source generators of air pollution, and we shall focus on the mobile-source policies. Public concern about the automotive contribution to air pollution began in California in the 1950s, and federal policy dates back to the Clean Air Act of 1970. This act required that CO, NO_x, and HC emissions per vehicle-mile traveled (VMT) be reduced by 1981 to a small fraction of their precontrol levels. Since then the standard has been tightened and is expected to require "99% emission-free" new cars by the 1999 model year (WSJ, 1997b; EPA, 1998).[2]

The targets and achievements of the 1970s are summarized in Table 5.2. The target reductions ran around 80–90%, the actual reductions on new model cars ran around 70–80%, and the actual emissions reductions for all cars ran around 30–60%. Since, during this period, total automobile VMT rose by 24%, this means that the total automotive emissions in 1981 were reduced from 1970 levels by only 42% for CO, 11% for NO_x, and 53% for HC.

The good news from these figures is that there was a sizable reduction in air pollution, at least with respect to CO and HCs, if not NO_x, and this reduction was almost certainly due entirely to the Environmental Protection Agency (EPA) regulations. Individual car owners had no more incentive in 1981 than in 1970 to

TABLE 5.2   Actual and Target Air Pollution Rates of U.S. Automobiles

	CO	NO$_x$	HCs
1970 (grams per vehicle-mile)			
Actual, new models	58.0	4.4	4.8
Actual, all autos	52.3	4.3	9.4
1981 (grams per vehicle-mile)			
Target, new models	3.4	1.0	0.4
Actual, new models	14.8	1.3	1.1
Actual, all autos	24.3	3.1	3.6
Percentage reduction:			
Target, new models	94	77	92
Actual, new models	74	70	77
Actual, all autos	54	28	62

Note. The CO standard has not since changed, but the NO$_x$ standard was lowered to 0.4 in 1994, and the HCs standard was lowered to 0.25 in 1994.
Source: Crandall et al., 1986.

voluntarily reduce their emissions or to demand more emission-efficient vehicles. The bad news is that the actual reductions fell far short of the targeted reductions, and air quality in many parts of the United States is still below the National Ambient Air Quality Standards (NAAQS). These so-called "nonattainment" regions consist roughly of the east coast from Virginia to Maine, the west coast from San Diego to San Francisco, and many of the major cities in between the coasts. The number of such areas has shown no sign of declining in recent years.

BENEFIT–COST ANALYSIS

Have the air quality benefits so far been worth the costs? Probably yes. (The details of the benefit-cost analysis are sufficiently complex to be relegated to the appendix to this chapter.) While benefit–cost studies of U.S. air pollution controls have varied widely in the past—some concluding that the benefits fall short of the costs—there is now strong evidence that many tens of thousands of deaths—perhaps hundreds of thousands of deaths—are prevented each year by our air pollution policies. If only 10,000 lives are saved each year by automotive air pollution controls, overall automotive air pollution policy definitely passes its benefit–cost test.

That the policy's overall benefits exceed overall costs does not prove that the policy has been the right one. It may have done too much or too little, and what it has done may have been achieved at too high a cost. We do not know much about the first issue—whether we have done too much or too little—but we do know that what we have done has *not* been cost-effective. To be cost-effective, we must make the marginal cost of pollution reduction the same for different cars, different policies, and different aspects of abatement. For the automotive part of the program, there are several ways in which policies have imposed high costs in one direction and ignored cheaper ways to alleviate air pollution in another direction.

FAILURE AT COST-EFFECTIVENESS

We turn now to five specific ways in which automotive air pollution policy could become more cost-effective. Some of these are complements to others, but for the most part, they are substitutes, listed in decreasing order of effectiveness.

1. *Emissions per mile versus vehicle-miles traveled.* EPA regulations have all been aimed at reducing emissions per mile; none have sought to reduce mileage itself. The total annual emissions of the entire vehicle fleet is, literally, the product of these two variables, emissions per mile and miles per year.[3] A cost-effective reduction in emissions would equate the marginal cost of reducing emissions by reducing emissions per mile with the marginal cost of reducing emissions by reducing miles per year. The EPA's narrow focus on only the emission rate means that any reduction in emissions has been achieved at an unnecessarily high social cost.[4]

If emissions are the problem, the correct policy attack is on emissions. An effective Pigovian tax is easy to conceive. Inspect every car periodically, identify its emissions rates of critical air pollutants, and levy a tax that is proportional to the emissions rates per mile times the miles driven since the last inspection (Mills and White, 1978; Harrington *et al.*, 1994–95).[5]

2. *New cars versus other vehicles.* The EPA regulates the maximum permissible rate of emissions of new cars but not of old cars. And the emissions requirements for new light trucks (including sport utility vehicles) and heavy trucks are much less stringent than those on new cars (Bradsher, 1997f; Blum, 1998). Total emis-

---

BOX 5.1 EPA's Brief Attack on Miles Driven
During the 1970s, when new-model emission standards still affected few of the cars being driven, the EPA despaired—with the legal prodding of the National Resources Defense Council—of reducing emissions through new-model standards alone. So EPA calculated how few miles cars would have to drive to move the nonattainment areas to attainment. Los Angeles, for example, was simply ordered to reduce its gasoline consumption by 82% by means of gasoline rationing! Needless to say, California challenged this order in the courts, and eventually the U.S. Congress called off this EPA approach to cars.

sions, however, are the sum of emissions from all cars and trucks.[6] Since only a small fraction of registered vehicles are replaced each year, this means that only a small fraction of registered vehicles will meet emission standards in the year in which they come into force. Indeed, as pollution-control costs push up new-car prices, consumers have an incentive to keep old cars longer and to switch to new light trucks, where the cost of meeting the less stringent truck regulations is lower. The average age of the U.S. auto fleet has increased from 5 years old in 1970 to 8 years old in the 1990s, and the fraction of noncommercial vehicles that are light trucks has doubled over that period. And light trucks and old cars are the worst polluters.[7]

The emissions tax previously suggested would solve this problem, since heavily driven, heavily emitting trucks and old cars would become heavily taxed. But there are other ways to accelerate the retirement of old cars:

a. A registration tax that rises with the age of the car. This is on the right track since the tax would rise with the typical car's air-polluting propensity. But it isn't the right Pigovian tax; think about why not (Q5.2). Also, it has such regressive implications for income distribution that it is rarely considered.

b. Government or industry purchase of old cars at a price above their economic value (called "cash for clunkers").[8] This is close to a Pigovian subsidy for the abatement of a negative externality. This avoids the regressive aspect of the tax in (a), but it has its own problems—it would require budgeted funds and it would be most successful in attracting cars that are little used or about to be scrapped anyway (so-called "zombie cars").[9]

c. Stiff auto inspections that either refuse registration to heavily polluting, and usually older, vehicles or require such expensive maintenance and repairs that the owners are induced to switch to newer cars. This is done in both Western Europe and Japan, partly for pollution reasons, partly for safety reasons, and partly as a stimulus for new-car sales.

d. Exemption from car-purchase taxes of buyers who trade in (for scrapping) a car that is over a certain number of years old. This is also done in many countries of Western Europe, again partly for pollution, partly for safety, and partly as a new-car sales stimulus.

3. *Attainment areas versus nonattainment areas.* All new cars must meet the same emissions standards. This imposes unnecessary costs in parts of the United States where the air is already sufficiently clean (the "attainment areas") and the benefits of reduced air pollution are small; these areas are nevertheless required to invest in the same high-cost emissions controls as are needed in places with unhealthy air (the "nonattainment areas"). As a result, at least half of American cars are overregulated (Grad *et al.,* 1975).

The emissions tax already suggested solves this problem since the size of the tax would be higher in nonattainment areas and lower, or even zero, in attainment areas. But there are other ways to address this problem, too. One way is a "two-car strategy," whereby low-pollution vehicles would not be required in attainment

---

BOX 5.2 CAFE and Air Pollution

The EPA mandates a maximum rate of emissions per mile for every car, whether it is fuel-efficient or not. Since emissions are roughly proportional to gallons in uncontrolled cars, this means that cars that use more gallons per mile need more extensive, and hence more expensive, emissions-control equipment. Presumably, the EPA chose the per-mile basis over the per-gallon basis in order to reinforce the CAFE efforts toward greater fuel efficiency (Khazzoom, 1988 and 1991). As a result, while the MPG of individual cars can vary a lot (within the need for a fleet average that meets CAFE standards), emissions per mile cannot vary, and hence emissions per mile should be independent of MPG.

All this is true for new cars. But, over time, the emissions equipment becomes less efficient as it goes undermaintained and underrepaired. There is a gradual reemergence of the basic relationship between emissions and gallons that is found for uncontrolled combustion. The effect of this breakdown of emissions-control equipment is stronger in fuel-inefficient vehicles. Thus, in fact, we find for old cars a negative relation between emissions per mile and MPG (Harrington, 1997). If CAFE boosted MPG, it helped to reduce air pollution as well.

---

areas. This approach is very second-best to the emissions tax since it limits itself essentially to a two-tier tax—a car either qualifies or it does not qualify. There are other problems with it, such as defining the relevant area: if the area is too small, suburbanized sprawl (and longer commutes from) just out of the high-car-cost areas would be encouraged, and if the area is too big, high-cost cars would continue to be required where they were not needed. Nevertheless, it would achieve a greater differential between the pollution standards in attainment and nonattainment areas.

4. *Car-specific versus fleet-average controls.* Costs of emission control are lower for some types of vehicles, engines, and pollutants than for others. Every new vehicle is nevertheless required to meet the same emissions standards. This suggests three ways to make policies more cost-effective:

a. CAFE-like averaging across different models of each manufacturer's fleet. If manufacturers could meet emissions standards on average, they would presumably exceed the standards on some models and fall short of the standards on others, depending on the relative costs of meeting standards. The same total emissions would ensue, but at a lower cost. The EPA does allow such averaging for heavy-duty truck engine manufacturers, but not for cars and light trucks.

b. Marketable pollution standards. Cost effectiveness could be further enhanced if, instead of averaging across each fleet, the EPA permitted averaging across the entire new vehicle market. Manufacturers that could meet standards cheaply could exceed the standards and sell their surpluses to other manufacturers that find it costly to meet standards. Estimates of cost savings from use of such marketable permits run as high as 20% (Kling, 1994).

BOX 5.3 Controlling Gasoline Emissions during Refueling
As air pollution from auto tailpipes has become tightly controlled, concern has shifted to controlling gasoline vapor (HC) emissions during refueling (OTA, 1989). There are two ways to do this: (1) the installation of a vapor-recovery system on service station gasoline pumps (called "Stage II" controls), and (2) the addition of vapor-control devices on each new vehicle (called "onboard" controls).

The two systems are equally effective in controlling HCs, they cost almost exactly the same dollars per pound of pollution prevented, and neither system adds anything useful once the other system is installed.

Which policy makes more sense? Clearly Stage II controls, for two reasons. One, they can be installed immediately whereas onboard controls would only become effective gradually, as new cars replace the old cars that do not have onboard controls. Two, Stage II controls can be targeted into the worst air quality nonattainment areas whereas onboard controls would eventually be in all cars whether the area they were being driven in needed the extra pollution prevention or not.

Politically, the petroleum industry fought the Stage II controls, the automobile industry fought the onboard controls, and environmentalists demanded one or the other. Guess how the U.S. Congress solved the dilemma. It mandated *both* systems![10]

---

c. Averaging across pollutants. Some engines and some fuels meet some air pollution standards very easily and others only very expensively (Sperling, 1995).[11] The EPA could offer trade-off rates between pollutants so that manufacturers could exceed some standards in order to fall short of others. The trade-off rates could be adjusted over time to attain the desirable mix of pollution abatement.

5. *Pollution standards in theory versus in practice.* New cars meet the EPA emissions standards "in theory" but not always in practice.[13] The discrepancy arises in several ways:

a. New models are certified as meeting emissions standards through EPA testing of preproduction prototypes.[14] There is no close monitoring to ensure that production vehicles continue to fully meet these standards, and while cars are supposed to continue to meet the standards until they have been driven 50,000 miles, few are actually tested to that extent. The EPA itself has estimated that new cars in practice emit at two to four times the allowed rate (Crandall *et al.*, 1986; Krupnick, 1993).

b. Emissions-control equipment does not operate very efficiently under the conditions of much of actual automobile usage. The backbone of the control system is the catalytic converter, which is placed between the engine and the tailpipe and removes pollutants from the exhaust stream. But catalytic converters only function efficiently when they are warmed up, and one-half of all auto trips in the United States are of less than 5 miles (Nadis and MacKenzie, 1993).[15]

BOX 5.4 The Transition to Market Incentives

In the early 1990s, California made two changes in its auto air pollution policy. One was the much heralded (and since rescinded) electric-vehicle mandate, whereby an increasing fraction of the vehicles sold had to be electric in future years. The other, much less publicized change, was the low-emission vehicle (LEV) program that allowed auto manufacturers to average, bank, and trade emission standards.

By averaging, the auto sellers can average pollution rates across their entire fleets rather than having to meet them for each model. In this respect, it means the CAFE averaging procedure has been extended to emissions. By banking, it permits manufacturers who exceed the standards in particular years to accumulate the surpluses in order to cover possible shortcomings in the future. Since the standards are becoming ever more restrictive year by year, this encourages manufacturers to get ahead of the standards when they are less strict and hence can be met at lower cost.[12] Finally, by trading, it permits manufacturers who more than meet the standards to sell their surpluses to other manufacturers who have failed to meet the standards.

Each of these changes makes the California auto air pollution reductions more cost-effective.

---

c. Most owners of cars have no incentive to keep their cars' catalytic converters and other pollution control equipment in working order. Repair and maintenance costs are borne entirely by the owner, while the benefits of the improved air are received by other people. Only in urban areas with substandard air (i.e., the "nonattainment areas") are owners required to submit to periodic inspections to ensure that their cars continue to meet the emissions standards, and even for these, the tests are often rudimentary, friendly, failed by few, not required of older cars, and with a ceiling on any mandated repair costs.[16]

As just seen, while there is much scope for making old policies more cost-effective, it is also interesting to look at some of the new directions that automotive air pollution policies are taking:

1. *Less polluting fuels.* The Clean Air Act Amendments of 1990 not only established still tougher "tailpipe" standards for automobiles but also mandated the increased use of "reformulated" fuels in nonattainment areas. There are a wide range of such fuels—oxygenated fuels, compressed natural gas, methanol, and ethanol—all of which are capable of reducing smog-producing emissions. The problem is that all are costly in the production cost of the fuel, or in the adaptation cost of the vehicle, or in their potential for polluting groundwater, or in the reduction in convenience to the user.[17]

2. *Battery-powered electric cars.* Long available as curiosities, electric cars are gradually appearing as contenders in the marketplace. Their social (but not private) advantage is reduced externality cost—the generation of the electricity they use to recharge their batteries can be done in plants located away from densely populated

BOX 5.5 "Cup-Lip Slippage"

Pigovian taxes should be levied directly on the activity generating the external cost. When they are levied on something else, distant but "sort of related," there is room for "many a slip." Examples of such "cup–lip slippage" abound in the gasoline/pollution area.

Recall that pickup trucks, sport utility vehicles, and minivans must maintain a fleet average fuel efficiency of 20.7 MPH. But consumers are currently buying so many of the high-horsepower, fuel-inefficient versions of these vehicles that Ford, GM, and Chrysler are all having serious trouble meeting these CAFE standards. In the past, automakers have resorted to lower prices in order to induce customers to buy their fuel-efficient vehicles, but this of course hurts profits. What to do?

In an effort to encourage the use of alternative fuels—such as ethanol—the government decided to *assume* that "flex-fuel" vehicles, those which can also be operated on ethanol, will in fact be operated half the time on gasoline and half on ethanol.[18] The government then counts the miles per *gasoline* gallon for the alternate fuel in calculating the overall MPG for CAFE purposes.[19] What this all boils down to is that a vehicle with an MPG of 20 (using gasoline only) ends up counting as a vehicle with an MPG of 33 if it is capable of running on ethanol. Chrysler has already started producing such vehicles, and GM and Ford will also shortly (Bradsher, 1997a; Reitman and Christian, 1997; Job and Lankard, 1998).

The "flex-fuel" system will add some $300 to the cost of these vehicles—though less as a "learning curve" kicks in.[20] Who do you think will pay this $300—the buyers of the flex-fuel vans or the buyers of the other Ford and Chrysler vehicles? There are now only 40 retail outlets in the entire nation that pump 85% ethanol, and while ethanol costs a little less than regular gasoline, it gets poorer mileage and hence raises the cost per mile of operating the vehicle. Not many of these vehicles will ever taste ethanol![21]

But why waste money on an engine that can burn a fuel that it will never be asked to burn? Ford has a better idea. It is planning to bring out a 3-ton, 20-foot van with twice the engine size of the typical minivan. It will get something like 14 MPG (Bradsher, 1997c). Will not such a gas-guzzler destroy any hopes Ford has of complying with CAFE standards? No. The wagon will be so heavy that it will not be defined as a "light vehicle" and hence its MPG will not be counted in that fleet average—and "heavy vehicles" are not subject to CAFE standards. Chevy is already selling such a vehicle (Bradsher, 1997f).

There is also talk about stiffening the air pollution standards for sport utilities and light trucks. But the proposed California law would exempt vehicles weighing more than 7000 pounds (Rechtin, 1997). See the possible cup-lip slippage?

and polluted areas. Their (social and private) disadvantages are high initial cost (two to five times as much as similar fossil-fueled cars), short range between recharges (one-third to one-sixth that of most fossil-fueled cars), and the need for frequent and expensive battery replacements (every 2 years, at a cost over $1000).[22]

3. *Hybrid cars.* Called "hybrid" because they use both a gasoline engine and an electric motor, these cars can attain fuel efficiency over 100 MPG by using a small engine and avoiding energy waste because of their steady operation. When greater power is needed, a battery-driven electric motor kicks in; when excess power is being produced, it is used to recharge the batteries.[23] The addition of a flywheel makes the vehicle even more fuel-efficient because power is not lost when the car is being braked (Lovins and Lovins, 1995). Like pure electric cars, fuel cost and air pollution per mile are low, but initial cost is still very high and the much greater number of parts raises the probability of breakdown.[24]

Each of these last three innovations—reformulated gasoline, electric cars, and hybrid vehicles—may have an important role to play in controlling air pollution in the near future. Currently, however, they are being pushed by regulatory "stick," with no consumer "carrot" to stimulate demand for them. Notice how each of the four cost-effective policy reforms we discussed earlier would encourage consumers to move toward these innovations: (1) an emissions tax, higher on more polluting gasoline, would be in effect a subsidy for reformulated gasoline and for vehicles that use less gasoline; (2) policies that raise the costs of old standard cars not only encourage their earlier discard but also increase the demand for cars that do not get taxed ever more heavily as they get older; (3) stricter standards in nonattainment areas increase the desirability of cars and gasoline that more cheaply attain those standards; and (4) tighter controls on catalytic converter longevity are in effect subsidies to cars that do not need such converters.

In short, past automotive air pollution policies have not been cost-effective. Improving these policies, even belatedly, would not only reduce the overall cost of achieving our current air pollution levels but would also stimulate the development of innovations that would further reduce the costs.

ALTERNATIVE POLICY

The current inefficiency of air pollution policy is not the result of political and bureaucratic blundering. The inefficiency arises because some parts of the United States (the nonattainment areas) have air so dirty that extensive restrictions on automobiles and their use are needed, but other areas (the attainment areas) do not need additional restrictions. Politically, however, it is always difficult to explicitly tax separate parts of the country differently—in this case by requiring antipolluting equipment, fuels, and/or taxes in some areas and not in other areas.

This political reluctance is curious. People and cars are in fact treated very differently in different areas of the country—except where federal law (or the Constitution) demands uniformity, states are presumably permitted leeway on both. If an area has dirty air, in the sense that on the margin people are willing to pay more than it would cost to clean it up, why would state and local politicians not

BOX 5.6 Getting the Lead Out

In the 1970s, lead became widely recognized as a serious health problem—and the catalytic converters being introduced to control air pollution could not work with leaded gasoline.[25] Most of the lead then in the environment came from motor vehicle exhausts. Lead was at this time also removed from gasoline in northern Europe, but by means of higher taxation of leaded gasoline and cars that could use leaded fuel (Borenstein, 1993). In the United States in the 1970s and 1980s, lead additives (which had been used to boost octane cheaply) were gradually removed by EPA directive. By 1996, lead and lead additives were prohibited from motor vehicle fuel (Nichols, 1998).[26] Two innovative incentive plans were offered gasoline refineries during the transition.

First, over 1982–1984, each refinery was given a maximum number of grams of lead per gallon of gasoline, which had to be attained on average across all refinery output—very like the miles per gallon average of CAFE standards. But the rule also allowed averaging across refineries, which meant that "lead rights" were marketable. Half of the U.S. refineries ended up participating in this market. Such averaging brings about more cost-effective gasoline production by getting the low-cost lead reducers to cut their lead use by more and the high-cost lead reducers to cut by less (Nussbaum, 1992).

Second, from 1985 on, as lead limits were seriously phased down, interrefinery averaging was disallowed, but refineries were permitted to "bank" their lead rights if they were able to reduce their lead use below their limits in any one period. "Banked" lead rights could be used later when lead limits had become more stringent. Again, this was cost-effective because it gave refiners more cost-cutting flexibility in the timing of their lead reductions without increasing the total amount of lead.

During the 1980s transition, the production costs of leaded and unleaded fuels of given octane were not much different, but one was usually much higher priced at the gas stations. Guess which one, and why (Borenstein, 1991) (Q5.5).

be anxious to propose laws that would achieve this? Californians have long imposed stricter pollution controls upon themselves than federal standards required. When, in other nonattainment areas, the politicians fight against changes that would further clean the air, is this not a clue that the marginal benefits are not perceived as exceeding the marginal costs?

The end result of all this is unfortunate. The actually implemented automotive air pollution policy has been way too costly for what it achieves, employing policies that are not cost-effective, achieving too little in some areas where the air badly needs further cleansing, and mandating high expenditure in other areas where the air is already quite clean.

It is always tempting for economics professors, and their students, to think synoptically—how would we like to do something if we could start over from scratch?

But, in fact, real policy proceeds incrementally—given where we are, what should we do next? This suggests a focus on marginal benefits and marginal costs of small changes from existing policy.

Imposing an emissions tax—and then gradually increasing it in nonattainment areas—is clearly the best way to approach the emissions problem. It would make the EPA certification of new models unnecessary—any car could be sold, provided its new owner was willing to pay the subsequent pollution taxes. Such a tax would cover all cars, not just new cars. It would give owners an incentive to keep their antipollution devices maintained and to discard old cars when this upkeep became expensive. (Look back at Box 2.3.) The tax rates could be varied according to the air pollution problems of particular areas. At the cost of strict and regular inspections, almost all other EPA policies about car emissions could be terminated.

BOX 5.7 Asbestos in Brake and Clutch Linings

Asbestos linings have long been used in auto brakes and clutches. Workplace inhalation of airborne asbestos fibers has long been known to cause asbestosis and cancer (Augustyniak, 1998).[28] As lower levels of exposure began to be seen as a danger, the EPA began working in the 1980s on a regulation to get asbestos out of construction and consumer products—but not necessarily all consumer products. In some forms, asbestos is relatively harmless, and in some products, substitutes for asbestos are relatively expensive.

Initially, the EPA proposed a permit system, whereby each user of asbestos received a permit entitling it to use roughly one-third as much asbestos as it had previously used. These permits could be used or sold or "banked" for use in later years, and the number of permits would be steadily phased down, eventually to zero. The idea was that users for whom asbestos substitutes were expensive would buy permits from users who could find cheap substitutes, and a cost-effective phasedown would be achieved.

In fact, however, the EPA ended up issuing a rule in 1989 with the traditional command-and-control elements whereby most uses of asbestos (including use in vehicle brakes and clutches) were phased down according to a fixed time schedule. The regulation was overturned by the courts, largely on procedural grounds. Serendipitously, disk brakes have since become cheap enough to have largely replaced asbestos linings.

By the way, the EPA also considered setting an excise tax on asbestos uses that posed health risks, with the size of the tax being proportional to the risks the use created. The proposed tax rates varied widely—for example, that on clutch facings was $0.02 per unit (with a cancer risk in the 1-in-a-billion range) and that on brake blocks was $0.31 per unit (with a cancer risk in the 1-in-10-million range).[29] Firms would presumably stop using asbestos if cheap substitutes were available, but would pay the tax and continue to use asbestos if substitutes were expensive. If the tax rates were set correctly, this system not only would have been cost-effective but also would have achieved the correct reduction in overall asbestos use. Nevertheless, asbestos-using firms would have preferred the permit system. Why (Q5.6)?

How big should such emissions taxes be? That depends chiefly on how many deaths are attributed to air pollution and how many of those deaths are attributed to the automobile. Current estimates of total air pollution deaths run around 100,000 per year. If as many as $1/10^{th}$ of these are attributed to the auto, that comes to $0.30 per gallon.[27] But that is on average. The marginal damage is near zero in attainment areas and may run well over $1.00 per gallon for a heavily polluting old car operating in an urban nonattainment area.

There are two serious disadvantages to this emissions-based tax. One, it is much more complex to administer than a simple tax per gallon of gasoline. Not only are administrative costs high but also tax evasion may prove a problem. Two, this emissions-based tax is even more regressive than a straight gasoline tax. While the poor drive fewer miles than the rich, they drive older, dirtier cars (Walls and Hanson, 1996). Adoption of an emissions tax should be accompanied by other tax changes that are sufficiently progressive to offset this regressivity. More on this in Chapter 17.

ENDNOTES

[1]We should also recognize, though not dwell on, agricultural productivity and forest growth losses due to air pollution. Ground-level ozone surely hurts crops, by amounts that have been variously estimated (in foregone consumer and producer surpluses), ranging up to $9 billion per year (French, 1989; MacKenzie et al., 1992). But most estimates run less than one-half billion dollars per year, and automobile-generated CO_2 may actually increase crop productivity (EPA, 1996c; Culotta, 1995).

[2]By "99% emission-free" is meant that the car produces only 1% as much (CO and HC) pollution as a 1960 car without a catalytic converter or other emissions-control equipment. By the way, notice also the word "car" in the text. Minivans, pickups, and sport utility vehicles, already 40% of the family-owned vehicles, are exempt from the proposed new regulations and will be permitted to emit nearly *six times* the pollution of new cars (Bradsher, 1997h). These regulations, by making new cars relatively more expensive, will further encourage the switch to "light trucks." Will overall pollution be reduced (Q5.1)?

[3]Note that the EPA's effluent limit is set per mile, not per gallon. When fuel efficiency increases, it simultaneously permits automakers to increase emissions per gallon and encourages drivers to drive more miles by lowering the marginal private cost of driving (Khazzoom, 1988 and 1995).

[4]Strictly speaking, it is possible that the least-cost reduction in emissions is achieved by cutting only emissions per mile and not at all miles per year. But that result would require that the marginal cost of reducing emissions by cutting out the *first* mile exceeded the marginal cost of reducing emissions by cutting out the *last* emission per mile.

[5]Alternatively, a tax on gallons, with the tax rate proportional to a periodically monitored emission rate per *gallon*, would come to the same thing. Since both require periodic emissions testing of vehicles and a tax rate that depends on the emission rate, which tax is preferred depends basically on whether it is administratively more convenient to measure and tax mileage or gallons. The advantage of the tax on gallons, compared to the tax on miles, is that it could be reduced for gasoline that is designed to be less polluting.

[6]Total emissions also includes all other internal combustion engines. Supposedly, one can drive a new car from Washington, D.C., to New York City and back and emit less pollution than while mowing one's lawn (Johnston, 1997). A new outboard motor releases unburned hydrocarbon at 40 times the rate of a new car. And a heavy truck emits as much pollution as 50 cars (Cushman, 1998c).

[7]"Light trucks" include minivans, sport utility vehicles, and pickups.

[8]You might ask why private firms would buy old cars in order to scrap them. Possibly for favorable publicity. But in Los Angeles, firms that buy and scrap old cars collect emissions-reduction credits that let them postpone the reduction of emissions from their factories and refineries (Fialka, 1997).

[9]Whether such a policy is effective or not depends greatly on what kind of transport is adopted after the old car is sold; if the seller just keeps another dirty old car alive longer, little is gained (OTA, 1992; Hahn, 1995; Alberini *et al.*, 1994 and 1996). Suppose, however, that everyone who sells a clunker then buys a new car (and drives exactly as much as before). The social benefits are clear: reduced gasoline consumption (since new cars get better mileage) and reduced emissions (since new cars pollute less). But what are the social costs of the program? And don't say it is what the government pays to the clunker-owner (Q5.3).

[10]The Clean Air Act Amendments of 1990 do permit the EPA to "revise or waive" the Stage II requirements as soon as onboard systems are "in widespread use."

[11]"Lean-burn" and two-stroke engines, for example, produce less carbon monoxide and hydrocarbon emissions than conventional internal combustion engines, but they also produce nitrogen oxide emissions in excess of the standards.

[12]Earlier pollution reductions are, in a social benefit sense, greater pollution reduction benefits. Look again at Q5.3 if you aren't sure why.

[13]Since the penalty for a new model's failure to meet the emission standards—that no such cars may be sold—is too harsh to be credible, manufacturers can complain that they are unable to meet the standards and get that year's standards softened or deferred. In that sense, some new models have not even met the standards in theory, at least not completely and on time.

[14]It is apparently difficult for the EPA to test under exact driving conditions. Diesel truck engines, for example, pass tests that do not represent realistic driving conditions and then emit *twice* as much pollution on the road as the regulations permit (Cushman, 1998a; Stoffer, 1998b). Ford, General Motors, and Honda, have all been fined at various times for designing engines that pass the tests but pollute excessively in practice (Wald, 1998b).

[15]A 5-mile trip emits over 80% as much (HCs) as a 10-mile trip (Kessler and Schroeer, 1995). Frequent short trips cause air pollution not only because of the cold start but also because of the "hot soak"—fuel evaporation from the still-hot engine after the trip has ended.

[16]Fewer than one-third of the states require regular emissions inspection of big diesel-powered trucks and busses (Martin, 1998). And diesels spew out particulants, the principal cause of death from air pollution (see the Appendix to this chapter).

[17]As an indication of the extra cost, New York City is encouraging its taxis to switch to natural gas. For each switch, the State offers a subsidy of $4000–6000 and Ford offers $5000 more. The City "hopes" 5% of its taxi fleet will be natural-gas-powered by the year 2000. One drawback to conversion: there is only *one* natural-gas fueling station in the City (though two more are planned).

[18]Ethanol is a corn-derived fuel additive, and it now receives a subsidy of more than one-half billion dollars per year. This subsidy keeps the ethanol retail price competitive by covering half the total production costs (MacKenzie, 1994). Do you find it curious that fuel additives that do not involve agricultural products are not subsidized (Noah, 1995)? To review your basic economics, figure out the impact of the ethanol subsidy on (1) the price of corn itself, (2) the price of other crops that are substitutes in production for corn, and (3) the price of other products that are substitutes in consumption for corn (Q5.4).

[19]A formula may help. Write the actual MPG on gasoline as MPG_g, and write the actual MPG on ethanol as MPG_e. But ethanol is only 15% gasoline, so its MPG per *gasoline* gallon is $MPG_e/0.15$. The official mileage, MPG★, is given by

$$MPG\star = \frac{2}{1.00/MPG_g + 0.15/MPG_e}.$$

For vehicles with $MPG_g = 20$ and $MPG_e = 15$, MPG★ $= 33.3$. If this formula eludes you, look back at Q4.5.

[20]Recall what is meant by a "learning curve." When a new product is first manufactured, the average cost is usually high, but, as each additional unit is produced, engineers and workers "learn" ways to make the product more efficiently. As a result of these continual small improvements, average cost often comes down dramatically, typically by some 20% with each doubling of production. To illustrate, consider a product where 100 units are produced this year, at an initial average cost of $10 per unit. Assuming a growth rate of output of 10% per year, then "learning" at 20% (per doubling of cumulated output) will yield the following path of average cost:

Year	Output	Cumulated output	Average cost
0	100	100	$10.00
1	110	210	7.87
2	121	331	6.80
3	133	464	6.10
4	146	610	5.58
5	161	771	5.18

Average cost has come down by nearly half within 5 years.

[21]For publicity purposes, the White House bought 30 of these vehicles, but they ran on conventional gasoline for some time while staffers searched for the District of Columbia's 2 ethanol pumps (McAllister, 1998).

[22]New York State has adopted a mandated percentage of electric vehicle sales. As of August 1997, each automaker had to find a way to sell 1 electric vehicle for every 49 nonelectric cars sold in the state—and be selling 10% electric by 2003 (Dao, 1997). Of course, no automaker has yet come close to this target (Austin, 1998). But fortunately for them, the U.S. 2nd Circuit Court of Appeals has meanwhile struck down the law, declaring that it "was out of step with the national standard and was a burden to car makers" (Grace, 1998).

[23]This is called a "parallel hybrid." A "series hybrid" car uses a small gasoline engine to generate electricity and uses an electric motor to drive the wheels.

[24]Recently, the U.S. Army introduced a hybrid Humvee (see Box 4.6). The reason? When it runs on its batteries, it is virtually undetectable by sound or infrared sensors. It also gets 18 MPG (more than twice that of the standard Humvee), which means it can carry smaller fuel tanks for the same range. The problem? Beyond its higher cost, there is a 540-pound loss in payload because of the large and heavy lead-acid batteries.

[25]Actually, lead was recognized as a health hazard 3 centuries ago. In 1696, Dr. Eberhard Gockel noted the high death rate of monks who "sweetened" their sour wine with syrups boiled in lead pots. For fear of losing sales of the Duchy's biggest export, the Duke of Wurttemberg then banned all lead-based wine additives—the world's first legislation on toxic substances (Eisinger, 1996).

[26]The EPA estimates the annual benefits of the removal of lead from gasoline as 5000 fewer deaths, 150,000 fewer cases of child brain damage, and 1.7 million fewer cases of hypertension (Nichols, 1996). And the cost is trivial, as it turned out that unleaded gasoline was only slightly more expensive to produce.

[27]The 100,000 lives figure comes from the appendix to this chapter. The $0.30 figure equals 0.10 times 100,000 lives per year times $3 million per life divided by 100 billion gallons per year. The $3 million per life figure is explained in the appendix to Chapter 7. The estimate of the appropriate gasoline tax has been rising in recent years as more and more evidence accumulates on deaths due to air pollution; the estimate was only half as high as recently as 1994 (Viscusi *et al.*, 1994).

[28]Roman mine owners noted the high mortality rates of their slaves in asbestos mines and required them to wear pig bladders to cover their mouths and noses.

[29]The value of a life lost to cancer from asbestos was assumed to be $3 million for these tax rates. See the appendix to Chapter 7.

Appendix: Social Benefit–Cost Analysis of Automotive Emmisions Controls

"Documentation is like sex:
when it is good, it is very, very good;
and when it is bad, it is better than nothing."

Dick Brandon

The cost of the emission-related controls on new cars consists of several things, each of which has been estimated by different studies (summarized in McConnell *et al.*, 1995). The major component of these costs is the initial equipment, which runs $650–$1350 per car (all dollar figures, recall, have been converted to 1995 prices, and the annual maintenance costs have been put in present value terms).[1A] For a steady-state output of some 10 million cars per year, this means a total annual cost for the automobile antipollution program of something like $10 billion.

What are the benefits of this program? This is much more difficult to estimate, for it requires a series of very difficult and very uncertain steps:

1. Estimating the actual automobile emissions reduction. As we have already seen, the emission standards, even if they were met fully and on time by all new cars, would greatly overestimate the extent of the actual emissions reductions. The EPA's own estimates of the extent to which their auto regulations reduced pollution in 1990 (compared to a no-control scenario) are:[2A]

	\multicolumn{5}{c}{*Pollutant*}
	CO	*NO$_x$*	*Hcs*	*SO$_x$*	*PM*
% change	-56	-47	-66	+1	-30

2. Estimating the impact on ambient air quality of these emissions reductions. Emissions are a flow variable, air quality is a stock variable, and it is the latter that

is relevant to health (and other) outcomes. The impact of the flow of emissions on the stock of air quality is not simple to model, depending both on the natural terrain and winds of the region and on other background factors.

3. Estimating the benefits of the improved air quality. These are primarily health benefits, but they also include reduced damage to vegetation, reduced damage to buildings, metals, and textiles, and improved "aesthetic" qualities (that is, being able to see further and better). All are difficult to measure. For mortality benefits, there has begun to appear convincing epidemiological evidence of significant changes in death rates in response to changes in air quality, and these have been measured, so one can make estimates of the number of deaths averted by reducing pollution levels.[3A]

4. Estimating people's willingness-to-pay for the health (and other) benefits of improved air quality. Since air quality over a city is a pure public good, there are no observed market values on which to hang WTP estimates.[4A] Indirect estimates are sought. Some examples of such indirect approaches are: (1) the extent to which house prices are higher or wages lower in areas with cleaner air; (2) the extent to which "averting" expenditures (e.g., on soap, paint, and air conditioners) are reduced where the air is cleaner; and (3) the extent to which medical costs and lost sick-day wages are reduced with improved air quality. (More on this in the appendix to Chapter 7.)

The EPA's own evaluation of these last two steps (for all sources of air pollution reduction (except lead), for health effects only, and for 1990) is as follows (EPA, 1997):

Result	Pollutant	Number of cases avoided (thousands/year)	WTP per case avoided ($ thousands/case)
Mortality	PM	112–257	$5500
Chronic bronchitis	PM	674	296
Respiratory			
Hospitalized	PM,NO$_x$,HCs,CO	200	10
Acute	PM,NO$_x$,HCs	130,000	0
Restricted activity	PM,NO$_x$,HCs	22,600	0

Note: 0 means less than $500 per case avoided.

When one puts together these four uncertain steps, the resulting estimates are fraught with uncertainty. The EPA estimates cited in the preceding table amount to a health benefit of $0.6–1.4 *trillion* in 1990. While these benefits are estimated for all air pollution reductions, both mobile-source and stationary-source, they are nevertheless huge (when compared to our earlier estimate of cost of mobile-source reductions, in the ballpark of $10 *billion*).

The EPA study is the most recent and the most compendious of U.S. air pollution benefit–cost analyses. It is also the most sanguine about the net benefits of the program. Other studies have concluded that the *complete elimination* of man-made smog in American cities would yield much smaller annual benefits—one study added them up to less than $10 billion, but that was done before the discovery of epidemiological evidence of fatalities due to particulate matter (Freeman, 1982).

The major source of uncertainty in studies like these is ignorance about the effect of small changes in air quality on health. There is agreement now that particulate matter kills, but the estimates of the how many deaths still range widely—perhaps only 112,000 per year according to the EPA study. The range of these life-saving numbers can be used to get an idea of the uncertainty of such benefit–cost analyses.

Most of the people who die from episodes of bad air quality are over the age of 65, and yet their lives are valued in the EPA study at $5.5 million per life. Throughout this book, we will be using values of life between $1 million and $5 million (see the appendix to Chapter 7 on why and how we value lives saved). But for elderly people, with few quality years left, it is arguable that the lower-bound value of life should be used. Making that change and assuming that air pollution policies save only 112,000 deaths per year would lower the EPA health benefit estimate from mortality reduction to "only" $112 billion.

Go a step further. All the deaths from air pollution are attributed to particulate matter. EPA controls are estimated to have reduced particulate matter by nearly 70% in 1990 (compared to what it would have been without controls), but automobile policies contributed only 2% of that reduction. If we attribute only 2% of the averted deaths to cars, then the benefit of the automobile part of the air pollution policy consists of only 2000–5000 saved lives in 1990, for a monetary benefit of something in the range of $2–25 billion.

In short, the U.S. automotive air pollution policy probably does pass its benefit–cost test, but it may not pass by much—certainly not by the margin that the EPA study suggests (EPA, 1997).

ENDNOTES

[1A]Some estimates of the additional costs of emissions equipment reach nearly $2000 per car (again, in 1995 prices and in present value) (Crandall et al., 1986; Rutledge and Vogan, 1995). Why so large a range? Two reasons exist. One, because the new equipment is mandated, its cost is not explicit but buried in the price of the whole vehicle, and different efforts at the cost estimate differ widely. Two, there is a serious difference of opinion about how the emissions equipment affects maintenance costs.

[2A]The main problem with sulfur in the gasoline is not emissions of SO_x—cars contribute little to the "acid rain" problem. Rather, the problem is that the sulfur can damage emissions-control devices. American gasoline has the highest sulfur levels of all the industrialized countries. Removing 90% of the sulfur from gasoline would cost some 5–10 cents a gallon (Fialka, 1998).

[3A]Epidemiological studies examine the changes in death rates in different U.S. cities, counties, or states as a function of the difference in air quality in those places.

[4A]Recall that a public good is a nonrival and nonexcludable good. Nonrivalness means that one person's consumption of the good in no way diminishes the next person's consumption of the same good, and nonexcludability means that it is impossible to prevent someone from consuming the good. Air quality is a classic example of a "pure public good" because it really is almost completely a nonrival and nonexcludable good.

CHAPTER 6

Global Warming

> *"More than any other time in history,*
> *mankind faces a crossroads.*
> *One path leads to despair and utter hopelessness.*
> *The other, to total extinction.*
> *Let us pray we have the wisdom to choose correctly."*
>
> **Woody Allen**
> *My Speech to the Graduates*

There are two kinds of air pollution to which automobiles contribute. The one we were discussing in the last chapter is *local* air pollution, the low-level carbon monoxide, smog, and particulate matter that damage the health of nearby residents. The second kind of pollution, which we will consider in this chapter, is the high-level, stratospheric change that may be occurring as a result of the increased burning of fossil fuels on the planet.

Burning fossil fuels releases carbon dioxide (CO_2), which does not contribute to low-level air pollution but does contribute to the trapping of solar heat that would otherwise be reflected from the earth back into space.[1] This heat trapping thus contributes to a warming of the earth's surface, which in turn could dramatically affect the planet and our life on it in several ways. Two possible effects are especially important for the United States:

1. Higher global temperatures would lead to a melting of the polar ice caps, raising the levels of the oceans by as much as 25 feet over the next few centuries. For the United States, this would mean that almost all our oceanside cities would become submerged, and much coastal farmland would be lost.

2. Ocean currents, storm patterns, and rainfall would be greatly altered. For the United States, this would mean insufferable summer heat, drought, and crop

loss in the south and southwest, although it would also mean milder winters and better crops in the north.

We have known about this problem for a century—a Swedish scientist, Svante Ahrrenius, warned us about it in 1898. We know that the problem could be immense. And we also know that the automobile's contribution to total human-caused CO_2 releases is not negligible. Transport accounts for nearly one-third of the current releases of CO_2 in the United States and other industrialized countries, and it already accounts for nearly one-fourth of the releases of the globe's poorer countries.

But is the problem immense? Indeed, is there going to be a problem at all? On these questions there is still a great deal of scientific controversy—and, accordingly, economic controversy about what to do about what, when, how, and where (Cline, 1992; Nordhaus, 1994).

Why is there controversy? Three basic facts are clear: (1) human-made CO_2 releases have been accelerating over the last century; (2) CO_2 is a "greenhouse gas" that traps solar heat; and (3) the earth has warmed over the last century (by about 1 degree Fahrenheit). The controversy arises from four other facts: (1) human-made releases of CO_2 constitute only about 3% of the total annual global CO_2 releases, the rest being from oceans, forests, and volcanoes; (2) many parts of the earth have not warmed over the past century—there has, for example, been no trend in the average temperature of the United States over this period; (3) global climate changes of the kind we are now experiencing have occurred, and reversed themselves, many times in the past; and (4) the forecasts of the extent

---

BOX 6.1 Annual Average Household CO_2 Emissions

Roughly half of the CO_2 emissions of the United States are from automobiles and residences. The major sources of these nonindustrial emissions are shown in the table below on a per capita basis.

Use	Unit	CO_2 per unit	Units consumed	CO_2 emissions
Automobile	Gallon	20	400	8000
Electricity	KWH	2	3600	7200
Heating				
Natural gas	Therm	12	200	2400
Oil and coal	—	—	—	1000

Note. KWH, kilowatt-hour. One therm = 100 cubic feet = 100,000 BTUs. BTU, British Thermal Unit. CO_2 is measured in pounds. Consumption and emissions are per annum. Sources: Bureau, 1995; EPA, 1995b; Hinrichs, 1996.

of global warming are based upon theories and assumptions about which reputable scientists disagree (Stevens, 1996).

While there is still scientific uncertainty about exactly what is happening, a clear majority of scientists are certain that something is happening. As the Intergovernmental Panel on Climate Change (IPCC) of the United Nations Environmental Program (UNEP) puts it in its summary,

> Our ability to quantify the human influence on global climate is currently limited. . . . Nevertheless, the balance of evidence suggests that there is a discernible human influence on global climate. (Houghton *et al.,* 1996)

Still, many respected scientists caution that it is not at all clear yet that human activities have begun to warm the planet—or how bad global warming will be if and when it arrives (Kerr, 1997).

"ROBUST" POLICY

Normally, where scientists are uncertain, economic policymakers would be quiet, arguing that no policy is appropriate until the benefits and costs of policy action are clearer. But policy postponement may not be the correct choice, even when the potential damages may be centuries away, if today's activities may be irreversibly contributing to future disaster.

Assuming, to take the argument a step further, that today's CO_2 emissions are already causing serious and irremediable external damage to the welfare of future generations, what should be done? The United States emits roughly one-fourth of the planet's CO_2—and more than twice as much per capita as Western Europe.

BOX 6.2 Too Soon versus Too Late

Statisticians like to talk about Type I errors versus Type II errors. Assume scientists have a hypothesis and some data to test it. There are two possible mistakes they can make in their analysis. One, the data in their sample will lead them to reject the hypothesis when they should have accepted it (Type I error). Two, the data will lead them to accept the hypothesis when they should have rejected it (Type II error).

These errors may crop up in global warming policy, too. The Type I error is rejecting the hypothesis that global warming is occurring, and doing nothing, when global warming is in fact occurring, and we shall later be burned for our inactivity. The Type II error is accepting the hypothesis that global warming is occurring, and contracting our standard of living in order to reduce CO_2 emissions, when global warming is in fact not occurring, and we shall later find that we have squandered an opportunity to raise the welfare of the billions of people currently living on the planet.

Nearly one-third of U.S. emissions comes from motor vehicles. Any global reduction in CO_2 emissions probably involves America's cars.[2]

Current automotive air pollution policies do not address this issue—they focus on the low-level pollutants, CO (carbon monoxide, not carbon dioxide), HC, and NO_x. The only policies that can directly attack the automobile side of the global warming problem are (1) those that reduce CO_2 emissions per mile driven and (2) those that reduce driving miles. About this, if little else concerned with global warming, there is a "wide measure of agreement" (Stevens, 1995).

When it is not absolutely certain that something should be done, we should be sure that whatever we do is "robust." Robust actions are those that "would be beneficial in the worst case, not harmful in other cases, and not very costly to take" (Lave, 1988). Robust actions also involve gradual changes in policy, for two reasons. One, sudden clampdowns on energy-using activities would mean the possibly premature and certainly expensive scrapping of fairly new capital equipment. Two, gradual change, properly signaled, would spur invention and investment in more appropriate technology, also reducing the cost of the transition.

In our search for robustness, let us consider three approaches to policy. The first is further increase in the fuel efficiency of the kinds of cars we now drive, those with an internal combustion engine. Increases in fuel efficiency would indeed reduce emissions of CO_2, but these would be expensive and would have to be sizable to achieve much; one study asserted that fuel efficiency would have to rise to 70 MPG by the year 2015 just to keep CO_2 emissions at their 1990 levels (Resolve, 1995). Nor would the long-awaited electric car solve this problem, for it does not do away with the burning of fossil fuel (unless of course the electricity is generated by hydro, wind, solar, or nuclear energy). The electric car merely relocates the fuel burning from the vehicle itself to an electric-power-generating station. This may help with urban air pollution if the electricity is generated outside the city, but it does not reduce the impact of driving on global warming—indeed, it could actually worsen it since coal is worse than gasoline for CO_2 (Renner, 1988).

A second approach to reducing greenhouse gas emissions is the development and adoption of totally new kinds of vehicles, those that do not burn fossil fuel at all and hence do not produce CO_2. Surprisingly, such cars are already available. Vehicles can be powered by fuel cells in which hydrogen reacts with oxygen to produce electricity, with only water as the waste product.[3] Fuel-cell vehicles are comparable to the current gasoline-powered vehicles in their speed of refueling, range, and rate of acceleration, but they contribute neither to local air pollution nor to greenhouse gases (Sperling, 1995).

Alas, such vehicles are not yet ready for the marketplace. Technically, they are old hat—fuel cells were used to provide the electricity for space missions in the 1960s. Today, fuel cells are considered 10 times too expensive to be practical—not long ago they were considered 1000 times too expensive (Krebs, 1997). Optimistically, if a rapid learning curve applies, and average cost falls 20% with each doubling of cumulated production, fuel-cell vehicles could undersell electric

BOX 6.3 Comparison of Available Alternatives to Gasoline

All of the currently available alternatives to gasoline are more expensive than gasoline. The greater expense does not usually reside in explicit variable costs—most of the five alternatives in the next table would add little to a car's fuel and maintenance costs. The greater expense resides in the initial capital costs of the vehicle itself or of the fuel distribution network.[4]

All the alternative fuels are derived from either corn, coal, or natural gas, and all of these inputs are securely available in the United States or from secure, nearby foreign sources. All make some contribution to the air pollution problem. But none do much, if anything, for global warming—after all, they all involve burning that releases carbon dioxide.

Fuel alternative	National security	Air pollution	Global warming
Oxygenated gasoline	Raises oil imports	Much better	No effect
Ethanol (from corn)	Uses U.S. corn output	Slightly better	About the same
Methanol	Uses Canadian or U.S. natural gas	Slightly better	About the same
Natural gas	Uses Canadian or U.S. natural gas	Much better	Slightly better
Electric vehicle	Uses U.S. coal or natural gas	Much better in cities	Depends on how the electricity is generated

Sources: GAO, 1990; OTA, 1990; MacKenzie, 1994; Resolve, 1995.

battery-powered vehicles and be only 30–40% more expensive than gasoline-powered cars within a decade (Williams, 1994).

The third approach to global warming policy addresses the need to reduce driving. Three pricing approaches suggest themselves: (1) taxes based on VMT, (2) taxes based on MPG, or (3) taxes based on gasoline usage. Of these three, greenhouse gas emissions are most closely related to gasoline usage. Taxing higher VMT gives no direct incentive for consumers to drive more fuel-efficient vehicles, and taxing lower MPG gives consumers no direct incentive to drive fewer miles. Thus, the best choice is higher gasoline taxation.

Actually, what would be really appropriate here would be higher carbon taxes. There is no good reason to discriminate between different means of burning fossil fuels. Such a fee, based on the carbon content of different fossil fuels, would raise the relative prices of all carbon-intensive goods and services and would lead to a cost-effective reduction in U.S. carbon emissions. Cost effectiveness on a global level would require that the same tax be assessed everywhere—or that a global system of marketable carbon permits be established.

What are the prospects for a near-term, coordinated international agreement on the curbing of greenhouse gas emissions? Essentially zero. This is "the tragedy of the commons" writ large.[5] Each country bears all of the costs of reducing its carbon emissions but garners only a small fraction of the benefits, and most of those benefits do not accrue until a politically, if not geologically, distant time. Most of the carbon is generated by the industrialized countries, but they stand to lose the least by global warming, simply because so small a part of their national output is dependent on temperature. The world's developing countries are heavily dependent on agriculture and forestry, are tropical, and do stand to lose greatly by higher temperatures and reduced rainfall. But their present citizenry is so poor that they are unlikely to want to deflect much investment to the welfare of their, not to mention our, future citizens. The Montreal Protocol on CFCs (see Box 6.4) will not be soon repeated for CO_2—the stakes are "two or three orders of magnitude greater for fossil fuels" (Schelling, 1991). For the United States to cut its CO_2 emissions to 85% of their 1990 levels by 2010—as the West European countries suggested at the Kyoto Climate Change Conference in 1997—we would have had to cut our emissions to roughly *half* of the level they would reach at the current annual growth rate (Economist, 1997a).

The industrial nations did, in fact, gather at Rio de Janeiro in 1992 to sign a climate change treaty. A voluntary goal was set to reduce greenhouse gas emissions to 1990 levels by the year 2000; 170 nations, including the United States, signed the treaty. Greenhouse gas emissions continued everywhere to grow. And so the nations gathered again, in 1997 in Kyoto, to negotiate a protocol to the Global Climate Change Treaty. Again they set targets—targets that the United States won't come close to meeting.

How can I be so sure that the United States will fail to meet its Kyoto target? We agreed in Kyoto to cut our greenhouse gas emissions to 7% below our 1990 emissions by 2012. Our greenhouse gas emissions have been growing at 1.3% per year in recent years. This means that by 1997 our emissions were already almost 10% above the 1990 level. At that growth rate, by 2012, our emissions would be about one-third above the 1990 level. So getting 7% below the 1990 level would mean a 30% cut below what we are headed for in 2012 at present growth rates.[6]

The administration thinks we can do this—the 1998 Comprehensive National Energy Strategy says that "by 2010, you may be driving a car that gets 80 MPG, emits virtually no pollution, has the acceleration, driving range, safety, and other performance characteristics to equal the best of today's cars—and is still afford-able" (DOE, 1998). *You* might be, but most Americans will not. A 30% reduction of greenhouse gases from automobiles by 2012 requires that *every new car sold in the United States be a fuel-cell vehicle within a decade.*

BOX 6.4 Autos and the Ozone Layer

The other global air pollution problem is the depletion of the ozone layer, which increases human exposure to ultraviolet radiation and hence causes skin cancers. All this is much less affected by motor vehicles—basically only through their air-conditioning systems, which have long used chlorofluorocarbons (CFCs) as a refrigerant. By international treaty, the use of these ozone-damaging CFCs (commercially known as Freon) is being phased out, production and import having ceased in 1995 in the United States (Hammitt, 1998).

Cars built since 1993 use a substitute refrigerant that currently costs more to produce than Freon but for which a learning curve is expected; for example, every doubling of the cumulated production of CFCs reduced the per-unit cost by one-fourth (Barbier *et al.*, 1991). Old cars, however, face a choice between retrofits that may cost more than $1000 (how much depends on the age of the car and the reliability sought) and periodic searches for some of the dwindling remaining supply of Freon, the price of which has risen from $4 per pound in 1994 to over $20 per pound today (Halpert, 1993; Sawyers, 1996; Lucchetti and Stern, 1996). Auto air-conditioning systems on average need to replace about 1 pound of coolant each year.

The federal government has put an excise tax of nearly $6 per pound on the sales of the remaining Freon supplies. Has that tax (compared to no tax) raised, lowered, or not affected the price of the remaining stocks of Freon (Q6.4)?

In Mexico and other Third World countries, Freon production can continue until 2005, so Freon is still relatively cheap there. So it is hardly surprising to learn that the second biggest smuggling problem reported by the U.S. Customs Service (after guess what) is Freon (Missoulian, 1996; Warrick, 1997).

COST-EFFECTIVE CO$_2$ REDUCTIONS

Suppose, however, to push the argument another step forward, the world community somehow agreed that CO$_2$ emissions should be reduced. Reduced automobile use in all countries, but especially in very automobilious countries like the United States, would almost certainly be one of the most cost-effective ways of doing it. The proof follows. It is long and messy, but grit your teeth, for we may be saving a planet.

Automobiles emit about 20 pounds of CO$_2$ per gallon of gasoline used. That is 0.01 tons of CO$_2$ per gallon. The price of gasoline is currently about $1.20 per gallon, and American motorists consume about 100 billion gallons per year. The short-run price elasticity of demand for gasoline is about 0.5 (in absolute value). With just this information, we can calculate how many fewer gallons of gasoline we would consume and how much less CO$_2$ we would emit at various (additional) gasoline tax rates.

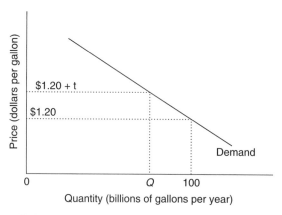

FIGURE 6.1   Effect of Gas Tax on Price and Quantity

Look at Figure 6.1, which shows the demand curve for U.S. gasoline and two intersection points. The point to the lower right shows current consumption, about 100 billion gallons per year at a price of about $1.20 per gallon. (This $1.20 includes current gasoline taxes of about $0.25 per gallon.) The point to the upper left shows a hypothetical consumption, Q, at a price that includes an additional gasoline tax of t per gallon. Recall the formula for arc price elasticity between two points on a demand curve,

$$0.5 = \left. \frac{(100 - Q)}{(100+Q)/2} \right/ \frac{t}{(2.40+ t)/2}, \qquad [6.1]$$

where 0.5 is the (absolute value of the) price elasticity.

We then solve Equation [6.1] for Q in terms of t:

$$Q = (240+50t)/(2.40+1.50t). \qquad [6.2]$$

The amount by which a tax of t reduces gasoline consumption is

$$100 - Q = (100t)/(2.40+1.50t). \qquad [6.3]$$

If we multiply Equation [6.3] by 0.01, we get the reduction in CO_2 in billions of tons per year.

The cost to consumers of this loss of gasoline is the foregone consumer surplus. Recall the area of the trapezoid that measures this: the rise in price (t) times the average of the quantity before and the quantity after the tax increase, $(\frac{1}{2})(100+Q)$. Using Equation [6.2] for Q, we find the change in consumer surplus to be

$$- (240t+100t^2)/(2.40+1.50t). \qquad [6.4]$$

The new tax has two effects on government tax revenue. First, it adds tax revenue because the tax rate is higher (by t) on all gasoline sold (Q). But second, it reduces tax revenue because the old taxes (about $0.25 per gallon) are no longer collected on the gasoline that is no longer sold ($100 - Q$). Thus, the net change in government tax revenue is

$$+ tQ - (100 - Q)/4. \qquad [6.5]$$

Substituting for Q with Equation [6.2], the net change in tax revenue is

$$+ (215t+50t^2)/(2.40+1.50t). \qquad [6.6]$$

The total social cost (TSC) of the new tax is the lost consumer surplus minus the gained net tax revenue:

$$TSC = (25t+50t^2)/(2.40+1.50t). \qquad [6.7]$$

Divide that by $[(0.01)(100 - Q)]$ to find the total social cost per ton of CO$_2$ reduction. Use Equation [6.3] to eliminate the Q, and we end up with a TSC of $(50t + 25)$ dollars per ton.

Now consider some specific value for the additional tax rate, say, 10 cents per gallon. Equation [6.3] tells us that this tax will cause a decline of 3.92 billion gallons of gasoline per year, and hence a decline of 39.2 million tons of CO$_2$ per year. Equation [6.4] tells us that this tax will cause a loss of consumer surplus of $9.80 billion per year. Equation [6.6] tells us that this tax will cause a net increase in tax revenue of $8.63 billion per year. The total social cost is $1.18 billion, or about $30 per ton of CO$_2$ saved.[7]

The solid line of Figure 6.2 shows the results of doing the preceding calculation for many different tax rates, with millions of tons per year of CO$_2$ saved on the horizontal axis and TSC per ton of CO$_2$ saved on the vertical axis. The dotted line in that figure shows the same thing for an assumed price elasticity of 1.0, roughly the long-run price elasticity of gasoline. There is also an indication in this figure of the magnitude of the additional tax rate per gallon that is needed to achieve the various levels of CO$_2$ reduction.

BOX 6.5 Air Pollution and Global Warming
The catalytic converter effectively breaks down the nitrogen oxides that contribute to smog and local air pollution. In so doing, however, it creates nitrous oxide, benign in smog creation but 300 times more potent than carbon dioxide as a greenhouse gas. Moreover, as catalytic converters get more efficient at eliminating smog creation, they produce ever more nitrous oxide. Trade-offs again! As Sheila Lynch (executive director of the Northeast Alternative Vehicle Coalition) lamented: "It's, like, clean is not green." (Wald, 1998a)

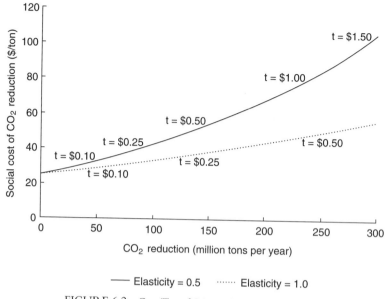

FIGURE 6.2   Cost/Ton of CO_2 Reduced by Gas Taxation

In the short run, up to 100 million tons per year of CO_2 reduction can be achieved at a cost of less than $40 per ton. In the long run, up to 200 million tons per year can be achieved at a cost of less than $40 per ton. How does this compare with other means of cutting CO_2? It compares very favorably. Such things as electric-vehicle research, expanded use of mass transit, early retirement of coal-fired plants (replaced with nuclear plants), natural gas vehicle subsidies, urban tree planting and rural afforestation programs, ethanol gasoline subsidies, and cogeneration of electricity and heat all cost more, sometimes much more, than reduced gasoline usage (OTA, 1991a; Policy, 1996).

FINAL THOUGHTS

There is not yet consensus as to when or even whether we should start fighting global warming. But if and when we decide to do that, costs under $40 per ton of carbon dioxide removed are clear winners. Higher gasoline taxation would be a very cost-effective way to start.[8] Fuel-cell vehicles will not become competitive within the next decade, and subsidizing such vehicles enough to make them competitive would not be as cost-effective as a gasoline tax. The cheapest way to reduce automobile-emitted CO_2 is to reduce driving—worrying about global warming and worrying about energy security come to the same policy end, gasoline taxation.

ENDNOTES

[1]CO_2 is not the only gas that contributes to global warming, but it is the most important one and the only one to which autos are a major contributor.

[2]Why the "probably" in that sentence (Q6.1)?

[3]You may recall your high school chemistry class where you applied electricity to break water down into hydrogen and oxygen. The process can be reversed. Hydrogen and oxygen can be combined to make electricity and water.

[4]Diesel fuel is the exception. The engines are comparable in cost, the fuel is usually slightly cheaper than gasoline per gallon, and diesel engines get 25–50% better fuel economy. This makes conversion of the passenger fleet to diesel a winner from the viewpoint of both CO_2 emissions and private fuel cost. Unfortunately, exposure to diesel fumes greatly increases the risk of lung cancer.

[5]In case you have not yet learned about "the tragedy of the commons," here is a brief outline of the problem. The "commons" was land in European medieval villages that was owned by no one and that could be used by any local farmer. People used it to graze sheep. When a farmer grazed his sheep, he reaped the benefit of fatter sheep, the more the better. As the human and sheep population of the town grew, this free access eventually meant overgrazing in the sense that the commons lost its ability to replenish itself from one year to the next. Overgrazing imposed an external cost on all who used the commons, because it then took longer for it to be used again for grazing. Free access to the commons reduced the total amount of grazing that could be done. Today we use the term "commons" for any resource where individual decisions and free access lead to overuse. Try to see the tragedy of the commons as a kind of "Prisoner's Dilemma" (look back at Box 4.2) (Q6.2). In the case in the text (global warming), CO_2 emissions play the role of grazing sheep and countries the role of shepherds.

[6]Don't take my word for it—do the algebra (Q6.3).

[7]To make sure you followed all that, do it through yourself with a price elasticity of, say, 1 in Equation [6.1] (Q6.5).

[8]By the way, the other clearly cost-effective global policy would be the reduced deforestation of tropical forests (Nordhaus, 1991).

Highway Safety

CHAPTER 7

An Overview of Highway Safety

"It's not that I'm afraid to die.
I just don't want to be there when it happens."

Woody Allen

The United States has the lowest highway death rate per vehicle-mile traveled (VMT) of any country, but it has one of the highest numbers of highway deaths per capita of any country.[1] Around 40,000–50,000 Americans die on public roadways each year. That number has remained roughly constant for the past quarter-century although during that period there has been a doubling of the number of licensed drivers, a doubling of the number of registered vehicles, and a doubling of the number of vehicle-miles traveled.

A few background statistics are in order. There are many numbers to play with since the automobile has been causing well-documented deaths for a century. (The first auto-related death, in 1898, is said to have been a person lighting a match in order to see if there was gasoline in the tank.) Half of those who are hurt or die on highways are below the age of 21 years, although they make up only 30% of the U.S. population. Indeed, 16 to 21 year olds make up only 9% of the licensed drivers in the United States, but they are the drivers in 18% of the fatal crashes. Cars are the leading cause of death in this age group (Viscusi, 1993). Unskilled manual workers are more likely to die than skilled or professional workers. Rural roads, nighttime, bankruptcy, and alcohol have all been regularly associated with higher highway death rates (Adams, 1985).

While pollution and congestion get most of the automotive publicity, all this highway death and damage is also a serious economic cost. Depending on how one values the lives that are lost on the highway—see the appendix to this chapter—highway accidents cost $150–350 billion per year, of which about $50 billion is property damage and $20 billion medical costs (Blincoe, 1996). Not all of this, of course, represents externalities—about half is damage done by drivers to themselves and their own property.

Many die each year on highways. But many die also in other ways—the total American deaths due to heart disease, cancer, stroke, and pneumonia each exceed in number the highway toll. So just how serious is highway death as a public health problem in the United States? One way to put highway death in this broader perspective is to look at the policy guidelines of the National Contingency Plan (NCP), which sets criteria for the cleanup of Superfund sites, and the U.S. Congress, which sets cancer limits for foods and pesticides. They state that the maximum acceptable concentration levels of carcinogens should pose a lifetime cancer risk exposure to an individual of not more than something between 1 chance in 10,000 and 1 chance in 1,000,000 (Hird, 1994). By contrast, the lifetime highway death risk of the average American is about 1 chance in 100.[2] To reach 1 chance in 10,000 of death on the highways would mean reducing auto-related deaths to about 1 per day in the entire United States. Currently, highway deaths occur at the rate of 1 every 10 minutes.[3]

THE THEORY OF HIGHWAY DEATH

Rather than further elaborating on the empirical evidence, let us develop a theory of highway death by exploring the following hypothetical "game." Consider an enclosed sports arena that can seat, say, 10,000 people. Seat 100 people randomly around the arena. Now bring in a blindfolded machine gunner with 100 bullets in the gun and let him (or her), while spinning dizzily, empty the magazine toward the seats. Some very unlucky spectator might be hit more than once, some will be hit once, but most will probably not be hit at all. The exact number is not important for the theory, but, as a guess, let us say that 1 is hit—that is, since 1% of the seats are occupied, it seems likely that 1% of the bullets will hit occupied seats, or rather the occupants of these seats.

Now comes the theory. Suppose we doubled the number of people occupying seats, from 100 to 200. Again the gunner with 100 bullets cuts loose. How many will now be hit? Most people would guess twice as many as before. Since 2% of the seats are now occupied, it seems plausible that 2% of the bullets will hit occupied seats. Doubling the number of people doubles the number of deaths.

Go back to the attendance of 100. Suppose that we now doubled the number of bullets in the gunner's magazine, and again cut the whirling-dervish shooter loose.

Each person's probability of being hit is doubled. Since, when 100 bullets were fired, only 1 person was hit, it is reasonable to guess that 200 bullets would probably hit 2 people. Doubling the number of bullets doubles the number of deaths.[4]

Going from this hypothetical arena to the nation's highways, where spectators become the entire nation's population (N), and the bullets become registered vehicles (V), we can summarize the preceding theory of highway death (D) as

$$D = aV^bN^c, \qquad [7.1]$$

where, according to our earlier speculations, we hypothesize that the exponent coefficients, b and c, are each very close to unity.[5]

ESTIMATES OF "SMEED'S LAW"

The empirical work on Equation [7.1] was begun by R. J. Smeed in 1949, when he fitted that equation in logarithmic form to the 1938 traffic data of 20 (largely European) countries (Smeed, 1949).[6] The equation that best fit the data was

$$D = 0.0003V^{1/3}N^{2/3}. \qquad [7.2]$$

Most curiously, the estimates of the two exponent coefficients were not each 1, as we theorized, but rather they *summed* to 1. This means we can rewrite Equation [7.2] as

$$D/V = 0.0003(V/N)^{-2/3}. \qquad [7.3]$$

This equation is telling us that if population doubles and vehicles double, with vehicles per capita thereby remaining constant, highway deaths per vehicle will not change. Equation [7.3] is the form in which "Smeed's Law" is usually expressed.

The Smeed regression has been repeated many times, for different geographical areas and for different times, and it has borne up well. Figure 7.1 shows the international highway death data for years around 1980, and the original 1949 Smeed equation still fits those data very closely.[7]

Figure 7.2 shows the U.S. highway death data for the years 1947–1991, and the original Smeed equation fits those data pretty well. However, two kinds of deviations will interest us shortly: (1) the break in the early 1960s in the longtime downward trend in the rate of deaths per vehicle, and (2) the fact that all the points are below the Smeed curve from 1975 on.

Figure 7.3 shows the U.S. highway death data by state, and these data definitely do not follow Smeed's Law. The highway death rate is below the Smeed prediction in all but one state, but that we would have expected from Figure 7.2. What is surprising is that there is no downward tilt in the state data—states with sparse population and high numbers of vehicles per capita have no lower deaths per vehicle than densely populated, urban states. And the variation in deaths per vehicle among the states is not easily explained—Mississippi (MS) is neither the largest nor the most sparsely populated of the states.

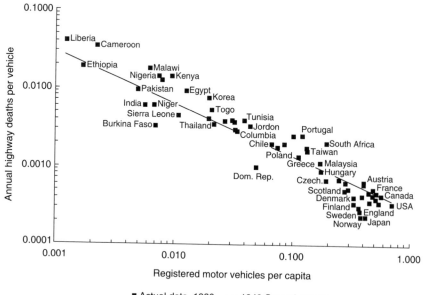

FIGURE 7.1   International Highway Death Comparisons

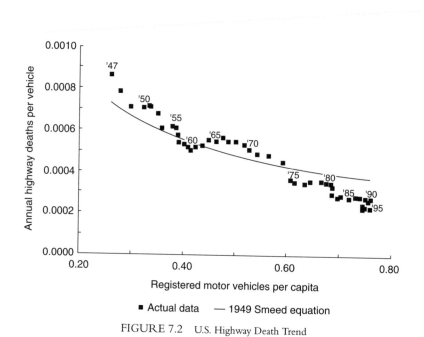

FIGURE 7.2   U.S. Highway Death Trend

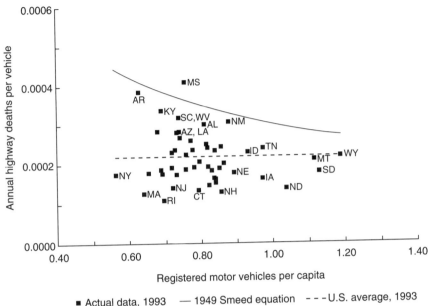

FIGURE 7.3   U.S. State Highway Deaths, 1993

FINAL THOUGHTS

In short, Smeed's Law is at best a rough first approximation. But it is still worth pondering why death rates per vehicle decline as the number of vehicles per capita increases across countries and over time. Two explanations suggest themselves:

1. *Learning.* In our hypothetical sports arena example, as we increase the number of bullets, people might well recognize that their chance of death was rising and begin to hide under their seats, get behind other spectators, or wear bullet-proof vests. As the number of vehicle registrations increases, people develop "street smarts." Both pedestrians and drivers learn the importance of taking greater highway care, and they also learn *how* to take greater care.

2. *Opulence.* Car demand is income-elastic, so when the number of vehicles per capita differs over time, the greater number of cars is usually indicative of greater opulence. With opulence comes urbanization, and city highway fatalities are lower because cars move more slowly and hospitals are nearer. With opulence come also better roads, better emergency medical systems, newer and safer cars, etc. Richer people buy more of most things than poorer people, including more expected longevity—which is partly purchased by caution, both as drivers and as pedestrians. All of these income-related forces offset the tendency for more vehicles to cause more deaths. It may not be just a coincidence that Mississippi, the

---

BOX 7.1 Highway Deaths per What?

Clearly, in a growing economy, highway deaths have to be measured per *something* if they are to be meaningful. Most people argue that Smeed's calculations of deaths per capita or deaths per vehicle are obsolete and that, as a measure of the lethality of vehicles, vehicle-miles traveled (VMT) is the better divisor. (Data on VMT were generally not available when Smeed's original work was done.) For example, a recent newspaper article on highway fatality trumpets that the "total number of deaths changed hardly at all [in 1997], but the death rate [per VMT] fell because of the relentless increase in traffic" (Wald, 1998c). This is a little like saying that we are beating lung cancer despite increased smoking because the death rate per cigarette is declining.

We remain consistent with Smeed by using registrations in Figures 7.1, 7.2, and 7.3. In any case, the difference is not important; VMT per registered vehicle—akin to cigarettes per smoker—has changed by barely one-half of 1% per annum in the last half-century, though it has been rising rapidly in the last decade (see Figure 3.1).

---

state with the highest rate of deaths per vehicle, is the *lowest* state in income per capita and *second-lowest* in educational expenditures per primary and secondary school pupil.

All this overview suggests that we can view highway death—or its obverse, highway safety—as a function of two things: (1) the driving environment, that is, the inherent "safeness" of vehicles and roads, and (2) the driving process, that is, the ability and carefulness of drivers themselves. We will look first at the physical, or engineering, aspects of vehicle and highway safety in the next chapter.

ENDNOTES

[1]South Africa wins the dubious distinction of the highest number of highway deaths per capita, with nearly 1 out of every 2500 citizens dying each year on highways; Portugal is second with 1 out of every 3300; and several West European countries are virtually tied with the United States at 1 out of 6000–6500. To be precise, "highway death" is defined as a death on or beside a public roadway, with the death (1) attributable to an accident involving a motor vehicle and (2) occurring within 1 year of that accident.

[2]Can you show the relationship between the probability of dying on the highway in any given year and the probability of so dying over the course of a lifetime (Q7.1) ?

[3]Why do we focus here on deaths rather than on accidents? Partly because death is clearly the most costly accident that one can undergo, but mostly because the data are more accurately collected—many accidents go unreported, for a variety of reasons, but deaths are almost always reported.

[4]This last statement is not quite accurate. Let D be the number of deaths, N be the number of spectators, S be the number of seats, and V be the number of bullets. Then, the number of deaths (D) is given by

$$D = N\{1 - [(S-1)/S]^V\}.$$

Doubling N does indeed double D, but doubling V slightly less than doubles D. This follows from the fact that there is always a probability that a bullet will hit an already dead spectator—no matter how many bullets you use, you cannot kill more than the entire population of the arena.

[5]The parameter, a, is called a scaling factor. In the machine gunner example, a was assumed to be 0.0001.

[6]By logarithmic form is meant the following:

$$\ln D = \ln a + b \ln V + c \ln N.$$

Smeed's equation is linear in (natural) logarithms, which made it easier to estimate statistically.

[7]Note that both axes of Figure 7.1 are in logarithmic scale.

Appendix: The Value of Life

"A single death is a tragedy.
A million deaths is a statistic."

Joseph Stalin

Most people have an instinctive distaste for thinking about "the value of life"—especially when one is talking about the termination of a particular person's life. When we talk about highway accidents, however, there are two important differences between those lives and the lives of, say, convicted murderers on death row. One, the lives in question are not yet identified, and two, the policy changes we are considering will move the probability of death by small amounts, not from zero all the way to one. These two differences make small changes in the rate of highway fatalities much easier to discuss than capital punishment for a particular convicted murderer.

Still, it is hard for most people to say that we should undertake a policy if it costs less than x dollars per expected life saved and not undertake the policy if it costs more.[1A] It may be hard, but for three reasons it is essential that we make ourselves willing to do this.

1. When we make decisions that marginally affect our expected longevity, we do not act like we value our lives infinitely: we play contact sports, we scuba dive, we hang glide, etc. We even walk, bicycle, and drive.[2A] If there are finite private pleasures that are worth some risk to your life, then this means that you are implicitly placing a finite value on this risk. If we value small changes in longevity fi-

---

BOX 7A.1 Making Risky Decisions
To get you thinking about risks that involve your own life, consider the following example. You are single and live in Town A, which has bad air quality and a high crime rate. Your risk of dying from an air-pollution-caused disease is 20 in 100,000 higher than in the average American city, and your risk of dying in a violent crime is 2 in 100,000 higher than the national average. You now have the opportunity of a costless move to either Town B or Town C, which are *exactly the same* to you as Town A except in two respects. Town B has the same crime problem as Town A, but the air quality is better, and your risk of dying from the air pollution is reduced to only 15 in 100,000 higher than the American average. Town C has the same air quality as Town A, but the crime rate is lower, and your risk of dying in a violent crime is reduced to only 1 in 100,000 higher than the national average. Would you prefer to move to Town B or to Town C? (Pretend you have *no* preferences about *how* you die.) Think about it, make a decision, read on through this appendix, and then come back and think again.

---

nitely in our private behavior, it would be inconsistent of us to value such small changes infinitely in our public decisions.

2. If all life were socially of infinite value, then any public policy that saves a life is worth doing, regardless of its cost. For example, banning the car would be justified! The corollary of this is that all policies that do not save lives will be pushed to the bottom of the public agenda—and probably just crowded out of consideration, given budgetary realities. Do we want to see the end of all free primary education in order to find the cure for a disease that strikes 1 person in a billion? If we are to make choices between life-saving policies and non–life-saving policies, we must put a value on the lives the life-saving policies save.

3. When we undertake public policies to save lives, we pay for them through taxes or foregone public expenditures elsewhere. This makes people worse off, and hence many eat less, work harder, drive older cars, worry more, and spend less on health care. All of these changes affect their probability of death. Estimates, albeit very rough, suggest that every time the government spends something between $5 million and $15 million, it costs one expected life because of reduced private expenditures on longevity-enhancing goods and services (Wildavsky, 1979; Keeney, 1990 and 1997; Viscusi, 1996).

Given that we need estimates of the value of life, how do we get them? Actuaries might suggest that the amount of life insurance tells us something about how one values one's own life, but use of such a number would mean that public policies are worthless if they save the lives of bachelors, because most bachelors neither need nor carry life insurance. Lawyers might suggest that the present value of all future earnings tells us the value of one's life, but use of such a number would mean that public policies are worthless if they save the lives of the retired or the disabled, because these people anticipate no further earnings.

Economists reject these approaches to the value of life and ask, instead, how much people are willing to pay for their own lives. And not with a gun in your ear and a mugger growling, "your money or your life"—that would bring us back to the identified life and a zero-versus-one probability. Rather, ask how much people are willing to pay for a small reduction in their probability of dying (Schelling, 1968).

Suppose, for example, that an inoculation were available that would reduce a person's chances of dying this coming year of some disease by 1 chance in a million. Suppose further that the average person were willing to pay x dollars for such an inoculation. Then if a million people were inoculated, one expected life would be saved, and their total willingness-to-pay (WTP) would be x million dollars. In a WTP sense, x million dollars is what these million people would be willing to pay to save 1 expected life.

A little algebra is in order. The formula implicit in the preceding paragraph is

$$x = (\Delta p)(V_L),   \text{[7A.1]}$$

where x is the life-saving monetary value of the policy, Δp is the reduction in each person's probability of death, and V_L is the monetary value each person implicitly puts on his or her own life. Each person's V_L will of course be different, but for public policy purposes we must pick some average, socially acceptable value. Then the social benefit of a policy that reduces the risk of death can be readily calculated (in theory) as

$$(\Delta p)(V_L)(N),   \text{[7A.2]}$$

where N is the number of people for whom the risk is reduced. In the inoculation example of the preceding paragraph, Δp was 0.000001, V_L was x, and N was 1,000,000.

But how big is x? Evidence is all around us. Whenever people demand money in order to undergo additional risk of death or spend money to reduce their risk of death, they are offering information about the WTP for expected longevity. Studies have looked at a wide variety of such choices. How much higher are wage rates in more risky occupations? Who buys smoke detectors? How much would people pay for cancer-detecting checkups? How much more do houses cost in areas free of life-threatening air pollution? How much discount due to lesser safety is there in used-car prices? And so on.

The figures vary from study to study, but the vast majority yield estimates between $1 million and $5 million per expected life saved (Dillingham, 1985; Fisher et al., 1989; Viscusi, 1996). Here, whenever we do benefit–cost analyses of life-saving devices or policies, we shall examine this entire range of WTP figures.[3A]

Don't forget to go back to Box 7A.1 and think some more about whether you made the right decision there (Q7A.1).

BOX 7A.2 Contingent Valuation

Another way of getting estimates of the value of life is simply to ask people what they would pay to avoid certain basic risks to life. Because the hypothetical payment is contingent on a change in risk, this questionnaire method has become known as "contingent valuation." While internal consistency checks can be made, the basic problem remains that what people say is not necessarily what people do. Below are three examples of contingent valuation questions.

1. You are planning on winter break in Florida. Suresafe Air will get you there and back for $400. Suresafe has a record of fatally crashing only 1 out of every million flights. You could also go on Flipflop Air, which is just as convenient except for one thing—Flipflop has a record of losing 1 flight out of every 100,000. What is the *smallest discount* below $400 that would make you willing to fly Flipflop instead of Suresafe?

2. After graduation you are offered a job by InterCorp, and you can choose to work in either Wagadaga or Yartakarta. You like the idea of living in either of these two places equally well. Then your new employer points out that while Wagadaga is safe, Yartakarta has anti-American terrorist activity—there appears to be 1 chance in 1000 that an InterCorp employee will be killed in any given year by such activity. InterCorp offers you $40,000 in annual salary for the Wagadaga location. What is the *least addition* to that salary that would make you willing to work for InterCorp in Yartakarta instead of Wagadaga?

3. You rent and you live alone. You are considering installing a smoke detector in your apartment. Smoke detectors last 5 (guaranteed and maintenance-free) years and then have to be replaced. Statistics, which you believe, say that some 7000 Americans are trapped in potentially fatal home fires each year and that the probability of dying in such a blaze is reduced by *half* if the residence is equipped with a smoke detector (Dardis, 1980). What is the *most* you would be willing to pay for a smoke detector?

The value of your life implicit in each of the three above questions is: (1) 55,555 times your answer to the first; (2) 1000 times your answer to the second; and (3) 16,000 times your answer to the third. Work it out (Q7A.2). Are your three implicit valuations sensible? Are they consistent?

ENDNOTES

[1]Recall what is meant by "one expected life." It is the change in the probability of death times the number of affected people. For example, if a cutback in the fire department of a city of 100,000 people raises the probability of a fire-related death from 0.00002 to 0.00003, then the cutback causes one expected death, that is, $(0.00003-0.00002)(100,000) = 1$.

[2]Businesses also have to make decisions about expected lives saved or lost, at least implicitly, because they have to decide which potentially life-saving gizmos to add to their product. But they hate to admit it. A 1973 memo surfaced recently that declared it to be a General Motors policy to add safety features only if they cost less than so many dollars per expected life saved. That memo now features prominently in court cases as proof of GM's heartlessness (Ingersoll, 1998).

[3]This is the value of one's life to one's own self. We ignore, though we should not, the fact that relatives and friends also value a person's life. Indeed, each "life" has attributes of a public good.

CHAPTER 8

Vehicle Safety

"There are lots of nutty people on the road,
including myself—
I'm a very absent-minded driver,
so [vehicle] safety was very important to me."

Marcie Brogan
(who commutes 40 miles daily in a Hummer)

Highway fatalities per vehicle-mile traveled declined steadily from the 1920s through the 1950s. This decline was not the result of any concerted government effort to force the manufacture of safer cars. Despite their belief that style, not safety, was what sold cars, manufacturers were steadily improving the safety of their vehicles. State regulations of cars did little more than formalize existing practices, such as requiring the headlights, windshield wipers, and rearview mirrors that automakers were already adding.

In the 1960s, however, the death rate on highways began to rise (see Figure 7.2), probably because Americans were just beginning to become accustomed to the new multilane, high-speed Interstate highways and because the baby boomers were just beginning to drive.[1] Ralph Nader's *Unsafe at Any Speed*, published in 1965, condemned auto manufacturers for callous disinterest in safety and sparked public interest in the subject. In 1966, Congress passed, without a single negative vote, the National Traffic and Motor Vehicle Safety Act and the Highway Safety Act, empowering the National Highway Traffic Safety Administration (NHTSA, pronounced "*nit*-sah") to promulgate rules that would force manufacturers to build safer vehicles. Between 1966 and 1974, dozens of standards were set for automobiles to make them less prone to crash and to better protect passengers when they did crash.

BOX 8.1 Safer Highways

Some of the improvement in highway safety has to do with improved highway design over the past half-century (Friedland *et al.*, 1990). Often, when a particular spot has suffered a particularly bad accident record, it is labeled a "black spot" and made safer through upgrading the road, adding lanes, installing traffic signs, etc. There is usually a great reduction in the accident rate there in the years following these improvements (Adams, 1995). Does this decline in accidents properly measure the impact of the highway improvements (Q8.1)?

In 1969, the highway death rate began again to decline, and indeed it has fallen in almost every year since then. How much of this decline can be attributed to the safer design and better equipment of vehicles? How much did these improvements add to the cost of making and operating vehicles?

COSTS AND BENEFITS OF SAFETY

An estimate of the added cost due to safety regulation is in principle straightforward. It consists of three things: (1) the initial manufacturing and installation cost of each new piece of safety equipment; (2) the greater fuel cost due to the weight the new equipment added to vehicles; and (3) a downward adjustment of those costs to allow for a learning curve, whereby manufacturers steadily cut costs as they accumulate more and more experience in production. Between 1966 and 1975, the heyday of new safety regulations, the cost of a new car rose somewhat over $1000 (in 1995 prices) because of newly mandated safety equipment; the present value of the added fuel and maintenance costs raises the total safety cost to about $1500 (Crandall *et al.*, 1985). Learning curve estimates are harder to make, but they might halve this cost.

The benefits of safety regulation are, most importantly, lives saved and serious injuries avoided or mitigated. Any measure of benefits must estimate these. The problem is that to estimate the reduction in death and injury one must not only know how many there actually were but also how many there would have been in the absence of the auto safety program. Obviously, since there has been a long-term downward trend in highway accidents and deaths, even before federal safety efforts began, we must separate the effects of trends from the effects of the new safety regulations.

One simple way to do this for highway deaths is simply to calculate the trend over time in highway deaths before 1965 and extrapolate this trend into the years after 1965. This assumes that the downward trend would have continued unchanged had there been no program. Then, the difference between this predicted death figure and the actual number of deaths each year is an estimate of the lives saved due to the program. One such careful estimate is reproduced in Table 8.1 (Crandall *et al.*, 1985).

Evidence like that of Table 8.1 supports the hypothesis that safety regulation after 1966 saved lives of passenger-car occupants. Table 8.1 suggests something approaching 2000 fewer highway deaths occurred on average in each year over 1966–1980, compared to a continuation of the pre-1965 trend.

Any benefit–cost (B/C) analysis of U.S. auto safety policy depends critically on this estimate of the number of lives saved—and on the value we put on those lives (see the appendix to Chapter 7). The annual net benefits are positive or negative according to whether $2V_L N_L$ (that is, the dollar's worth of deaths and injuries prevented) is greater or smaller than $C_V N_V$ (that is, the dollar's worth of costs incurred to prevent the deaths and injuries), where: 2 is a multiplier to raise the life-saving benefits by 100% to account for the dollar value of injuries prevented or made less serious; V_L is the value of each life saved; N_L is the number of lives

TABLE 8.1   Predicted and Actual Highway Deaths, 1966–1980

	Average number of highway deaths per annum			
	1966–1970	1971–1975	1976–1980	1966–1980
Total deaths				
Predicted	50,717	55,576	56,151	54,148
Actual	54,500	51,860	50,440	52,267
Lives saved	−3,783	3,716	5,711	1,881
Passenger-car occupant deaths				
Predicted	35,698	40,632	42,401	39,577
Actual	35,480	31,420	28,500	31,800
Lives saved	218	9,212	13,901	7,777
Pedestrian and bicyclist deaths				
Predicted	8,929	8,638	7,904	8,490
Actual	10,518	10,840	10,100	10,486
Lives saved	−1,589	−2,202	−2,196	−1,996
All other highway deaths				
Predicted	6,394	6,855	6,819	6,689
Actual	8,502	9,600	11,840	9.981
Lives saved	−2,108	−2,745	−5,021	−3,291

Notes: The three categories are exhaustive, and the actual deaths add to the total. Different trend equations were used, however, so that the predicted deaths do not exactly add to the total. "All other highway deaths" are predominantly on motorcycles and other unregulated vehicles.

Source: Crandall *et al.*, 1985.

saved each year because of the safety program; C_V is the increased cost per vehicle of the safety regulations; and N_V is the number of new cars sold per year.

Let's explore the magnitudes of these numbers. N_V is around 10 million; C_V is estimated to be anywhere between $750 and $1500; and V_L is between $1 million and $5 million. Then the critical value for N_L—that is, the value of N_L that makes the annual net benefits just positive—is somewhere between 750 and 7500 lives saved per year. All estimates of N_L are above 750, but many are below 7500, so this simple B/C calculation indicates why different researchers differ so greatly on the economic efficiency of the enhanced federal auto safety program of 1966–1974.

BEHIND THE BENEFIT–COST ANALYSIS

The preceding B/C calculation is for the whole safety package that has been added to cars. Implicitly, if we consider this a B/C analysis of the federal NHTSA program, we are assuming that no safety features would have been added otherwise—neither mandated by the states nor chosen by consumers. The B/C analysis of just the safety features *not wanted* by consumers might be very different and would be very hard to do.

Furthermore, some parts of the federal safety program are better than other parts. Increasingly, B/C analysis has played a part in the adoption of safety standards. For example, the NHTSA recently rejected a rollover standard for sport utility vehicles because it would cost more than $300 million per year and would be expected to save barely 30 lives per year—the cost per life saved was considered too high (Frame, 1996a). Many of the federal auto standards cost much less per life saved—for example, the Office of Management and Budget (OMB) estimates that the cost per life saved has been only $0.1 million for passive restraints in cars and for getting asbestos out of brake linings, $0.2 million for collapsible steering columns, $0.4 million for fuel system integrity standards, and $0.8 for seat cushion inflammability and for side impact standards.[2]

But we have so far considered only the impact of increased auto safety on total highway deaths. Notice in Table 8.1 that the estimate of lives saved of passenger-car occupants is nearly 8000 per year over 1966–1980, but that over 5000 lives were lost, mostly deaths of pedestrians, bicyclists, and motorcyclists. Most studies of the impact of auto safety find this offsetting impact: while the program saved lives *inside* the safer cars, those on the highway *outside* of these safer cars suffered increased death rates.

RISK COMPENSATION

Economic theory offers an explanation of these outcomes (Lave and Weber, 1970; Peltzman, 1975). The theory is called "risk compensation." In words of few sylla-

---

BOX 8.2 Less Than Life-Saving, But More Than Profitable

Not all NHTSA standards save lives; many just reduce the number and cost of fender benders. The center high-mounted stoplamp (CHMSL), one of the few new standards introduced since the mid-1970s, displays a particularly impressive benefit–cost success. Because they are mounted at the trailing driver's eye level, are brighter, and are not confused with parking lights and turn signals, the new stoplamps have reduced the number of rear-end collisions by about half. The cost of each additional CHMSL is less than about $6, which means, in a steady state of 10 million cars being sold each year, that the cost is $60 million per year.

The NHTSA estimates that $600 million in damages are saved by accidents avoided each year and another $80 million saved because the accidents that do occur are at reduced speeds and hence lower severity. The benefits of the CHMSL are more than 10 times the costs even without monetizing the cost of the 40,000 injuries prevented each year (NHTSA, 1983).

But CHMSLs save few lives. If we were to value life-saving infinitely in our public policymaking, CHMSL would go to the end of the queue—along with all other policies and projects that benefit us in valuable, but other than life-saving ways.

---

bles, the theory states that safer cars will be driven less safely. Conversely, drivers in unsafe cars or unsafe conditions will drive more carefully.

To keep the analysis simple, think of the typical driver as having only two goals in life, excitement and longevity. Excitement means, among many other things, driving fast and hence driving less carefully; longevity means, among many other things, driving carefully and hence driving less fast. Thus, this stereotypical driver faces a trade-off between speed and care, and hence between excitement and longevity. How does the acquisition of a safer car affect the complete set of choices available to the driver? The driver is better off in the sense that he or she can now choose more excitement or more longevity, or more of both, than before.

Will drivers mostly choose more excitement or more longevity when offered these new options? It depends on the preferences of the driver. But it seems a good guess that the typical driver will choose some more of each—more excitement *and* more longevity. This is good news for the car occupants, whose death rates will go down, but bad news for other cars, pedestrians, and cyclists, whose death rates will go up owing to the greater speeds of the safer cars that crash into them.

So far, we have implicitly been talking as if all drivers were alike in their attitudes toward excitement and risk. We all know that this is not so. On the highway there are—to put it traditionally, simply, and sexistly—"Dangerous Dans" and "Nervous Nellies" (Hemenway, 1993). When placed in a safer car, Nervous Nelly will take advantage of the opportunity to live a lot longer, with maybe a little more excitement. But Dangerous Dan will use the opportunity to achieve lots greater excitement, with maybe a little more longevity—for himself, though not for others he meets on the road.[3]

Note that this theory of risk compensation applies to a particular individual in two different circumstances. If you went out on a highway and observed, as cars went by, whether the drivers were wearing seat belts or not and whether they were driving cautiously or not, you would probably find that most people were either wearing a seat belt *and* driving cautiously (the Nervous Nellies) or not wearing a seat belt *and* not driving cautiously (the Dangerous Dans). It might seem at first to be a refutation of the theory—belted people driving more carefully than unbelted people. But each of the drivers you observed was a different person with different preferences, not the same person in different circumstances.

Aw, come on, you're saying. That's just theory. But, study after study supports the risk-compensation hypothesis. A few are gathered here:

1. Canada records accidents by the model year of the vehicle. Calculate the ratio of accidents involving cars of model year m in calendar year t (A_{mt}) to the total number of registered cars of model year m in calendar year t (V_{mt}), and compare this ratio (A_{mt}/V_{mt}) for different years (t) and different model years (m). The average ($t - m$)-year-old car had one-fourth more accidents for $m > 1964$ than for $m < 1964$ (Peltzman, 1975).

2. In North Carolina in 1968, 27% of the registered autos had the new safety equipment. These cars "accounted for" 34% of the accidents, but the fraction of these accidents involving an occupant's death was 15% less for the newer cars (Peltzman, 1975).

3. In Virginia in 1993, 44% of the cars on the road had driver-side air bags. In single-car crashes where only the driver died, 48% of the cars had driver-side air bags; in single-car crashes where only occupant(s) died, 69% had driver-side air bags; and in multiple-car crashes where one car had a driver-side air bag and the other did not and where someone died, the State Police determined that the air-bag-equipped car was the "initiator" of the accident in 73% of the cases (Peterson *et al.,* 1995).

4. Cars with air bags run up higher insurance claims for personal injuries than those without (WSJ, 1993). For example, when a given model of a car has a driver-side air bag added in a given year, its share of industry personal injury claims rises significantly in that year (Peterson *et al.,* 1995).[4]

5. Drivers of small cars fare worse in multicar crashes than do drivers of big cars. Given a multicar crash, the driver of a 1-ton car is two and a half times as likely to be killed as a driver of a 2-ton car. But accident rates for 1-ton cars are only 72% of the accident rates for 2-ton cars, and drivers of small cars get killed less often than drivers of big cars in single-car crashes. It is hard to resist the conclusion that drivers of small cars drive more carefully because they recognize that they are more likely to be seriously hurt if they crash (Evans, 1985; Chelimsky, 1991).[5]

6. In the Indianapolis 500, speeds have increased greatly over the century. The winning average speed was 75 MPH in 1911 (the first race) and had risen to 186 MPH by 1990 (the fastest race). But the death rate of participants has declined slightly over this entire period. If the cars (and the track) had not become safer,

the ever-higher speeds would have meant a rising trend of deaths; if the speeds had not gotten higher, the ever-safer cars would have meant a falling trend of deaths. The logical conclusion is that the Indy drivers were willing to take their ever-safer cars on the ever-safer track to ever-higher speeds.

7. When traffic lights are introduced at a road intersection, the number of right-angle crashes is (unsurprisingly) much reduced. But the number of rear-end, left-turn, and side-swipe crashes increases, leaving the overall accident rate roughly unchanged (Box, 1970).

8. Antilock brake systems (ABS) are designed to prevent yawing. While ABS has been long heralded as a dramatic contributor to auto safety, cars equipped with ABS have so far failed to display lower rates of accidents and fatalities. Comparisons were made between identical models in the year before they had ABS and in the year after ABS became standard equipment. Crashes and fatalities were lower for ABS-equipped cars in multiple-vehicle incidents, especially on wet roads, but in single-vehicle incidents, the ABS-equipped cars had much worse crash and fatality outcomes (Frame, 1996b; Kahane, 1994). Drivers of cars with ABS may be simply misusing the new systems out of ignorance, but another plausible explanation is that they are feeling safer and hence driving more aggressively.[6]

BOX 8.3 Do Consumers Care about Vehicle Safety?
Ever since Henry Ford II stated that "safety doesn't sell," there has been debate about whether consumers are willing to pay for safer vehicles. The recent history of all-terrain vehicles (ATVs) provides some evidence.

Four-wheeled ATVs began to be marketed in 1983, and evidence quickly accumulated that they were safer than the earlier three-wheeled ATVs. By 1986, four-fifths of the new ATV sales were of four-wheeled vehicles, despite the fact that they cost a few hundred dollars more. In 1988, the Consumer Product Safety Commission (CPSC) arranged a consent decree with ATV producers to no longer sell three-wheeled ATVs. New four-wheeled ATVs continued to be made, and the secondhand market for both kinds continued.

What happened to the relative price of three-wheeled and four-wheeled ATVs in the secondhand market after 1988? If they were imperfect substitutes, and the implicit safety information was disregarded by consumers, then the increased scarcity of three-wheeled ATVs should have driven their relative price up. If, on the other hand, they were highly substitutable, and the new safety information was valued by consumers, then the relative price of three-wheeled ATVs should have gone down. In fact, the relative price of the used three-wheeler did go down, suggesting that consumers took advantage of the new safety information (Rodgers, 1993).

Production of single-engined private planes has essentially ceased in the United States because of high accident rates and the rising insurance costs to manufacturers. What do you think has happened to prices of secondhand single-engine private planes (Q8.2)?

> **BOX 8.4 CAFE, Emissions, and Vehicle Safety**
>
> In order to meet CAFE standards, auto manufacturers have reduced the weight of the average new car in the United States by some 500–1000 pounds. This in itself increases highway death since occupants of small cars are at greater risk in accidents than are occupants of big cars.[7] This weight loss is probably the cause of several thousand extra highway deaths each year. One study estimates the resulting trade-off to be, per year, 200–400 lives lost and 500 million gallons saved—roughly 1 fatality for every 2 million gallons (Crandall and Graham, 1989). Thomas Sowell called this "really trading blood for oil" (Johnston, 1997).
>
> Then, in order to meet safety and emission standards, auto manufacturers have added a few hundred pounds back on to the weight of the average new car, thus increasing its fuel consumption. Roughly, this added weight converts a 28 MPG car into a 26 MPG car (Lave, 1981; Crandall *et al.,* 1985; NRC, 1992).

9. One Sunday in September 1967, Sweden switched from driving on the left side of the road to driving on the right.[8] Highway death rates attained an all-time *low* during the next few months (Spolander, 1968; Adams, 1985 and 1995). The same temporary drop in highway fatalities occurred when Iceland later made the same switch (Wilde, 1982).

The advantage of safer cars is clearly eroded by two factors: (1) drivers drive less safely when they are driving safer cars and in safer conditions, and (2) as a result, nonoccupants are at greater risk on the highways. Again, in words of few syllables, belted and bagged drivers are belting and bagging more bikers and walkers. If you want to understand accidents and deaths on the highway, it appears that it is at least as important to examine drivers as vehicles—and we shall do just that in Chapters 9 through 13.

RECALLS

Before leaving the subject of vehicle safety, however, it is interesting to look at what has happened at the NHTSA over the last two decades:

> Since the mid-1970s, NHTSA has instead [of requiring greater safety technology for new automobiles] concentrated its statutory power to force the recall of motor vehicles that contain defects related to safety performance. It has retreated to the old . . . form of legal regulation—case-by-case adjudication—which requires little, if any, technological sophistication and which has no known effects on vehicle safety. (Mashaw and Harfst, 1990)

Over the past two decades, the NHTSA has ordered the recall of some 5 to 10 million vehicles per year.

The costs of recalls are often great, and the benefits often small. Studies, as usual, vary, but the estimates suggest that 5–15% of all auto accidents involve vehi-

BOX 8.5 When Big Vehicles and Small Vehicles Collide
As small vehicles have gotten smaller, drivers have turned more and more to light trucks (which category includes sport utility vehicles and vans). Being big and sturdy, these light trucks are safer for their occupants in a crash. But the occupants of ordinary cars are at greater risk of fatality when they crash with one of these large vehicles (Lerner, 1993; Bradsher, 1997b and 1997d; Brown, 1998). See if you can show that if f is the fraction of the vehicles on the road that are light trucks, then the probability that a two-vehicle crash involves a light truck and a car is $2f(1-f)$, which is maximized at $f = 0.5$. Ironically, one-half is getting to be the actual fraction of light trucks on America's roads (Q8.3).

When big trucks hit cars, it is even worse for the cars, which is the reason the law requires truckers to do serious training before piloting an 18-wheeler. Training courses are offered by private schools, and they last from 1 day up to 6 months, at the end of which the schools themselves administer the exam for commercial drivers licenses (Prager, 1998). Worried? Worry some more. Many students' tuitions are paid by trucking companies or the U.S. government, but they will not pay unless and until a student passes the exam. Ninety-five percent of them do pass, compared to a pass rate for ordinary drivers licenses that ranges from 46% (in Washington) to 86% (in Illinois).

cle failure of some kind. This means that if all defective vehicles were recalled, all owners responded, all defects were fully corrected, and no new defects were introduced in the process, highway deaths might be reduced by some 2000–6000 per year. This would be no small achievement on the highway safety front.

In fact, however, not all defects are spotted, nor are all potential recalls ordered. Only half the eligible vehicle owners respond to recall notices by returning their cars for repair. Most of the accidents involving "vehicle failure" are caused by inadequate maintenance, not by any inherent defect in the vehicle. Dealer repair of defects is often slipshod and, since they sometimes involve extensive disassembly of the car, "could introduce more hazards than are eliminated" (Mashaw and Harfst, 1990). One wag suggested that more accidents have happened on the trips to the dealer for recall repairs than would have been caused by the defects themselves.

There has been one major exception to this change of emphasis from safety equipment to recalls. This exception concerns seat belts and air bags, to which we turn in the next chapter.

ENDNOTES

[1]The term "baby boomers" refers to the people born during 1945–1960. United States birth rates were high then, and this meant a rising proportion of U.S. drivers were new, teenage drivers in the 1960s and early 1970s.

[2]Currently, the OMB sets a limit of $2.7 million per life saved for use in B/C analyses of policy changes throughout the federal government. But that limit is exceeded in many EPA cases; cost per

life saved often runs over $10 million, and sometimes over $100 million (Van Houtven and Cropper, 1996). Some regulations by the Occupational Safety and Health Administration (OSHA) run even higher—for the 1987 regulation of formaldehyde, the cost has been estimated at nearly $100 *billion* per expected life saved (Viscusi, 1996).

[3]This distinction between people in their attitudes toward risk and their valuation of their own lives shows up in other aspects of life than driving. For example, studies of wage rates and the risk premium in them have shown that people in high-risk jobs (with annual fatality rates on the order of 1 in 1000) value their lives at less than $1 million, while people in low-risk jobs (with annual fatality rates on the order of 1 in 10,000) value their lives at more than $4 million (Viscusi, 1996).

[4]Is it possible that bad drivers, knowing they are bad drivers and hence at risk on the highway, rush out to buy cars equipped with driver-side air bags? Then we would expect that the air-bag effect would be large at first but would get smaller over time as more and more models became so equipped; the data do not show this (Peterson *et al.*, 1995).

[5]Of course, these data are also consistent with a different explanation, that bad drivers know they are bad drivers and buy big cars so they will not get killed in their more frequent crashes.

[6]In a controlled experiment of ABS, part of the Munich (Germany) taxi fleet was equipped with ABS and part not. Drivers were randomly assigned to the two types of vehicles. Over the next 3 years, those with ABS had slightly higher accident rates than those without (Aschenbrenner and Biehl, 1994).

[7]The effect of car size on highway death rates is huge. According to an Insurance Institute for Highway Safety study, small new cars (wheelbase <95 inches) experience 296 occupant deaths per million vehicles while large new cars (wheelbase >114 inches) experience only 110. The figure for large new utility vehicles (wheelbase >120 inches) is even lower, 90 (IIHS, 1997).

[8]European left–right conventions date back at least 700 years. Early conventions were local and varied from city to city, but they tended increasingly toward carriages-to-the-left and pedestrians-to-the-right (facing oncoming carriages). The international convention of driving on the right in continental Europe was prompted by the French who, after the Revolution, made the formerly privileged carriages also go on the people's side (Young, 1996).

Seat Belts and Air Bags

"A common mistake that people make
when trying to design something completely foolproof
is to underestimate the ingenuity
of complete fools."

Douglas Adams
Mostly Harmless

Technically, there is no question about the life-saving advantages of equipment that mitigates the impact of the "second collision"—the collision when drivers and passengers are being thrown around the auto interior or out of the vehicle. The questions are why so many drivers and passengers choose not to utilize these devices when they are available and what public policy should do in response to this disuse. The history of the U.S. policy response to seat belt disuse over the past quarter-century is instructive.

Manual seat belts differ from almost all other safety features of autos in one important way: to be effective, manual seat belts require the cooperation of drivers and passengers. Unused seat belts most definitely fail anybody's benefit–cost (B/C) test.

THE BENEFITS AND COSTS OF SEAT BELTS

Seat belt assemblies became available in American cars as optional extra equipment in the 1950s, and more than half the states required their installation even before the NHTSA was formed. In 1967, the NHTSA mandated lap ("two-point") seat belts in all new models as one of its first safety regulations and mandated lap and shoulder ("three-point") seat belts in the front seats soon afterward. As a result, in the early 1970s, there were cars on the road with a variety of belt equipment, including none, and with a variety of belt usage, including none.

This provided a "natural experiment" on seat belt effectiveness. To a social scientist, for whom controlled experiments that vary one thing at a time are usually impossible, a "natural experiment" is a situation in which one factor happens to change significantly while other important factors remain relatively constant. One can then conclude with some confidence that any observed changes in related other things were caused by the one factor that changed significantly. Even here, one must be careful. Not everything else is exactly unchanging. Sunny days cause picnics, and not the reverse—of that we can be sure; but do high grades cause student enthusiasm, or does student enthusiasm cause high grades? Also, one must be careful of the "post hoc, ergo propter hoc" fallacy.[1]

From this natural experiment, evidence quickly began to mount. This evidence was unanimous. Lap and shoulder belts, when used, have proven quite effective in preventing fatal injury in severe motor vehicle crashes. Nearly half of the deaths of front-seat (driver or passenger) occupants in potentially fatal accidents are prevented (Table 9.1).[2] Since the initial cost of installing each lap and shoulder harness is less than $30, it is hard to see how they could fail a B/C test.

A very simple B/C calculation will suffice to make the point. For cars that last, say, 10 years, the cost per year of a driver-side belt system is roughly $3. The life-saving benefit of wearing a seat belt outweighs this cost if

$$(0.45)(p)(V_L) >< \$3, \qquad\qquad [9.1]$$

where 0.45 is the percentage reduction in fatality, conditional on a potentially fatal crash, p is the probability that the driver will become involved in a potentially fatal crash during the year, and V_L is the value the driver puts on his or her own life. The probability that the average car driver will actually be killed in any year is about 0.0001, so the probability that the average driver will be involved in a potentially fatal accident is somewhat greater than that. Even accepting $p = 0.0001$,

TABLE 9.1   Life-Saving Effectiveness of Different Restraints

Restraint system	Life-saving rate (%)
Lap and shoulder belt only	45
Air bag only	15
Both lap/shoulder belt and air bag	50

Note: These life-saving rates are for front seats.
Sources: Viano, 1991; Lawson, 1991; Evans, 1986 and 1990.

we find that wearing a seat belt provides benefit in excess of cost if only V_L is as great as $67,000!$[3]

But many people would not buy seat belts if they were optional and do not wear seat belts when they are available. In 1983, when seat belt usage was voluntary everywhere in the United States, only 14% of drivers (and front-seat passengers) used them.

Why do people not use seat belts when they are so effective? Ignorance is not the answer—the only people who "ought to know better" than unbelted drivers are heavy smokers. Are time and discomfort the answer? Discomfort is hard to measure, but time is not. Consider a driver who values his or her own life at V_L and whose relevant driving-time hourly wage is P_t. This driver gets into and out of the car an average of 5 times a day, every day of the year, and takes 10 seconds to buckle and unbuckle each time. At what value of V_L would the life-saving benefit of buckling up not be worth the time "wasted" with the buckling? Now, the benefit of seat belt usage outweighs the cost if

$$(0.45)(0.0001)(V_L) >< \$3 + (5)(365)(10)(1/3600)P_t. \qquad [9.2]$$

It is not difficult to think of values of V_L and P_t which make seat belts privately unwanted. For example, consider a P_t of about $8 (that is, about two-thirds of the average U.S. hourly wage); then the critical value of V_L is about $1 million, at the bottom of the value-of-life range we are considering (Blomquist, 1979).[4]

THE BENEFITS AND COSTS OF AIR BAGS

There is now widely available in the United States a third alternative to belting or not belting (and driving totally unprotected)—namely, the air bag. Air bags automatically inflate when the car crashes and thus provide a protective cushion between the front-seat occupant and the car. Though they were invented in the 1950s, only in the last decade have they begun to appear in cars because of their great expense. All new cars from now on will be equipped with two air bags. The fact that auto manufacturers have been adding air bags at a faster pace than the government has mandated suggests that people are now willing to pay their added cost, and studies support this (Mannering and Winston, 1995).[5]

What kind of person would refuse to belt up but would pay an extra $150 or so for each air bag? Consider, for example, a driver who values his or her own life (V_L) at $5 million and whose value of time (P_t) is $50 per hour. His or her seat-belt-usage B/C (inequality [9.2]) fails, but the air-bag-purchase B/C succeeds since

$$(0.15)(0.0001)(\$5 \text{ million}) > \$15, \qquad [9.3]$$

where 0.15 is the reduction in the probability of fatality due to the air bag alone, conditional on a potentially fatal crash (see Table 9.1), 0.0001 is again used as the probability of becoming involved in a potentially fatal crash during the year, $5 million is the value this person puts on his or her life, and $15 is the annual cost of an air bag assuming the car lasts 10 years.

Figure 9.1 shows the regions of values of V_L and P_t that lead a rational B/C maximizer to the various choices among seat belt and air bag. There are four possible choices—neither, seat belt only, air bag only, and both. Which choice a person makes depends on how that person values his or her own life (V_L) and the price of his or her time (P_t).[6] As U.S. public policy moves toward mandating both seat belts and air bags, "we" collectively are in effect saying that people may not value their lives at less than $3 million and may not value their time at more than $20 per hour.

So far, we have been assuming that while people differ in how they value their own lives and their own time, all people face the same risk of a potentially fatal accident. In fact, different drivers drive differently and thereby generate very different highway risks for themselves. People who voluntarily belt themselves tend to drive more carefully than those who do not wear belts. Unbelted drivers have 50% more crashes than belted drivers and, of course, die more frequently per crash; they also drive drunk more often and commit more traffic violations.

In Chapter 8, we introduced Nervous Nelly and Dangerous Dan. Nervous Nelly leaps at the chance to wear seat belts (and buy air bags, too) and then drive a wee bit faster with her seat belt snugly fastened about her. Dangerous Dan just does not wear his seat belt, or he halfheartedly fastens it and then drives faster or more recklessly. Forcing Dangerous Dans to wear seat belts or buy air bags therefore has two offsetting implications for highway safety:

1. It would reduce their deaths a lot, given their basically high propensity for crashes. For example, putting seat belts onto Dangerous Dans should save even more lives per seat belt than do the voluntary seat belts now embracing the safely driving Nervous Nellies.

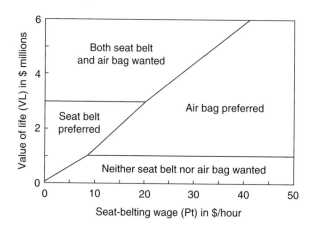

FIGURE 9.1   Air Bag versus Seat Belt versus Nothing

2. Forcing Dangerous Dans into greater safety in one respect may induce them to drive less safely in other respects. Consider mandating seat belts, for example. Putting belts around Dangerous Dans might simply make them drive faster and have more numerous and more serious crashes—risk compensation again. Maybe fewer Dans would die per crash, but the greater number of crashes might more than offset that. And the additional crashes of the Dangerous Dans would also kill pedestrians, motorcyclists, and other drivers (some belted, some not).

MANDATING SEAT BELT USE

Let us return to the decision of many people not to use seat belts. American public policy has essentially not accepted this decision. One possible reason is that U.S. policy assumes that those who fail to use seat belts are simply irrational and should be protected from their irrationality. As evidence for this argument, we might cite the groups who, relative to others, most often reject seat belts: males (and cigarette-smoking females), the poor, the uneducated, the young, and the drunk.

A second possibility is that U.S. policy accepts the private rationality but steps in because the resulting highway deaths generate negative externalities for other, also rational, citizens. For argument's sake, take the view that the lives unbelted drivers endanger are their own, to have or to have not. Nevertheless, highway suicide does generate negative externality of two kinds. One, not only are friends and relatives saddened by such an event, but even strangers are hurt by the knowledge of senseless and premature death. Two, dying on the highway incurs many social costs for which the dead do not privately pay (namely, police, medical, congestion, and litter costs beyond what is covered by the deceased's family or insurance).

Whatever the reason, "we" collectively have been unwilling to accept people's private decisions not to protect themselves from the consequences of their accidents. A review of the actual policies undertaken over the past quarter-century is interesting.

When the NHTSA first began to think about ways to thwart the no-belt choice, auto manufacturers suggested an ignition interlock that would prevent a car from being started unless all its passengers were properly restrained. The interlock was fairly cheap, less than $200, and completely effective, unless disabled by the user. It first appeared in the new models of 1974. Unfortunately, many of those who preferred not to buckle simply disabled the interlock, and many others screamed loudly at this invasion of their something or other. The uproar caught Congressional attention. The interlock disappeared by the 1975 model year (Mashaw and Harfst, 1990).

Somewhat later, automatic seat belts were mandated. Attached to rails above the front-seat doors, these are shoulder belts that swing back across the seats when the doors are closed. They are cheap, costing little more than manual lap and shoulder belts, and they were used nearly twice as much as manual belts. That they were not 100% used is attributable to the fact that they are readily detachable and thereby turned into manual or unused belts. The lap belt still needs to be attached manually, so many users are only restrained by the automatic shoulder belt, which is even less valuable in a crash than the early lap-only belts. The bottom line on these "passive restraints" is that to be equivalent to a manual lap and shoulder system, they require greater cost in initial equipment and just as much cost in time and discomfort; but they do provide somewhat greater protection for those who would take no active part in the manual system. They are disappearing in favor of air bags.

Behavioral, rather than technical, modification has also been sought. Beginning in 1976 in Canada (Ontario) and in 1985 in the United States (New York), front-seat car passengers were required by law to attach their lap and shoulder belts. By the end of 1986, over half the states had such laws; today, all but one does.[7] Such laws quickly more than double usage, typically from under 25% to over 50%. The cost is lower than the ignition interlock or the automatic seat belt, involving no equipment change, few enforcement resources, and only the time and inconvenience of those least inconvenienced by belts—those seriously inconvenienced will risk the low-expected-cost fines instead.

States have added mandatory seat belt laws at different times and with different types of enforcement, providing a "natural experiment" in the laws' effects. The interstate effects by seat belt law have been dramatic, as Table 9.2 shows (Bureau, 1993). Overall, mandatory seat belt laws have reduced front-seat fatalities by nearly 10% by pressing protection on some people who would not have otherwise worn manual belts (Wagenaar *et al.*, 1988). Of course, most estimates of lives saved by new belt use assume that compulsorily belted Dangerous Dans continue to drive with the same care as they did when they were unbelted. But there is evidence that they do not—nonoccupant highway deaths rose in many of the states that

TABLE 9.2   Seat Belt Laws and Highway Deaths

	Primary	Secondary	None
Number of states	10	26	14
Motor vehicle deaths			
1985	11,194	29,071	5798
1991	9,800	25,972	5479
Percent decline	−12	−11	−6
Deaths avoided	672	1,454	—

Notes: "None" refers to states that had passed no mandatory seat belt law by 1 January 1991. Recall that no mandatory seat belt law had been passed in any state before 1985. The "deaths avoided" figures (672 and 1454) are estimates of the number of 1991 highway deaths that were prevented by achieving 11 and 12% fatality declines instead of 6% (as in states that did not mandate seat belt usage).

mandated the wearing of seat belts (Evans and Graham, 1991). Moreover, mandatory seat belt laws still leave a third of the (front-seat) passengers unprotected.

MANDATING AIR BAGS

Under mandatory seat belt usage, many people still go unbelted, and fatal accidents occur to belted people. Air bags can reduce deaths in both circumstances. Does this justify mandating air bags? A social benefit–cost analysis that ignores people's preferences about longevity, time, bags, and belts might simply ask if the expected value of the lives saved by air bags is greater than their cost. How many lives are saved by air bags? For the 30% that do not wear seat belts, deaths in a potentially fatal accident are reduced by 15%; for the 70% who do wear seat belts, deaths in a potentially fatal accident are reduced by 5% (see Table 9.1) (Kahane, 1996). The life-saving benefits of mandatory air bags exceed the costs if

$$[(0.15)(0.30) + (0.05)(0.70)](0.0001)(V_L) > < \$15, \qquad [9.3]$$

where we again assume the probability each year of a driver being in a potentially fatal accident to be 0.0001 and the annual cost of an air bag to be \$15. The air bag passes its social B/C test if the societal V_L is about \$2 million or higher. Not a clear call.

BOX 9.1 Mandatory Child-Restraint Seats?
We mandate the use of automotive child-restraint seats in all states, and estimates consistently show great reduction in child injury and death, at least when the seats are properly used—which they often are not (Wagenaar, 1985; Wald, 1996). The NHTSA considers the child-safety seat "one of the most successful auto safety innovations," saving kids' lives at a cost of only a few hundred thousand dollars per expected life saved (NHTSA, 1985).

Nevertheless, the Federal Aviation Authority (FAA) decided *not* to require the use of child-safety seats in commercial airplanes (Wald, 1995). Why? Air crashes are different, and belts are much less effective as lifesavers there. But the main reason for the FAA decision involved the extra cost to parents of paying for the child's seat (since a parental lap is no longer a free option). Proponents of such child-restraint seats claimed that 2 baby lives would have been saved by such seats since 1987; the airlines, opposing such a requirement, claimed that if babies needed to have and pay for their own seat, more parents would drive instead of fly, and 8 additional baby deaths would occur per year on highways (Kolstad, 1989; McKenzie and Lee, 1990).

Incidentally, studies show that *ownership* of auto child-restraint seats rises with higher family income, but *use* of the seats falls with higher family income. Surprised (Q9.2)?

BOX 9.2 Mandatory Motorcycle Helmets?

Motorcycling is a dangerous way to travel. Motorcycles account for only 1/200th as many vehicle-miles as cars in the United States, but they account for 1/20th of the highway deaths—a death rate that is one order of magnitude higher (NHTSA, 1994). Can mandatory helmets help?

Another natural experiment. Before 1967, only 10 states mandated the wearing of motorcycle helmets. About half of the motorcyclists wear helmets when they are not required; virtually all wear them when they are required (Waller, 1995). The federal Highway Safety Act of 1967 empowered the withholding of highway funds from states without such laws, and 37 states quickly passed such a law. Motorcyclist fatalities per registered motorcycle fell by nearly half (Muller, 1980; NHTSA, 1980). California was one of the states that did not comply, and, when its highway funds were threatened, the law was repealed; 28 states then repealed their mandatory motorcycle helmet laws.

Motorcyclist fatalities per registered motorcycle rose by nearly half (NHTSA, 1980). But they rose by a larger percentage in states that did not repeal their mandatory helmet laws than in states that did repeal them (Adams, 1985)!

Motorcyclist fatalities *per registered motorcycle* are lower in the states without helmet laws than in the states with them (Teresi, 1995; Adams, 1995). On the other hand, motorcyclist fatalities *per motorcycle accident* are higher in the states without helmet laws than in the states with them (de Wolf, 1986). Why? Try risk compensation (Q9.3).

By the by, a larger fraction of the serious auto accidents involve head injury than do serious motorcycle accidents. Does this suggest mandatory helmets for auto drivers and passengers?

Unfortunately, air bags can cost lives as well as save them. Some people, mostly children and small women, have been killed by the force of the air bag inflation. Net, the NHTSA estimates that, through 1996, passenger-side air bags had "saved" 144 adults and "killed" 35 children (Nomani and Taylor, 1997). Other observers, including one GM safety researcher (who got in trouble with the company for saying it), think that air bags may have *increased* the average risk of death in a crash (Evans, 1997). As a result, two air bag modifications are being made: some people are getting permission to install on–off switches so they can deactivate the air bags, and some automakers are installing air bags that deploy less forcefully and do not deploy at all in low-speed collisions (Wald, 1997a and 1997b).[8]

Before leaving the subject, we should remind ourselves again of the two countervailing forces on the safety of added safety equipment: (1) as cars become more expensive because of this equipment, people will tend to keep old cars longer, and the oldest cars have the least safety equipment, and (2) as cars become safer, risk compensation may lead drivers to drive less carefully, which endangers not only themselves but their passengers and nonoccupants. There is more than a little truth to the waggish comment that if you want highway safety, do not install air bags, install swords (Bedard, 1994).

ENDNOTES

[1]Translation: After this, and therefore because of this.

[2]"Potentially fatal accidents" are those in which people will die if they are protected by neither a full seat belt nor an air bag.

[3]Throughout this section, we will ignore the possibility that a buckled seat belt or an air bag reduces the severity of a nonfatal accident. In fact, they of course do reduce the severity of injuries. So what we are getting is a lower-bound (or most conservative) estimate of V_L.

[4]The relevant wage (P_t) must be about $44 for the critical value of life (V_L) to be at the top end of the range, that is, V_L must be $5 million.

[5]Consumers were not always willing to pay for air bags. General Motors offered optional air bags in some 1974 cars. GM spent $80 million on them and sold only 10,000—$8,000 per bag!

[6]It is left to the masochistic reader to work out the precise equations for the lines in Figure 9.1. You can do it if you try—all the necessary data have been given (Q9.1).

[7]Enforcement is either "primary" (in a few states), which means that police can stop a car for a seat belt infraction, or "secondary" (in most states), which means that seat belt fines can only be levied on cars which have been stopped for other reasons. Not surprisingly, usage is somewhat higher with primary enforcement. Aggressive primary enforcement could get American seat belt usage up to that of Canada, Australia, and much of Western Europe—over 90%. Evidence for that statement comes from North Carolina, where $25 tickets pushed seat belt usage up 20 percentage points (to 83%) in just 2 years. If seat belt usage in the United States were everywhere 83%, it is estimated that over 4000 lives would be saved per year (Nomani, 1997).

[8]Such "depowered" air bags are more effective for seat-belted occupants than are current U.S. air bags. The extra force in American bags is there to better protect the *unbelted* occupants (Mathews, 1998). Another interesting trade-off!

Legal Liability and Insurance

"Do not look where you fell,
but where you slipped."

African Proverb

In principle, legal liability for one's external damages should "internalize" the external costs and induce drivers to take the proper amount of care in their driving and to cause no more than the optimal amount of highway damage. In fact, problems arise due to damage measurement, risk-aversion, bankruptcy, moral hazard, and the existence of automobile liability insurance, all of which act to reduce the effectiveness of the legal approach to highway safety.[1]

"STRICT LIABILITY"

Let us consider a legal system that places "strict liability" on drivers for the external damage they do. By strict liability, we mean that the driver can offer no excuses—if a pedestrian is run down by a car, the driver is held liable. For simplicity, we will consider only one kind of external damage, that of causing an accident that kills a pedestrian on the highway. All highway deaths are assumed to be correctly valued at $3 million. Drivers can drive at fast, medium, or slow speeds, and drivers get more benefit from faster driving, either because of the intrinsic thrill or because of the reduced time spent getting places. Hypothetical annual expected outcomes are shown in Table 10.1.

BOX 10.1 When Do You Stop Carrying Collision Insurance?
While liability insurance to cover damage you do to others is mandated almost everywhere, the extent to which you insure your car for damages you yourself do to it—collision insurance—is always optional. Those who own new cars almost always carry collision insurance; those who own clunkers rarely do. When do you stop carrying collision insurance as your car gets older?

If you look at your annual collision insurance cost and divide it by the current resale value of your car, you will get the implicit estimate of the insurance company of the probability that you will "total" your car during the coming year.[2] It will astound you. Are these just high profits? Not necessarily. In addition to the costs of running the insurance company, collision-insured cars do tend to cost more than uninsured cars because: (1) accident-prone drivers are more likely to carry collision insurance; (2) more repair gets done if the car is insured; and (3) repair costs are higher if the car is insured. Think about why each of these three things is true—and think in terms of adverse selection and moral hazard (Q10.1).

So, at some point after the resale value of your car gets low enough that your finances could tolerate its "totaling," it is time to save the very high cost of the collision insurance. Exactly when depends upon the extent of your risk-aversion.

The driver must make a decision on how fast to drive. All three speeds yield positive net benefits relative to the alternative of not driving, but the net benefit is maximized at "medium" speed—the net benefit from going at medium speed is $125 (i.e., $425 minus $300), higher than the net benefit of going at either fast or slow speeds. Fast driving too greatly increases the expected court cost, and slow driving too greatly reduces the benefits of driving. This decision to drive at a medium speed is also the correct social decision, given how we value lives. The driver drives at the optimal speed not because the driver is concerned about killing other people but because the expected court settlement acts as a Pigovian tax that internalizes the externality.

Notice how critically this optimal outcome depends upon the value of life selected by the courts or the jurors. If the courts set the value of a life at $4 million, the expected court costs would rise by one-third, to $600 for fast driving, to $400 for medium driving, and to $200 for slow driving. The rational maximizing driver would now choose to drive slowly. Because the courts have decided that life is more precious, drivers end up driving more slowly and killing fewer pedestrians.

What if we all have agreed that life should be valued at $3 million, but juries are generous and award $4 million in cases of pedestrian death? Then, drivers will drive slowly when they should have been driving at medium speed—society's valuation of life is essentially a decision about the optimal speed limit (more on this in Chapter 13). People will take too long to get places and too few pedestrians will be killed.

TABLE 10.1   Expected Benefits and Costs of Driving

Driving style	Driver's benefits	Probability of a death	Expected court cost
Fast	$500	0.00015	$450
Medium	$425	0.00010	$300
Slow	$250	0.00005	$150

Note. The driver's benefits are measured relative to the benefits of the next best alternative to driving—e.g., relative to busing or walking. The expected court cost equals the probability of causing a death times $3 million, the assumed court valuation of the lost life.

It seems curious to say that "too few" pedestrians would be killed—surely the now-surviving pedestrians are better off with this lower pedestrian death rate! We should not, however, be looking at the highway carnage from an ex post viewpoint when identified dead people would, if they could, pay huge amounts to change their situations. From an ex ante viewpoint, the pedestrians would have been willing to pay only $150 to have the probability of highway death reduced from 0.00010 (with medium-speed drivers) to 0.00005 (with slow drivers). But the jury's erroneous life valuations have caused drivers to go slowly and thereby forego $175 of benefits (i.e., $425 minus $250). The drivers who lose by the excessive jury valuations could, in theory, bribe pedestrians to let them return to medium speed (with a sum between $150 and $175), and everybody would be better off. The correct valuation of life is critical, and our courts and juries cannot be expected to always get it right.

SOME COMPLICATIONS

Notice also that the preceding outcome is optimal (with the correct value of life) only if drivers are risk-neutral. All the calculations were conducted with expected values and hence all are based on the assumption of risk-neutrality. In Table 10.2 we repeat Table 10.1, this time spelling out the actual possible outcomes rather than just calculating the expected outcomes—with the court settlement for killing a pedestrian being again set at the (assumed) correct value of $3 million. The benefits of driving at different speeds pale in comparison to the driver's costs if a pedestrian is killed. If this possible loss of nearly $3 million weighs heavily on the driver's decision how to drive, as it should if the driver is risk-averse, then the driver may choose to go slowly (or take the bus!) even though driving at medium speed is socially optimal.

TABLE 10.2   Actual Benefits and Costs of Driving

Driving style	Driver's gross benefits	Net benefits of driving if	
		No death	Yes death
Fast	$500	$500	−$2,999,500
Medium	$425	$425	−$2,999,575
Slow	$250	$250	−$2,999,750

Few drivers in fact have assets of $3 million, so that Table 10.2 is not an accurate picture of the outcomes. Suppose the total assets of the driver are, for example, just $1000. Then a realistic table of the outcomes is given in Table 10.3, where the driver simply pays over those assets and declares bankruptcy if a court case comes up. Notice now that expected net benefits are maximized by driving fast (and declaring bankruptcy if a pedestrian is hit). Bankruptcy is generally thought to be a humane policy that prevents entire lives from being shattered by a single mishap or mistake. But an unfortunate by-product of the possibility of bankruptcy here is a distortion of the driving decision.

So far, we have not considered the possibility that the pedestrian might be partly or completely at fault when an accident occurs. The driver is "strictly liable." The problem is one of moral hazard—the possibility that pedestrians will not be sufficiently careful if society arranges that they are fully compensated for any damages they sustain.

Death is quite final, and it is hard to argue that moral hazard arises when it is the dead pedestrian's family, not the pedestrian, who is "compensated." But for lesser damages, such as broken legs or concussions, it is very possible that pedestrians will cross streets during the "don't walk" sign if their medical bills will be certainly and automatically compensated by the driver who hits them. The law attempts to counter this problem with the concept of "negligence," whereby the driver is *fully* liable only if the driver is negligent (in our example, the car is going too fast) *and* the pedestrian is not negligent.

If drivers can purchase auto liability insurance, and the competitive insurance companies know accurately how the drivers they insure will drive, then well-off, risk-averse drivers will want such insurance.[3] The cost of insurance to the driver will exactly equal the probability that the driver causes a death times the $3 million that the insurance company will have to pay if a death occurs.[4] Then the driver's insurance costs will exactly equal the expected court cost of Table 10.1, and the driver's decision on how to drive will continue to be optimal—that is, to drive at medium speed, with the driver's net benefits maximized at $125, with gross benefits of $425 and insurance premiums of $300.[5]

Individuals become better off by reducing their risk when they buy insurance. You might wonder why the insurance companies are not worse off for assuming

TABLE 10.3   Benefits and Costs of Driving, with a
Bankruptcy Option

Driving style	Net benefits of driving if		Expected net benefits
	No death	Yes death	
Fast	$500	-$500	$499.85
Medium	$425	-$575	$424.90
Slow	$250	-$750	$249.95

this risk. They are saved by the magic of the law of large numbers. If you flip a coin once, you will either win or lose—there is nothing in between. But if you flip a coin 1000 times, you can be about 95% certain that you will get between 470 and 530 heads—95% of the time, the outcome will be within 6% of the mean. If you flip it 1 million times, you can be 95% certain that you will get between 499,000 and 501,000 heads—95% of the time, the outcome will be within 0.2% of the mean. Insurance ends up being one of the most risk-free of all industries! Since auto insurance companies are so secure in their profit, regardless of accident rates, did you ever wonder why they act as if they had an interest in highway safety (Q10.2)?

But what if insurance companies cannot tell how a driver will drive after buying insurance? The moral hazard problem again arises. If insurance premiums are everywhere $300 (because the company thinks everyone will drive at medium speed), then the net benefits of drivers are, for fast speed, $200 ($500 of gross benefits minus $300 of insurance cost); for medium speed, $125 ($425 minus $300); and for slow speed, -$50 ($250 minus $300). Drivers will choose to drive fast, pedestrian deaths will rise, and insurance companies will lose money.

Insurance companies do not stay in business if they lose money, so they will have to find ways to adjust the premiums they charge individual drivers so that on average each driver's premium covers his or her expected cost in court to the insurance company. But the adjustment is not instantaneous—the tight link between driver behavior and court costs is weakened by the intervention of insurance. In the long run, a driver's insurance costs may reflect the driver's behavior, but in the short run, drivers can literally get away with murder. To the extent that insurance rates do not reflect driving ability and behavior, insurance removes the incentive for drivers to drive with socially optimal care.

ACTUAL AUTO INSURANCE POLICIES

This has been a long theoretical excursion. There are also some interesting institutional and empirical aspects of auto insurance, to which we now turn.

In the United States today, there are two kinds of automobile insurance:

1. *Traditional liability insurance.* This follows the model discussed previously. Those whom a driver injures sue the driver's insurance company; the company pays (how much often depending on whether the victim was also negligent) and then adjusts the rates which the driver must pay in the future. About two-thirds of the states maintain this kind of insurance.

2. *"No-fault" insurance.* Each driver's insurance covers the driver's *own* claims, not those of the other people that he "comes in contact" with. No resources are wasted trying to assess blame and collect compensation from others.

These are radically different systems—in theory. No-fault insurance addresses three of the more serious shortcomings of traditional insurance: (1) the final compensations go more to lawyers than to victims, (2) too many resources are wasted in the lawsuits, and (3) too much time elapses before victims start receiving the money. The disadvantage of no-fault insurance is that it drives yet another wedge between the care with which one drives and the private cost of driving. As a result, under no-fault insurance, the saved legal fees are partly offset by higher accident rates (Flanigan *et al.,* 1989; Devlin, 1997).

In fact, in the United States, the two insurance systems are not as different as they sound. In Michigan, for example, the idea of no-fault insurance applies only to minor cases. If, in an accident, there occurs death, disfigurement, or dismemberment, then the traditional liability lawsuits are permitted, and huge "pain-and-suffering" awards can be added to the more readily measurable damages. In other

---

BOX 10.2 "Pay-at-the-Pump" Auto Insurance

In some countries (South Africa, for instance), the government directly pays compensation for personal and property damage in highway accidents—without regard to fault and without recourse to courts or insurance companies—funding it through a special excise tax on gasoline. If we had such a system in the United States, covering current minimum liability levels, the insurance tax would range up to 50 cents per gallon, depending on exactly how much insurance was provided (Segal, 1993; Sugarman, 1994; Wenzel, 1995; Khazzoom, 1997).[7]

The advantages are clear: reduced billing costs for insurance companies, insurance payments more closely related to miles driven, and removal of the option for drivers to go uninsured. The disadvantages are also clear: creation of a new government bureaucracy, a shift of the insurance burden from urban to rural drivers (who drive more but now pay lower auto insurance rates), and the total divorce of drivers' insurance costs from their accident rates. Is it just coincidence that South Africa has the highest rate of highway deaths per capita in the world?[8]

Are low-income drivers better or worse off with pay-at-the-pump insurance (Q10.3)? Would previously uninsured motorists have more or fewer accidents with pay-at-the-pump (Q10.4)?

BOX 10.3 Gender and Auto Insurance Rates

Michigan has a "unisex" law (as do 4 other states) prohibiting insurance companies from discriminating between the sexes, which effectively leaves young women subsidizing the bad driving records of young men. In Michigan, for example, it is estimated that a typical young woman pays $400 more per year for auto insurance than she would pay in a comparable non-unisex state (Nordheimer, 1996).

Whether this is fair or not may soon become a moot issue, as young women drivers are getting worse with respect to their highway accident and death rates and are rapidly approaching the high rates of young men. In non-unisex states, as recently as 1980, 17 to 20-year-old women bought auto insurance at barely one-fourth the cost charged men in that age bracket; today, they are charged nearly two-thirds the men's rate. Why are young women drivers getting more like young men in this respect (Q10.5)? (Box 2.6 may give you a hint.)

---

no-fault states, lawsuits are permitted under even weaker criteria. So no-fault insurance is really only no-fault for accidents with small damages.[6]

The second way that no-fault coverage resembles liability insurance is in the setting of premiums for individual drivers. In theory, these rates would either be uniform for all or they would depend upon the driver's claims without regard for whether the driver was driving carelessly or not. In reality, in Michigan, for example, the insurance companies quietly argue fault among themselves, compensate each other where they agree it is appropriate, and then adjust the premiums of the insured drivers—just like the courts but without lawyers' fees. Since lawyers' fees absorb nearly one-third of all auto insurance premium payments, a strict national no-fault, no pain-and-suffering-compensation auto insurance plan could save the average American driver over $200 per year (McConnell *et al.,* 1997).

Auto insurance rates depend upon many things beside past driver claims (as they should—if rates adjusted immediately and fully to cover past losses, it would hardly be insurance). Statistical evidence is collected on driver claims by group and the insurance rates are set higher on the higher-risk groups. Who pays more? Those whose "principal garage" is in an urban area, those who commute to work, those who drive more miles, those who have garnered more moving violations, and the young. And auto insurers are now thinking about raising rates on sport utility vehicles and pickup trucks since evidence is piling up that they cause expensive liability claims (look again at Box 8.5) (Bradsher, 1997e).

The young pay more because they are involved in many more than average numbers of accidents—not until one reaches the age of 85 is the probability of an accident per mile as high as it is during the ages of 16 to 19 (Williams, 1994; Mathis, 1996). Auto insurance rates roughly reflect this; regardless of driving experience, the rates take steps down as drivers get older. In Michigan, for example, the rates come down at ages 21, 23, 25, 50, and 65. We turn again in Chapter 12 to this relationship between youth and highway death.

Those with large numbers of "points" from moving violations pay more because there is ample evidence that the two are related, on average. In Michigan, insurers are permitted to refuse insurance to those with six or more "points" because of their supposedly greater risk. Such drivers must get their insurance from a special state-operated, high-cost, high-priced, "high-risk pool." Though insurance rates there are extremely high, they are nevertheless subsidized through a tax on the insurance premiums of all other car owners.[9]

Finally, and interestingly, some insurance companies have recently discovered that the best single predictor of future insurance claims (beside age) is not moving violations or past insurance claims, but *credit-rating* (Birnbaum, 1994; Scism, 1995). Bankrupts apparently are terrible drivers. This may soon find its way into the general criteria for insurance rates.[10]

FINAL THOUGHTS

Auto liability insurance reduces the private cost of careless driving. In the 19th century, English common law actually forbade "carriage insurance" on the grounds that it would encourage reckless carriage driving. At a time when all carriage owners were rich and the accepted value of a peasant's life was low, this may not have been a bad idea. With automobiles today in the United States, however, these provisos no longer hold. Today, we not only permit, we even require, auto liability insurance because we collectively recognize that accidents occur from bad luck as well as from carelessness; the provision of insurance is a rational response of a risk-averse society when accidents occur by chance. But it does exacerbate the highway death problem when accidents occur from carelessness, for insurance reduces each person's private cost of careless driving.

In short, legal liability has the potential to make drivers take proper care. But there are lots of ways in which it fails in fact to achieve this potential. And auto liability insurance removes much of what incentive is left.

ENDNOTES

[1]Recall what is meant by the terms "risk-aversion," "risk-neutrality," and "risk-loving." Consider the following bet: you flip a coin 12 times. If it comes up heads at least once, you win $1; if, however, it never comes up heads—that is, there are 12 straight tails—you lose $4095. That is a fair bet in the sense that, if you made this bet over and over, thousands of times, then you would expect to exactly break even. But you have the chance to do it only once. If you do not want this bet, you are risk-averse; if you are indifferent about making the bet or not, you are risk-neutral; and if you would leap at the chance for such a bet, you are risk-loving. Ditto for the reverse game: if it comes up heads at least once, you lose $1, but if there are 12 straight tails, you win $4095. A risk-averse person does not want to bet, a risk-neutral is indifferent, and a risk-loving goes for it. Recall also what is meant by "moral hazard." When an insurance company promises to pay any losses you incur, there is always the risk to the insurance company that you will no longer take as much care to avoid losses. Insurance

companies worry about that and, indeed, try to factor allowance for it into the premiums they charge. Notice that what we earlier called "risk compensation" is simply a kind of moral hazard—when people are made to feel safer through the addition of safety equipment to their cars, they may drive those cars less safely. Finally, keep in mind the difference between adverse selection and moral hazard: adverse selection is *precontractual* opportunism, while moral hazard is *postcontractual* opportunism.

[2]To "total" a car means to incur so much damage that the insurance company simply gives you the going resale value of the car rather than undertaking the cost of putting it back in working order. Incidentally, insurance companies may declare a car "totaled" even if the repairs would cost less than the value of the car. Why? Partly because the insurers then get to resell the totaled car for parts and scrap, and partly to avoid the possibility of later additional claims. The sentence of the text is ignoring, for simplicity, both the possibility of lesser accidents than "totaling" and the "deductible" (i.e., the part of any repair cost that you yourself have to pay).

[3]Because of the bankruptcy option, the poor will often prefer to be uninsured. Consider the case we discussed earlier, where a person's wealth is only $1000. If this person drives fast, the expected cost of accidents is 0.99985 times $0 plus 0.00015 times $1000, or $0.15, while the cost of insurance would be $450. Even very risk-averse poor people may prefer to go uninsured. Such a market may in theory have a dual equilibrium. As more people go uninsured, the auto insurance rates of those remining insured go up; this induces still more people to choose to go uninsured. There may be two equilibria in this market: almost everyone driving insured and rates very low, and many people driving uninsured and rates very high (Schelling, 1978; Smith and Wright, 1992).

[4]We are ignoring the management costs of the insurance companies, and we are assuming that they are all big enough to reduce their risks to zero through "the law of large numbers."

[5]Drivers who have so little wealth that they preferred to drive uninsured and resort to bankruptcy in the case of an accident may well choose to drive fast. Thus, a law mandating insurance may also represent an effort to curtail excessively speedy driving.

[6]In countries with "pure" no-fault insurance—where all damages are collected from one's own insurance company and pain-and-suffering damages are never permitted—there is clear evidence of increased accidents (Gaudry, 1991).

[7]Drivers would still use private insurance companies if they wanted either collision insurance or liability insurance beyond the minimum mandated level. The insurance provided by pay-at-the-pump would, of course, be no-fault insurance.

[8]See Figure 7.1, and remember that the death rate per *capita* is equal to the product of the death rate per vehicle and the number of vehicles per capita. Before you place all the blame for South Africa's high rate of highway death on pay-at-the-pump insurance, recall that South Africa has the most inequitable income distribution in the world, and that may well have a lot to do with it.

[9]Why would the state government want to install such a tax and subsidy system (Q10.6)?

[10]But remember, those with little wealth are tempted to go uninsured. Higher premiums will encourage this temptation.

CHAPTER 11

Alcohol

"If you drink, don't drive.
Don't even putt."

Dean Martin

Alcohol is a major cause of highway crashes and highway deaths. How major a cause is uncertain.

Part of the uncertainty is a problem of defining cause. Every fatal vehicle accident has many causes. The immediate cause is that the vehicle came into violent contact with a pedestrian, with a bicyclist, with a large, immobile object, or with another vehicle moving in a different direction or at a different speed. One might ask why? Because the vehicle was being driven "recklessly." Again, one might ask why. Because the driver was drunk. Again, one might ask why. Because the driver was very upset over a recent divorce. What, then, is *the* cause of the accident: the laws of physics, reckless driving, alcohol, or divorce?

Another part of the uncertainty is a problem of defining drunkenness. Alcohol, like most drugs, requires ever higher dosages for regular users to achieve any given "kick." Evidence of this shows up on the highway: half of those arrested for "driving under the influence" (DUI) are 25 to 39-year olds, but alcohol-related fatal highway crashes are more likely to be caused by 16 to 24-year-old drivers (Bureau, 1995; Wagenaar, 1983). Nevertheless, the law defines drunkenness for driving purposes not in terms of behavior but in terms of the concentration of alcohol in the body fluids. Legally, in most states, a blood alcohol concentration (BAC)

129

BOX 11.1 Drunken Pedestrians and Highway Death

For nearly half the adult pedestrians killed in highway accidents, the BAC was 0.10% or higher. The U.S. National Academy of Sciences has considered two policies to reduce this toll: (1) tilt sidewalks so falling drunks will roll away from the street, and (2) scatter glowing powder on barroom floors so patrons who fall down walking home will be more highly visible to drivers (NAS, 1989). Hmmm. Drunks are twice as likely to be killed walking home as they are driving home. Perhaps a new motto is called for: "If you drink, don't walk!"[1]

---

less than 0.05% is acceptable, a BAC between 0.05% and 0.15% is "evidence of impairment," and a BAC above 0.15% shows the subject to be "under the influence" of alcohol.

Despite these difficulties, there is little doubt of the relationship. For nearly half the fatally injured drivers, the BAC was 0.10% or higher (Jacobs, 1989). The fraction of highway deaths considered to be "alcohol related" had risen steadily (as long as good statistics have been available) until the mid-1980s. In the last decade, something—policies, education, peer pressure—seems to have been paying off to discourage drunk driving.

TAXING DRUNK DRIVING

To the extent that drunk drivers are responsible for the deaths of others, there is definitely a negative externality. Since neither negotiation nor legal liability can provide a practical deterrent, some kind of Pigovian tax seems called for. But a tax on what? Presumably a tax per impaired mile equal to the extent to which a drinking driver raises the expected death rate (of other people) on the highway times the dollar value of each life so endangered. If all drunk driving trips were of the same length and had the same probability of killing someone (else), that probability is about 0.00002 (Kenkel, 1996). Valuing lives at $3 million each, this suggests a Pigovian tax of $60 per drunk driving episode (for deaths, it does not count other damages).

This $60 is not the fine if you are caught; it is the fine for driving drunk. It assumes 100% of drunk drivers are caught and convicted. In fact, the probability of being arrested is on the order of 0.0004—and the probability of being arrested *and* convicted is even lower (Ross, 1982). So the correct fine for conviction of drunk driving is something like $60/0.0004, which is *$150,000!*

In fact, we do not even try to hammer drunk drivers this hard, but rather levy modest penalties on those stopped and tested to have a BAC above a certain level. The tax may be levied in money, in time of incarceration, or in some other form of inconvenience—such as deprivation of driving privileges. The idea, it will be recalled, is that a Pigovian tax "internalizes" the external costs that emerge from drunk driving. A drunk chooses to drive intoxicated because he or she ignores the bad things that such driving may do to other people. In theory, a Pigovian tax on drunk driving lowers the driver's expected income in an intoxicated state, but not in a sober state, and thereby makes sure that the driver feels "internally" the otherwise external costs.

Before asking what is the appropriate size of such a tax, we should look first at two questions: (1) are Pigovian taxes likely to work at all in deterring drunk drivers, and if so, (2) in what form should such taxes be levied?

The theory of Pigovian taxes utilizes the economist's model of the rational consumer—that penalties on some socially obnoxious but privately enjoyable behavior will cause the consumer to choose less of that obnoxious behavior. There are many logical links between the penalty and the reduction in the obnoxious behavior: that we are rational, even when we are choosing drug addiction; that we are free, genetically and addictively, to choose the level of our drug consumption; that we can accurately and effectively implement our choice; and that we know the relationship between our consumption level and the expected tax that will be levied on us (Votey, 1988). To list these links is to cast doubt on them. Nevertheless, there is a consensus among studies that increased penalties, at least for many kinds of penalties, do in fact reduce drunk driving (Kenkel, 1993a; Chaloupka *et al.*, 1993; Jones, 1987; Falkowski, 1986).

MONEY FINE VERSUS JAIL TIME

If penalties for drunk driving are effective, what form should these penalties take? To a person considering drinking before driving, the expected monetary penalty is

$$q(F_m + F_t), \qquad [11.1]$$

where q is the probability of being caught, convicted, and punished, F_m is the money fine that must be paid, and F_t is the monetary value of the time fine (i.e., jail time). Note that two of the three variables in expression [11.1] use up society's resources (and government budgets) to impose: raising q above zero requires that governments devote resources to highway policing and to courtroom activity; and raising F_t above zero requires that governments construct prisons and operate them. On the other hand, F_m, being a money fine, uses up no resources; it is simply a transfer payment from drunk drivers to "all of us," and it generates government budget revenue.

Since money fines are perfect substitutes for time fines in expression [11.1] and are preferred by the rest of us, this suggests that we should exclusively rely on money fines as a Pigovian deterrent to drunk driving: few highway police, no jail terms, but huge money fines—huge enough to reduce the amount of drunk driving to the "optimal" level (Becker, 1968). This is like the $150,000 fine solution we laughed at a few paragraphs back. It is time now to look more carefully at the reasons why we laughed at it. There are four reasons:

1. Bankruptcy is an option. Poor drivers might feel free to drink and then drive, prepared simply to declare bankruptcy if and when a big monetary fine is imposed.

2. Very small values of q might fail to be perceived as even positive by potential drinker/drivers. Recall that the probability of a drunk driver being arrested and convicted is very very low.

3. Such a penalty structure would not prove tolerable. If drunk drivers were rarely apprehended but then threatened with, say, a $150,000 fine, the courts would overflow with contested cases, juries would refuse to convict, and judges would balk at sentencing. In the United States, as in other democracies, people feel that the punishment must fit the crime.

4. Money fines are not easily attuned to incomes; hence, if they are fixed amounts for all offenders, they are regressive taxes. On the other hand, time penalties represent more nearly proportional taxation and hence are politically more acceptable.[2]

In reality, therefore, penalties for drunk driving tend to involve some mixture of money, time, and inconvenience. Some econometric studies have shown that some penalties can be very effective in reducing highway fatalities. For example, a mandatory drivers license suspension of at least a year for the first DUI convic-

---

BOX 11.2 Could "Dry" Counties Have Higher Death Rates?

In some states, counties can individually choose whether or not to permit the public sale of alcohol. Texas, for example, has 53 "dry" counties and 201 "wet" counties. The county voters' decision to become "dry" effectively raises the price of alcohol since it forces buyers to drive further to buy it. What is the impact on highway death? There are three effects: (1) the higher effective price reduces alcohol consumption, which in turn decreases alcohol-related highway deaths; (2) the greater distances to places that sell alcohol reduce the number of trips made per unit of time, which in turn reduces the vehicle-miles traveled (VMT) and hence decreases deaths; and (3) the average distance per trip to buy alcohol is increased, which in turn increases the VMT and hence increases deaths. A Texas study found that "wet" counties experienced about two more highway deaths per million VMT than "dry" counties (Brown et al., 1996). But another study of Oklahoma counties found that the third effect dominated—that is, highway fatality rates were higher in "dry" counties.[3]

Only a few states limit the counties in which alcohol can be served, but every state limits the number of business establishments that can serve alcohol and the times when they can serve it. Do such laws reduce alcohol-related highway deaths (Q11.2)?

tion, if implemented by all states, as compared to being implemented by no state, would reduce highway fatalities by nearly 4000 per year; a law authorizing police to administer a prearrest breath test for alcohol, if implemented by all states, as compared to being implemented by no state, would reduce highway fatalities by nearly 3000 per year; and a law authorizing parties injured by a drunk driver to file a lawsuit against the alcohol server (called a "dramshop law"), if implemented by all states, as compared to being implemented by no state, would reduce highway fatalities by more than 2000 per year (Chaloupka *et al.,* 1993; Kenkel, 1993a; Sloan *et al.,* 1994). Sounds good. But other econometric studies find that the *marginal* strengthening of existing drunk driving deterrence policies would have no effect on either alcohol consumption or highway fatalities (Wilkinson, 1987).

Sweden and Norway routinely impose stiff penalties on drunk drivers, with both stiff fines and imprisonment. The result seems salutary. Though Scandinavians drink heavily, they do not drive while drunk. Unfortunately, it is not certain whether the Scandinavian law has caused the inhibition against drunk driving or the Scandinavian inhibition against drunk driving has caused the law (Ross, 1982).

ALCOHOL TAXATION

There is one alcohol-related policy, however, that shows up consistently as saving highway lives—an increase in the excise tax on alcohol. Unfortunately, such a tax is very ill-targeted as a Pigovian tax since it equally, and incorrectly, taxes nondriving drinkers.[4] Nondriving "responsible" drinkers cause no externalities at all—by the definition of "responsible"—and nondriving heavy drinkers cause relatively few external costs—"only" some medical care, sick leave, and family abuse. The driving heavy drinkers cause the most external costs—in highway carnage and property damage. One study concluded that highway externalities accounted for about four-fifths of all the alcohol-related externalities (Manning *et al.,* 1989).

Even though alcohol taxation is not well-targeted as a drunk-driving deterrent, it is widely accepted and used. So let's think about such taxes for a bit. Right away, two things are clear: (1) the tax should be the same regardless of the form in which the alcohol is consumed, since it is hardly the water, fizz, or flavorings that cause the external costs, and (2) the tax should be the same over time unless the external costs associated with alcohol are known to be changing over time. Neither of these are true of U.S. alcohol taxation.

We tax alcohol very differently depending on whether it is consumed as spirits (e.g., whiskey, gin, and vodka), wine, or beer. The alcohol content of spirits is taxed by the federal government at 21 cents per ounce, while the alcohol content of beer and wine is taxed at 9 cents per ounce, less than half as much tax per unit of alcohol.[5]

The federal excise tax rate on beer has only doubled since 1951, while the overall price level has increased by more than fivefold. So the real tax on beer per alcohol ounce has declined by more than half. But highway deaths in the United States have not declined much in total since World War II, and it is quite implausible to think that the number of beer-related highway deaths has fallen by anything like half.

Suppose we were to raise the excise tax on beer, first to the same level (per unit of alcoholic content) as the tax on spirits in 1951, and then raise it again by the amount of inflation since 1951. These two changes together would significantly raise the retail price of beer, significantly reduce beer consumption by the young, and significantly decrease the highway mortality rate of 18 to 20-year olds—perhaps *by as much as 50%* (Grossman and Saffer, 1986; Saffer and Grossman, 1987; Coate and Grossman, 1988; Kenkel, 1993b; Laixuthai and Chaloupka, 1993; Grossman *et al.,* 1993; Chaloupka *et al.,* 1993; and Ruhm, 1995).

Higher taxes on drinking or higher taxes on driving are tempting because they are so effective in reducing highway death. But we must remember, once again, that these are not the correct Pigovian taxes. Neither taxes drunk driving itself—one taxes drinking and the other taxes driving. From the strict viewpoint of alcohol-related highway death, it is still important to seek policies that deter not drinking *or* driving, but drinking *and* driving.

FINAL THOUGHTS

Perhaps technology will help. Even now, it is possible to install an ignition interlock system that prevents drunk drivers from starting a car.[6] And the search for better policies is not over. At the least, American fines for drunk driving should be raised periodically so as to keep their real value from declining. In New York, for example, the basic fine for a first-time DUI offender, $350, is little higher than it was when New York first enacted a drunk-driving law in 1910 (Jacobs, 1989).[7] Jail time is expensive to society, as we have seen, but house arrest with electronic monitoring is cheap. Car impoundment is cheap, too. And how about this: North Carolina seizes the cars of many drunk drivers and turns them over to the local school boards, which auction them off (Wald, 1997c; Blumenauer, 1998).

ENDNOTES

[1]And do not bicycle, either. Alcohol "is a factor" in about one-third of the 900 bicyclist deaths each year in the United States (Okie, 1997).

[2]Recall what is meant by "proportional" taxation. A proportional tax is one that takes the same percentage of people's incomes whether they are rich or poor. If everyone earned only wage income and worked 40 hours a week, then a tax of "two hours" would be a 5% tax for everyone, regardless of their wage rates. This simple demonstration ignores differences in workweeks and in nonwage income, which is the reason for the phrase, "more nearly," in the text. Finally, think about which, the money fine or the time fine, is the correct Pigovian tax (Q11.1).

[3]This is a good time to think more carefully about "simultaneity" problems in the data. Consider two possible scenarios. In scenario one, suppose Baptists tend to be teetotalers and tend to drive very carefully. Then, predominantly Baptist counties will tend to vote to be dry and will also have a low accident rate compared to wet counties. But this does not mean that changing a non-Baptist county from wet to dry will lower its accident rate. In scenario two, suppose counties with a significant minority of heavy drinkers tend to have lots of accidents, and the voter majority tends to vote dry in an effort to reduce the accidents. Suppose, however, that the basic problem of heavy drinking remains and that this switch to dry therefore has little effect on highway accidents; the county will continue to have a high accident rate compared to wet counties. But this does not mean that changing some other county from dry to wet will lower its accident rate. This second scenario reminds me of a famous Will Rogers line: "Oklahomans will vote 'dry' as long as they can stagger to the polls."

[4]Any alcohol tax aimed to deter drunk driving must be less than the marginal external cost of the expected resulting drunk driving since the tax is not only deterring drunk driving but also removing consumer surplus from those who drink and do not drive.

[5]There are also state taxes, on average about two-thirds the magnitude of the federal taxes. These vary across states as well as across liquor types.

[6]Would such solutions be politically acceptable? Recall the discussion of the 1974 ignition interlocks for seat belt use (in Chapter 9).

[7]Think what a $350 fine was in 1910! It is equivalent to a fine of over $5000 in today's prices.

CHAPTER 12

Youth

"Being young is a fault that improves daily."

Swedish Proverb

Highways—unlike cancer, stroke, and heart attacks—especially kill the very young, compounding the tragedy because, with each young person's death, more future years of life are lost. Drivers aged 16–19 are involved in 20 crashes per million miles traveled, as compared with 5 crashes per million miles for all other age groups combined (Williams, 1994). Male and female crash rates are becoming almost identical among 16 to 19 year olds (i.e., 21 per million miles for male drivers and 19 for female). Only drivers over 80 have higher crash rates than 16 to 19 year olds. Teenage passengers also die at high rates on the highway, usually in cars driven by other teenagers. Indeed, the highway death rate of teenagers compared to 30 to 34 year olds is twice as high for drivers and four times as high for passengers (Williams, 1987).

MATURITY AND EXPERIENCE

Why do so many young people crash and die on highways? It is at first surprising, given that their powers of athleticism—efficiency of coordination and speed of reaction—are near their peaks. The answer seems to be twofold: (1) immaturity and (2) inexperience. The two are closely related. Young drivers undertake risky driving practices partly because they fail to consider rationally the expected life they are endangering and partly because they have not yet learned how risky these practices are or how good drivers should react when crashes become imminent.[1] But lack of maturity and lack of experience are not exactly the same—a new 17-year-old driver is more mature than a new 16-year-old driver, but the two have identical driving experience.

New Jersey provides evidence of the relative importance of maturity and experience on highway fatalities. It is the only state that licenses no drivers until they are 17 years old. To think about the effect of this delay in driving, consider Figure 12.1. There are two curves shown there, relating highway fatalities per VMT to age. For drivers licensed at age 16, the relationship between fatalities and age is shown as curve ABC, declining over time as these drivers gain both maturity and experience.

What relationship between highway death and age would we expect if licensing were postponed a year? Two extreme hypotheses suggest themselves:

1. If maturity plays no role in these fatalities, and they are entirely caused by lack of experience, the relevant curve would be DE, which is the same curve as ABC but simply moved to the right by 1 year: 16-year-old lives are saved by the delay, but those savings are almost exactly offset by later deaths.

2. If experience plays no role in these fatalities, and they are entirely caused by lack of maturity, the relevant curve would be BC: 16-year-old lives are saved by the delay, and those savings are permanently gained because the new 17-year-old drivers are just as mature as the (surviving) drivers who were licensed a year earlier.

The evidence from New Jersey is very clear on which of these two extreme hypotheses is closer to the truth. Highway deaths of 16 year olds are of course much lower in New Jersey; comparison to nearby states shows how much— 4 highway deaths per 100,000 16 year olds in New Jersey compared to 18 per 100,000 in Massachusetts and 26 per 100,000 in Connecticut. The highway death

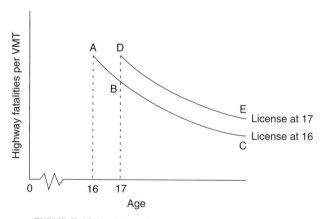

FIGURE 12.1   Drivers License Age and Highway Fatalities

BOX 12.1 Very Old Drivers and Highway Death

People's highway crash rate per VMT *never* climbs back to the height of the teenagers. But, because the very old are more fragile, their death rate per VMT is higher by the time they reach age 85 (Rigdon, 1993; Collins, 1998). And the problem is worsening—highway death rates per capita are rising for the elderly (Wald, 1998c).

The problem at this end of the age spectrum arises not from inexperience, but from incapacity. The solution is not learning, but quitting. How do you detect which older drivers are about to become hazards? Only 17 states (not including Michigan) mandate any sort of age-related license renewal testing (Mathis, 1996). And anyway, eye tests, written tests, and even driving tests all seem to be incapable of predicting who is about to become an over-the-hill highway killer (Zaidel and Hocherman, 1986).

Yale University researchers think they have found a way to predict which elderly drivers are most likely to cause auto accidents, namely, those who: (1) walk less than one block per day, (2) have foot abnormalities, and (3) perform badly when copying designs during mental tests (*New York Times*, 1994).

Sick joke: "Wouldn't it be nice if we all could die peacefully like Grampa, instead of terrorized and screaming—like his passengers?" We have a minimum legal driving age; should we have a maximum legal driving age?

---

rates of 17 to 20 year olds are only very slightly higher in New Jersey than in neighboring states, so there is little offset in highway deaths in later years (Williams *et al.*, 1983; Levy, 1990).

THE MINIMUM LEGAL DRIVING AGE

If delaying the licensing of drivers until age 17 saves lives, why don't more states do it? The answer, of course, is that there is a cost to saving these lives, namely, the lower welfare of the 16 year olds who are denied access to auto transport (without an older driver) for another year of their lives.

A benefit–cost analysis might ask whether the willingness-to-pay (WTP) of 16 year olds for the driving privilege is greater or less than the value of the lives saved. But think of the problems with doing such a B/C analysis. That it may be hard to estimate the average WTP of 16 year olds for the driving privilege is the least of these problems. Should we consider 16 year olds as rational adults—in which case they would have already considered their increased risk of fatality in their decision to seek a drivers license? Or should we consider 16 year olds as irrational children—in which case, why should we consider their WTP at all?

Notwithstanding the inconsistency, let us consider 16 year olds as irrationally ignoring their death risks but rationally having a socially meaningful WTP for driving. How high does this WTP have to be to make licensing 16 year olds a net social benefit? The WTP of the average 16-year-old driver is greater than the expected cost in lives lost if

$$\text{WTP} >< (2)(0.0002)V_L, \qquad [12.1]$$

where the 2 assumes that the costs of hospitals and injuries add 100% to the costs of lives lost, and the 0.0002 means that 20 more out of every 100,000 16 year olds die because 16 year olds are licensed to drive. We will assume the value of life (V_L) to be $5 million, at the upper end of our $1 million to $5 million range for V_L, since we are talking about *young* lives.[2] Then the average WTP must exceed $2000 to make licensing 16 year olds worth the carnage that they cause on themselves. And this simple B/C ignores the deaths of non-16 year olds who are killed by 16-year-old drivers.

Is the average American 16 year old (or the parents) willing to pay something over $2000 for a license to drive? Probably not. Indeed, there is evidence on this: in many European countries, young drivers need to spend several hundreds of dollars—in some countries, thousands of dollars—on courses and tests to become licensed, and few do. Even in America, driving has not always been an automatic right of teenagers—until 30 years ago at the University of Michigan, unmarried undergraduates under 21 years of age had *no* right to automobility (Peckham *et al.,* 1992; J. Berkley, personal communication).

GRADUATED LICENSING LAWS

Many states have sought means other than delayed licensing to reduce teenage highway death. These means go under the rubric of "graduated licensing laws" and apply special restrictions to novice teenage drivers. A few merit discussion:

1. *Drivers education.* Young licensees must have completed a special driving course. But high-school drivers education courses have never been shown to create any strong or lasting benefit in reduced highway crashes.[3] The skills learned in these courses almost inevitably run to parallel parking and not how to recognize, avoid, and survive imminent crashes. Unfortunately, the most significant effect of drivers education courses seems to be perverse. Such courses speed up the rate of licensing, and earlier driving means more early deaths (Robertson, 1980; Lund *et al.,* 1986). Curiously, in the face of the evidence of no improvement, insurance companies in many states give discounts to teens who have passed a drivers ed course. Why would they do this (Q12.1)?

2. *Adult presence.* Requiring young drivers to be accompanied by an adult greatly lowers crash rates, thereby providing further evidence that it is lack of maturity and not lack of experience that causes teenage crashes. Many states have introduced a probation period of 6 months during which new drivers must be accompanied by an adult.

BOX 12.2 Testosterone and Highway Death

Economics offers little help in explaining the greater proclivity of young males to crash automobiles, but biology does (Daly and Wilson, 1983). Added to immaturity and inexperience on the highway is the young male's search for domination over other males in order to establish lifelong privileged access to females. An extreme and stylized form of such activity is "chicken."

To play "chicken," two male teenagers drive toward each other at high speed on a single lane road. The assumption is that if one opponent swerves off the road and the other does not, then the non-swerver's display of bravery supposedly wins the hearts of the females, and the swerver is doomed to celibacy. If both swerve, both are mildly embarrassed in front of the females. If neither swerves, there is a head-on collision, and both players are rendered incapable of interest in, or performance with, females for an extended period of time.

The payoff matrix is shown below; the two players are called A and B, with A's payoff given first and B's second. Here, the payoffs are not in dollars but in some measure of utility—with 1 being the utility of the worst outcome, and 4 being the utility of the best outcome.

	Strategies for B	
Strategies for A	Swerve	Do not
Swerve	3,3	2,4
Do not	4,2	1,1

Look at the strategy choices. If A thinks that B will swerve, A is better off not swerving (4 > 3), and if A does not swerve, B is indeed better off swerving (2 > 1). This is a possible equilibrium outcome in the sense that neither can improve his payoff by changing strategy. If A thinks that B will not swerve, A is better off swerving (2 > 1), and if A swerves, B is indeed better off not swerving (4 > 3). Again, this is an equilibrium outcome in that neither can improve his expected payoff by changing strategy. These are two possible outcomes (called pure strategy equilibria).

But there is also a third possible outcome. If A does not have a clue what B will do, A might choose to just flip a coin to make the strategy choice. If B is similarly clueless and also decides to just flip a coin, then neither can achieve a better expected payoff by doing something other than just flipping a coin. Work it out (Q12.2). So this randomized strategy equilibrium (called a mixed strategy equilibrium) is a third possible outcome.

When, however, this mixed strategy equilibrium emerges, both end up swerving one-fourth of the time, one but not the other swerves one-half the time, and neither ends up swerving one-fourth of the time. Of course, few actually "play" chicken, but to the extent that teen male highway driving involves elements of such a game, deaths will occur.

3. *Night curfew.* Less than 20% of teenage driving is done between 9 P.M. and 6 A.M., but 40% of their fatal crashes occur during these hours.[4] Nearly half of the states have some kinds of restrictions on night driving by young drivers. The laws in New York and Pennsylvania, where the strongest restrictions operate, have reduced crash involvements of 16-year-old drivers during curfew hours by over half (Preusser *et al.,* 1984).

4. *Zero alcohol tolerance.* Under this law, drivers under 21 years old lose their driving licenses if their blood alcohol concentration registers significantly above zero (greater than 0.02% in Michigan—barely one beer) when they are arrested. Under stimulus of federal law—which again threatens the withholding of highway funds—more than 40 states have passed "zero tolerance" laws. Studies of the first states to pass them have shown declines in accident involvement, especially at night, of the affected group (Dao, 1996).

Of these four ways in which teenage drivers are treated more strictly than older drivers, three significantly reduce teenage deaths. But note that these saved lives are not without cost. In each case, the welfare of the young driver is reduced because the driver's choices are narrowed. And the welfare loss matters—if it did not, we should be refusing drivers licenses to all young people.

THE MINIMUM LEGAL DRINKING AGE

So far in this chapter, we have been sort of pussyfooting around the major cause of teenage death on the highways, alcohol. It is not that teenagers drink so much

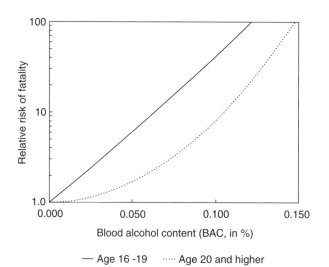

FIGURE 12.2   Risk of Death and Blood Alcohol Content

more than older people—they drink much less, whether or not they are driving—but the combination of learning to drive while learning to drink is deadly. Figure 12.2 shows the extent to which alcohol elevates the risk of fatal crashes by age.[5]

To examine how learning to drive and learning to drink interact, consider Figure 12.3. Assume that drivers begin driving, but not drinking, at age 16; then, if these drivers were never to drink, their learning curve would follow the line ABCD (just as in Figure 12.1). If the minimum legal drinking age (MLDA) were 18, then the fatalities curve of those who began drinking would jump up at age 18 from B to E, and thereafter follow the path EFG. If the MLDA were 21, on the other hand, the curve would continue to fall along ABC until age 21, jump up (for those who then choose to drink) to H, and thereafter follow the path HI.[6]

Raising the MLDA from 18 to 21 therefore has two effects: (1) highway deaths of 18 to 20 year olds decline (the area between the curves BC and EF), and (2) highway deaths of those aged 21 and older, who began drinking later, rise (the area between the curves FG and HI). Which effect dominates is an empirical question. Fortunately, two natural experiments have occurred over the past quarter-century.

Until 1971, one could not vote until one was 21, and most states had settled on a MLDA of 21 years. But, during the Vietnam years, men of 18 to 20 were extensively drafted and sent into a dangerous and increasingly unpopular war. If one could fight and die for one's country, it was argued, one should be able also to vote and drink. The 26th Amendment in 1971 extended the vote to 18 to 20 year olds, and 30 states (including Michigan) had lowered the MLDA to 18 by 1976.

Highway deaths of 18 to 20 year olds probably rose with these changes, but it is not at all clear by how much. Some estimates suggested that deaths of 18 to 20

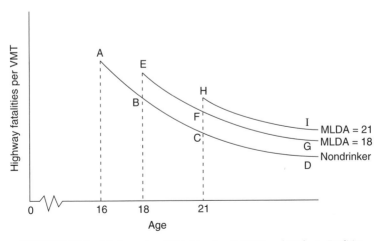

FIGURE 12.3   Minimum Legal Drinking Age (MLDA) and Highway Fatalities

year olds more than doubled, some suggested an increase of less than 10%, and others found no effect at all (Wagenaar, 1983; Cook and Tauchen, 1984; Asch and Levy, 1987 and 1990). As a natural experiment, the change in the 1970s of the state MLDAs was very unsatisfactory, occurring as it did at the same time as mandated vehicle safety equipment, mandated vehicle emissions reductions, and the OPEC gasoline price increase. It was hard to sort out the effects of each.

Despite the lack of consensus of professional studies, the public perceived a dramatic increase of teenage highway fatalities, and pressure was put on state legislatures to reverse the lowering of the MLDA. Beginning with Michigan in 1975, half the states had raised the MLDA to 21 years by 1984, and the Federal Uniform Drinking Age Act of 1984 provided for a reduction in federal highway assistance funds to states that had not raised the MLDA to 21 by 1988. Under this stimulus, all states (except Louisiana) have now complied.[7]

This has provided another natural experiment, as neighboring and hence presumably similar states raised their MLDAs at different times. The evidence was clearer in this experiment, as we would expect since there were fewer other major changes in factors influencing highway driving and safety. Almost all studies found, where MLDAs were raised from 18 to 21, a discernible, albeit modest, decrease in highway crash and death rates of 18 to 21-year olds (DuMouchel et al., 1987). In terms of Figure 12.3, the area between BC and EF is positive but small.

What about the area between FG and HI? Unfortunately, most studies found that much of the decrease in 18-year olds' crashes when the MLDA was raised from 18 to 21 was offset by an increase in 21-year olds' crashes (Males, 1986; Asch and Levy, 1990). In terms of Figure 12.3, area GFHI was almost as large as area CBEF. It appears that there is a "learning to drink and drive" effect that raises highway accidents of new drinkers, whatever the MLDA is.

If age (maturity) makes teenagers better drivers, but only experience makes them better drinkers (in the sense that their highway fatality rate comes down with years of drinking), this suggests to me that we might have gotten the order backward in the United States. Perhaps teenagers could start drinking early but not driving until much later when they have learned "how" to drink and are mature as drivers. Curiously, this is exactly how most European nations handle things: the MLDA is frequently as low as 16, but very few become licensed drivers until several years later.

PROHIBITION VERSUS TAXATION

What these studies seem to suggest is that while alcohol, youth, and accidents are closely interrelated, a higher MLDA is at best a partial solution to the problem. Indeed, prohibition of alcohol consumption for a group may encourage in some people the very lawlessness it attempts to prevent. During 1920–1933 (the "Prohibition" years), the United States outlawed the sale of alcohol everywhere and to everyone, and alcohol consumption declined by only 30–40% (Aaron and Munro, 1981; Miron and Zwiebel, 1991).

A prohibition, moreover, is the equivalent of an infinite excise tax. A Pigovian tax is appropriate where negative externalities are generated, but the size of the tax should equal the marginal external damage done. Whatever the highway slaughter done by 18 to 20 year olds and whatever the value we place on life, the appropriate tax is finite. To justify an infinite tax from an economic viewpoint, one must fall back on the argument that 18 to 21 year olds are ill-informed or ir-rational—in which case, why do they have the right to vote?

Probably the best *single* weapon for an assault on youth drinking, driving, and death, all studies agree, is still a higher beer tax. Teens predominantly drink beer, whether legally or not, and many deaths per year of 18 to 20 year olds would be averted by raising the real rate of alcohol taxation in beer up to the rate of alcohol taxation in spirits. That so many studies find a finite increase in the beer tax to be more effective in preventing teenage highway deaths than a supposedly infinite in-crease in the beer tax (that is, raising the MLDA to 21) may also be telling us something about the effectiveness of MLDA enforcement.

FINAL THOUGHTS

No single feasible policy seems able to reduce the deaths of young people on high-ways. A multifaceted approach, however, can add up to some success. Graduated driving licenses help. Stiffening the penalties for teenage driving offenses—and es-pecially for drinking-and-driving offenses—has probably been effective. Raising the MLDA to 21 has certainly reduced young highway death, and raising beer taxes would surely help.

ENDNOTES

[1]I once asked a divemaster why there is a minimum age for scuba diving, thinking it had something to do with physical lung or heart development. I was told that the very young would be fine divers physically, but they lack concentration, too often plain forgetting to check their depth, air, time, etc.

[2]Careful life–death analyses are beginning to recognize that the whole idea of valuing "lives saved" is crazy—since we never "save" lives, we merely postpone their end. This suggests the use of concepts like "the expected number of life-years extended," which of course is very large if the death of a healthy 16 year old is avoided.

[3]Nor have postlicensing driver training courses been effective in reducing vehicle accidents (Lund and Williams, 1985).

[4]Adults, as well as teenagers, suffer high auto fatality rates at night. Less than 1/20th of American passenger-miles are traveled between 11 P.M. and 4 A.M., but nearly one-third of the highway fatalities occur in these hours (Schwing and Kamerud, 1988).

[5]By relative risk is meant the probability of a fatal crash divided by the probability of a fatal crash when no blood alcohol is present. Thus, the curves in Figure 12.2 start (at the lower left) at 1; note that the vertical axis of Figure 12.2 is in logarithmic scale. Figure 12.2 shows that BAC raises the 16 to 19 year old's probability of a fatal crash, quickly and sizably, above that of older drivers (Mayhew *et al.*, 1986).

[6]I have drawn the figure so that the distance CH is about equal to the distance BE, but, if maturity matters, CH will be smaller.

[7]Louisiana did comply, but its Supreme Court found the law in violation of the state constitution.

CHAPTER 13

Speed and Highway Design

"In America, an hour is forty minutes."

German Proverb

Speed kills, they say. The case that it does so rests basically on the physical fact that when a moving body comes to an abrupt halt more damage is done the faster it was going. The counterargument is that if everyone on a well-designed road were going exactly 100 MPH (and staying in lane), no two cars would ever touch, much less become involved in a fatal accident. This latter reasoning leads to the conclusion that speed does not kill, variance does (Lave, 1985). Probably both theories are right: variance kills when speeds are high, and speed kills when variance is high (Levy and Asch, 1989; Wilkinson, 1987).

The question of whether speed kills is further complicated by changes between states and over time, in the quality of roads, in the distribution of driving across different kinds of roads and across different densities of vehicles and people, in the relationship between speed limits and actual speeds, and in the level of speed-limit enforcement. It is not so easy to prove that "speed kills."[1]

A NATURAL EXPERIMENT

Two natural experiments have occurred in the United States over the past few decades to help us address the question of how speed affects death on highways.

Recall that OPEC raised oil prices in 1973, and the need to economize on gasoline use was felt by U.S. policymakers. Knowing that the fuel efficiency of automobiles falls steadily as speeds rise above 50 MPH, the Emergency Highway Conservation Act of 1973 lowered the speed limit on Interstate highways to 55 MPH. An unexpected by-product of the resulting reduced average speeds was a noticeable decline in the death rates on Interstate highways.

This decline in the highway death rate generated two questions. The first asked whether the decline was caused by the reduced speed limit. If the answer was yes, then a second question asked whether the decline in fatalities was worth the costs. We will look at each of these questions in turn.

The evidence on the speed limit reduction and death is complicated by the fact that so many other factors affecting highway fatalities were also changing in the mid-1970s, such as gasoline prices, auto fuel efficiency, car size, vehicle safety hardware, and the degree of police enforcement of the new lower speed limit. Furthermore, any estimate of "lives saved" by the reduction of the speed limit must estimate a counterfactual: how many lives would have been lost had the speed limit not been lowered? Since highway death rates per VMT were falling steadily both before and during the period in question, it is clearly inappropriate simply to calculate the difference between the "before" and "after" deaths.

Accordingly, one should not be surprised to find that the econometric studies of this period are not unanimous on the influence of highway speed on highway fatalities. Estimates of the number of highway deaths prevented each year by the move from 65 to 55 MPH speed limits, holding other factors constant, are almost all positive, but they run from close to zero to as high as 9000 (NRC, 1984; Forester *et al.*, 1984; Jondrow *et al.*, 1983; Crandall *et al.*, 1986).

BENEFIT–COST ANALYSIS

Thus the second question arises: are these probably small but still positive life-saving benefits worth the time-wasting costs? Since the most contentious of the speed-limit changes were those for rural Interstate highways, let us look at a simple benefit–cost analysis of the speed-limit reduction from 65 to 55 MPH there. The principal benefit is lives saved, and the principal cost is the extra time spent driving. Total benefits are greater than total costs if

$$(450) V_L \gtrless (413 \text{ million person-hours}) P_t, \qquad [13.1]$$

where 450 is an estimate of annual lives saved on rural Interstates, V_L is the value of a life, 413 million is an estimate of the annual number of person-hours wasted by driving at the lower speed, and P_t is the relevant hourly wage rate.[2]

Recall that the opportunity cost of driving is usually thought to be a fraction of a person's working wage. Suppose we take the average value of driving time as one-third of the average U.S. wage rate (which is $12 per hour). Then the lower

BOX 13.1 To Speed or Not to Speed?

Is it wise to exceed the speed limit? It depends partly on what other drivers are doing. If "everyone else" is speeding, then there are three reasons for you to speed, too. First, of course, is that you get to your destination faster. Second, if there is truth to the argument that it is variance, not speed, that kills, you (and others) would be endangered by the existence on the highway of a slow-moving, law-abiding obstacle that all speeding drivers must circumnavigate. Third, since police resources are limited, your chance of being stopped and fined for speeding is low if lots of other cars are also speeding (Dixit and Nalebuff, 1991).

With these assumptions, the payoff matrix could be that shown below. Again, the two players are called A and B, with A's payoff given first and B's second, and the payoffs are ranked from worst (1) to best (4).

	Strategies for B	
Strategies for A	Speed	Do not
Speed	4,4	2,1
Do not	1,2	3,3

This leads to two possible pure strategy equilibria on the highway, one where "everyone" speeds and one where "everyone" drives at the prevailing speed limit.[4]

The implication for the police is that if a critical mass of drivers can be induced to drive within the speed limit, the equilibrium may flip from the "everyone speeds" equilibrium to the "no one speeds" equilibrium. In terms of the payoff matrix above, if the speed/speed payoff could be reduced from (4,4) to, say, (1/2,1/2) through a frenzy of radar, cops, sirens, and tickets, the do not/do not equilibrium becomes unique—and stable, even if the frenzy ends and the speed/speed payoff returns to (4,4). Does this suggest to you that periodic bursts of intense police enforcement of speed limits may be more effective than spreading out the same total enforcement resources smoothly over time?

---

speed limit passes its B/C test only if the relevant V_L is greater than about $4 million. This is on the high side of the $1–5 million range that we have been using, suggesting that 55 MPH may be too low a maximum for rural Interstate roads.[3]

ANOTHER NATURAL EXPERIMENT

One thing was for sure, it seemed as if nobody liked the lower speed limits on rural Interstates. That is not unexpected. Those who were being slowed up knew they were being slowed, and those who now lived to voice an opinion did not realize that the lower speed limit had saved their lives. Finally, the Surface Transportation and Uniform Relocation Act of 1987 authorized states to return to a 65 MPH limit on rural Interstates. By the end of the year, 37 states had taken advantage of this permission, providing another natural experiment.

Analysis of the raw data as states began to raise their speed limits from 55 to 65 MPH indicated that the death rate on rural Interstates rose as a result by about 20%, which means about 400 people per annum (Baum *et al.*, 1990 and 1991). This is very close to an average of the (highly varied) estimates of the number of lives saved per annum on rural Interstates as a result of the speed limit decrease 14 years earlier.

HIGHWAY DESIGN

It takes three to tango with highway death, the driver, the car, and the road itself. And roads are not an unimportant part of the dance. For example, the fastest speeds are driven on Interstates, but the fatality rate per VMT is twice as high on primary highways that are not Interstates, and even higher on secondary rural roads (FHA, 1994). How can this be? The answer is that speed is not hazardous on highways that are designed for speed.

Rural Interstates are designed for speed—banked turns, wide shoulders, median barriers, stronger guardrails, clear signs and lane markings, etc. Other rural primary highways are just not designed for speed. Either they are in bad repair or curvaceous or obsolete or carrying more traffic than they were designed for; and the end result is an elevated rate of highway death (Cushman, 1998b).

Interestingly, some studies of the post-1987 period are beginning to appear showing that the increased deaths on rural Interstates are offset by reduced deaths on other roads, presumably because the higher speed limit on rural Interstates has diverted traffic to them from other rural highways (Brown *et al.*, 1990; Friedland *et al.*, 1990; McCarthy, 1991). But other studies have shown that when speed limits are raised on rural Interstates, average speeds also rise on other roads, and hence that deaths do not fall on these other roads (Wagenaar *et al.*, 1990; Casey and Lund, 1992).

BOX 13.2 Right Turn on Red

In 1972, only 13 states permitted right turns at red lights. The federal Energy Policy and Conservation Act of 1975 offered funds to states that adopted the supposedly energy-saving policy of permitting such turns. By 1980, all states had such a law (Zador *et al.*, 1982). Make a list of the major *private* benefits and *private* costs to drivers of this change. Are there externalities that could make the *social* benefits and *social* costs different? What would you tell policymakers if it passed the drivers' private B/C tests but failed the social B/C test (Q13.2)?

FINAL THOUGHTS

In short, just saying "speed kills" is not enough. Speed also saves time. Moreover, the speed limit on rural Interstates has complex effects on both the usage of other roads and the speeds drivers travel on them. As states begin to use their newfound powers to set their own speed limits, the evidence for exploring these complex effects may begin to appear.

ENDNOTES

[1]Evidence that speed does not kill is often adduced from the experience of the German autobahns, which are mostly without speed limits and which suffer no higher rates of highway death than U.S. Interstate highways. But other factors are not held constant. In Germany, seat belt usage is greater than 90%, the minimum age for a drivers license is 18 years, and drinking-and-driving laws are much stiffer.

[2]In the original B/C analysis from which the text numbers were taken (Kamerud, 1988), account is also taken of a number of other factors: (1) property damages avoided by the lower accident rate; (2) productivity losses avoided by the reduced hospitalization of people injured but not killed; (3) medical costs avoided by the lower accident rate; (4) fuel savings at the lower speed; (5) greater enforcement and compliance costs; and (6) increased prices of goods because of the higher transport costs (higher truck driver wage costs far outweigh the fuel savings). We ignore all these here (but Kamerud (1988) estimates that they add up to a net annual cost of just over $300 million). Kamerud should have also considered: (1) the reduced air pollution generated by engines at the slower speed, and (2) the welfare losses to those who were induced either to give up trips altogether or to travel by alternative, less preferred means. (And note that if giving up trips means more hang gliding and skydiving, or if the less preferred means of travel is a highly curved, ill-maintained, two-lane road, *total* deaths could even rise as a result of lower speed limits on Interstates.)

[3]The 55 MPH speed limit more clearly passes a B/C test for "urban" (i.e., more densely driven) Interstates (Clotfelter and Hahn, 1980; Kamerud, 1988; Mannering and Winston, 1987); but even here, not all B/C tests agree (Forester *et al.,* 1984).

[4]As with the "chicken" game, there is also a mixed strategy equilibrium where each driver chooses at random to speed one-fourth of the time and not to speed the other three-fourths of the time. But it seems very unlikely to emerge in fact since the expected payoff of each driver is then worse than the payoff from either of the two pure strategies. Work it all out (Q13.1).

Other Automotive
Externalities

CHAPTER 14

Congestion, Roads, and Parking

"Traffic congestion has made high-speed freeway chases
sufficiently rare that they are now
covered on the six o'clock news. . . .
California motorists wasted
more than a million hours [per day]
as they waited in traffic,
despair inflating in the trunk. . . .
[T]he biggest waste of time by Americans . . .
since . . . Gilligan's Island went off the air."

Peter Newman

From the Land of Freeways Comes Car Culture Shock

There are 3 million square miles of land area in the continental United States, nearly 2% of which has been paved over for roads (Zuckermann, 1991).[1] Almost every acre of these roads has some potential alternative use and hence some opportunity cost. As a first shot at the cost of using this land for roads instead of the next best alternative, we might look at the value of the land—presumably it is the market's estimate of the capitalized value of the present and future stream of marginal product in its best alternative use.[2]

Two problems exist, however. First, we do not have much of a clue about the total market value of the public land under asphalt in the United States. Second, the preceding procedure would ignore the fact that roads not only use up land but also raise the marginal productivity of the land that surrounds them. We must not forget, after all, the very reason for roads: they lower the costs of transporting people and goods.

Note that if all roads were toll roads and all road investors had perfect foresight before making their investments, we could be sure that the willingness-to-pay (WTP) of road users fully covered the costs of the roads, including the opportunity cost of the land. But of course, all roads are not toll roads. Nor should they be. An uncongested road is essentially a public good, and welfare would be lost by

155

pricing it and thereby excluding persons with low WTP whose presence on the road would not impose any congestion costs.

CONGESTION

A congested road, on the other hand, is not a public good. It has become a commons, overused because all the benefits are captured by the individual user but many of the costs are borne by others. This is another negative externality of driving; the marginal social cost of driving exceeds the marginal private cost paid by each driver because each driver imposes costs of added wasted time and gas on other drivers.[3] And rush-hour congestion is getting worse every year in all major American cities. In Manhattan, for example, nearly a half-million cars enter each working day from New Jersey, and traffic during the Monday through Friday working hours *averages* only 6 MPH, down from 8 MPH only 6 years ago (Collins, 1997).

It is sometimes argued that congestion is not a true externality because drivers impose externalities on other drivers, not on nondrivers. But who bears the external cost is irrelevant. The point is that the cost is not borne by the driver himself or herself, and hence the driver does not consider the external costs when making decisions whether, where, and when to drive. And the cost of congestion is not just a little inconvenience here and there. Tens of millions of cars are involved daily with congested travel in the United States.

ARE MORE ROADS THE ANSWER?

There are two ways to approach the problem of congested roads, expand the supply of lanes until the congestion is gone or reduce the demand for lane space by some kind of rationing or pricing scheme.

Consider first the supply expansion route. New lanes initially reduce congestion, no doubt, but gradually what Anthony Downs has called the "triple convergence" moves in: (1) drivers who formerly used other routes begin to use the newly expanded and faster route (spatial convergence); (2) drivers who formerly avoided peak-hour travel because of the too great congestion resume their preferred rush-hour travel time (time convergence); and (3) some commuters who used to take the bus during peak hours now switch to driving since it has become faster (modal convergence). Thus, what has been called Downs' Law: traffic expands to fill the lanes available (Downs, 1992).

Capacity expansion cannot solve the congestion problem as long as drivers are not charged for the congestion they cause. Congestion is an externality, and the answer is a Pigovian tax. In the case of highway congestion, this means road tolls—tolls that are higher the greater the congestion. (The theory is developed in the ap-

BOX 14.1 If Congestion Is Really Worsening, Why Don't More Data Show It?

The evidence that congestion is worsening is not just anecdotal. There are serious estimates of U.S. congestion costs that exceed $100 billion per year (OTA, 1994; DOT, 1996). Vehicle-miles traveled increased at a rate of 3.7% per annum over the past three decades, but the miles of highway increased at a rate of only 0.9% per annum (GAO, 1989).

On the other hand, the data tell us that the average American spends less time commuting than he or she used to, and the average speed on urban highways is greater than it used to be (FHA, 1994).

Perhaps these data cannot be fully reconciled, but some reconciliation is possible. Three ideas follow. One, the average distance from residence to workplace has been declining—could Americans be reacting to congestion by moving closer to their workplaces?

Two, suburb-to-suburb commuting is replacing suburb-to-central-city commuting, partly because people and businesses have both moved out to locations that involve less congested commuting routes. Consider the following hypothetical numerical example.

Commuting route	1960		1990	
	Percent of commuters	Average time (min.)	Percent of commuters	Average time (min.)
Suburb–City	70	30	20	40
Suburb–Suburb	30	10	80	20

Over these three decades, the commuting time has increased on both kinds of commute, from 30 to 40 minutes on the suburb-city route and from 10 to 20 minutes on the suburb–suburb route. But the *average* commuting time has remained constant at 24 minutes!

Three, remember the gender changes in driving habits. More women work now, and hence more commute. People commute in order to get higher wages. Women face occupational discrimination and glass ceilings and hence, on average, earn lower wages than men. But women pay the same price for gasoline as men. As a result, women do not commute as far as men on average. The increasing labor force participation of women, therefore, lowers the overall average commuting distance and time (Gordon and Richardson, 1993).

pendix to this chapter.) It is sometimes argued that the congestion itself is a kind of toll, raising the cost of driving, and hence that a toll is unnecessary. But congestion is a very inefficient way of raising the cost of driving since it involves real resource costs. A tax (i.e., toll) is vastly superior because it involves mere transfers, with no real resource costs (except the costs of collection). The toll induces drivers to drive less on that road at that time and hence reduces the amount of wasted time and gasoline.

One traditional complaint about tolls is the very congestion that toll collection itself creates as cars slow, stop, and then accelerate at the toll booths. Technology is about to end this problem. Toll booths are becoming obsolete. Vehicles can now be equipped with prepaid transponders—about the size of credit cards—on windshields, and the tolls can be deducted automatically and electronically as the car goes by a toll station.

Another argument against tolls is that our highways are supposed to be "free ways"—though our forefathers seem to have neglected to write this into the Constitution. In fact, the meaning of "freeway" is that the traffic moves freely on it, without stop signs and traffic signals. Congestion stops roads from being freeways in this true sense.

There are other side benefits to a toll over congestion as a way to raise the cost of driving. Tolls reduce the trips made and speed existing trips up. Both of these effects reduce air pollution and gasoline demand. So tolls contribute to the alleviation of energy security, air pollution, and global warming worries. Furthermore, tolls reduce the political pressure to expand the number of lanes on congested roads and hence reduce public expenditures on roads. Nor is it just a matter of political pressure—the socially optimal number of lanes that need to be constructed and maintained is lower the smaller the peak-load rush-hour traffic.[4] The

---

BOX 14.2 Congestion in Third World Cities

While most of the cars on this planet are concentrated in the relatively few rich, industrialized countries—North America, Western Europe, and Japan—high income inequality, laissez-faire policy, and low road construction and repair budgets are rapidly creating serious congestion in the cities of developing countries.

Singapore has responded by levying a special toll on all vehicles that use the downtown part of the city during the highly congested (and highly air polluted) weekdays (Behbehani et al., 1984; Economist, 1994).[5] Other cities have responded with less market-oriented policies.

In Cairo, trucks are completely banned from entering the central part of the city by day, but cars are in no way restricted. In Bangkok, new multilane highways are built with high-interest foreign loans, but the government balks at charging a toll that would keep the new roads uncongested and provide revenue to repay the loans.[6] In Jakarta, several arterial roads are "three-in-one," which means that only cars with three or more passengers can use the roads at peak times.[7] In Calcutta, with perhaps the worst smog problem outside of China, "zero-emission" vehicles—rickshaws, pedal-cycles, and handcarts—are banned from use in the central city because they slow up auto traffic.

Think about the Cairo, Bangkok, Jakarta, and Calcutta approaches long enough to convince yourself that each is less cost-effective than the simple tax in Singapore.

BOX 14.3 The Correct Highway Congestion Toll

When a highway is congested, and traffic is slowed, each driver considering entry onto the highway thinks of the time price that will be personally paid there. But the driver does not consider the fact that the additional car will add to the congestion, slowing all the other cars on the highway by another second or two per mile. This is a classic external cost, and the classic Pigovian correction is a toll equal to the marginal external time cost that each new driver imposes on all the existing cars on the highway.

Try the following questions. Should the toll be lower for old cars in order to minimize the regressiveness of the toll-taxation? Should the toll be the same at different times of day, should it be higher at the highly congested times to discourage driving at these times, or should it be lower at the highly congested times to equalize the time-plus-toll price that drivers pay? Should the toll be set per car or should the toll per car be lower for cars with multiple occupants (to encourage carpooling) (Q14.2)?

---

proof is long and hard, but you should be able to uncover the intuition behind the proof (Q14.1).

Curiously, drivers do not like tolls, even though they reduce congestion. Why not? Because the tolls raise the private variable cost of driving (i.e., the sum of toll costs and congestion costs) even as they lower the social variable cost of driving (i.e., congestion costs only—the tolls are a transfer). Who then gains privately from tolls? Whoever gets the toll revenue. Is it possible to funnel the toll revenues back to commuters in such a way that they do not lose their incentive to avoid congested roads and times? Yes (Small, 1983). One obvious way is to earmark the toll revenues to improved maintenance of roads.[8] But the easiest way is simply to lower the gasoline taxes so that commuters who avoid congestion come out ahead and only commuters who fail to find alternatives to congested rush-hour travel times come out behind.

INCENTIVES TO CARPOOL

Tolls are levied per car, not per person, so there is an incentive to carpool or vanpool, which also reduces congestion.[9] Significant carpooling first appeared in the United States during World War II as a response to gasoline rationing and tire shortages. It declined in the 1950s and 1960s, when jobs as well as residences moved to the suburbs, real wage rates rose, and real gasoline prices fell. The fact that carpooling revived when the gasoline price leaped up twice in the 1970s indicates that there is some price elasticity there. One-fourth of commuters were sharing cars in the mid-1970s, but the fraction has now dropped below $\frac{1}{10}$th

(Bowles, 1998). Higher congestion tolls or higher gasoline prices due to higher taxes could reverse the long-term trend away from carpooling.

High-occupancy vehicle (HOV) lanes also encourage carpooling since they move faster. These lanes are reserved for cars with multiple (usually three or more) occupants. But HOV lanes are a second-best approach to congestion. To attract users, they must move faster. This means attracting few cars.[10] But, if few cars choose to use a designated HOV lane, then most of the cars that used to travel in N lanes are forced into N-1 lanes, further slowing speeds there. Overall, the *average* travel time of all commuters could be increased rather than decreased.

Some cities are trying to divert more traffic into the HOV lane by offering it as a "high-occupancy toll" (HOT) lane, where lone drivers can zing along with the high-occupancy vehicles, but only by paying a money toll (Bowles, 1998). Does this increase welfare? There are three groups to consider. One, the carpoolers who were alone in the HOV lane before may be slowed slightly by the addition of toll-paying solo drivers. Two, the new toll-paying drivers in the HOT lane must be better off or they would not have moved over. Three, those in the regular lane before, and who stay there, go a little faster because some drivers have switched to the new HOT lane. So two of the three groups gain, but carpooling in the former HOV, now HOV/HOT, lane is discouraged.

BOX 14.4 Alternatives to Tolls

Given people's dislike of tolls, some urban areas have tried alternatives, two of which we will look at here.

In some cities, a parking surcharge is levied on those who arrive at public or private parking spaces in the central city between 7 and 9 A.M. This, however, is hardly a perfect substitute for peak-hour road tolls. The parking tax is the same no matter how many miles the driver has traveled, so that people who cause 1 mile of congestion pay no less than those who cause 10 miles of congestion. Thus, those who cause the least congestion are taxed the most per mile, though they cause no more congestion per mile. While the parking tax may induce nearby residents to seek other travel times or modes, it does little to induce the distant commuter to move closer to the workplace.

Although technically an air pollution measure, "transportation control measures" have been required of large employers, each of whom must develop a series of measures to encourage carpooling among employees. The measures range widely, from simply providing information on alternatives to solo car commuting to subsidizing those who use buses or carpools. There is clearly potential for change here, but, alas, these measures in fact seem to have had little effect—in Los Angeles, for example, such employer efforts managed to increase the average vehicle occupancy of their commuting employees from an average of 1.22 to only 1.25 (GAO, 1993; Giuliano et al., 1993).

ROAD WEAR AND TEAR

Even on uncongested roads, vehicles incur unpaid social costs by wearing down the roadbed. When a motor vehicle uses a road, it imposes two kinds of wear-and-tear costs: (1) it hastens the day when the road begins to get bumpy, necessitating minor roadway repairs, lowering fuel efficiency, causing vehicle damage, and creating discomfort for road users, and (2) it hastens the day when the road needs to be completely repaved.[11] Each vehicle should be charged these marginal costs for efficient use, and it happens that charging the marginal cost will create just enough revenue to cover the cost of maintenance and the periodically needed repavement (Small *et al.*, 1989).[12]

In the United States, we do in fact attempt to charge these marginal costs, not through direct highway tolls but through gasoline taxes, which are indeed often called "highway user fees." The total of all federal and state gasoline taxes (and road tolls) is about $55 billion, and the total of all public road administrative, maintenance, and capital outlays is nearly $90 billion (FHA, 1994). This deficit of roughly $35 billion per year, translated to a per-gallon basis, amounts to some 35 cents per gallon.[13]

All motor vehicles, however, are not equal in the amount of damage that they do to roads. The gallons of fuel a vehicle uses is a bad measure of the highway damage the vehicle does. When an axle passes over a road, the damage depends upon the *cube* of the weight on that axle. This means that if you double the weight on an axle, the highway damage is increased eightfold (i.e., $8 = 2^3$). Trucks carry much more weight per axle than do cars. Typically, a truck will carry 10 times as much weight per axle as a car, and hence that truck will do 1000 times as much damage to the road (per axle). For practical purposes, road damage is done by trucks, not cars.

Since trucks and cars pay roughly the same gasoline taxes per gallon, this means that cars are more than covering their share of highway wear and tear while trucks and buses are not coming close to covering their share. Fuel taxes are a very poor proxy for the marginal cost of road wear. The tax should be on number of axles, weight per axle, and distance covered, but gasoline taxes only provide a decent proxy for distance covered. Trucks do pay higher registration fees than cars, and heavier trucks pay higher fees than lighter trucks. But, at the federal level and in most states, these fees are unrelated either to miles driven or to weight per axle.

Tires are also taxed and at higher rates the heavier the tire. This is a form of tax per mile since tires wear out with use. But retread tires are exempt from the tax even though trucks on retread tires cause the same damage to roads as trucks on new tires. And this tax also penalizes anyone who spreads the weight of a truck over more axles since that would mean buying more tires.

We do charge 6 cents more per gallon for diesel fuel (at the federal level—and a few states also charge more for diesel), but that does not begin to cover the differential damage done by trucks, the dominant users of diesel fuel. But sky-high

TABLE 14.1   Actual and Marginal-Cost Truck Taxes

Truck type	Tax rate per mile	
	Actual	Marginal cost
Standard 3-axle semi	0.071	1.149
4-axle truck-trailer	0.072	0.572
Standard 5-axle semi	0.076	0.222
6-axle semi with trailer	0.086	0.150

Note. The actual tax rate is the U.S. average and includes both fuel taxes and registration fees, converted into a per-mile basis. All vehicles are assumed to have the same gross weight (40 tons) and are assumed to be driven on intercity routes with no congestion.
Source: Small *et al.*, 1989.

diesel taxes are certainly not the answer. Diesel engines run on a variety of fuels, and substitution is possible. The answer must involve taxing trucks periodically by odometer reading, adjusted by weight per axle and number of axles.

How much tax would trucks need to pay to cover their highway wear-and-tear cost? Table 14.1 shows that the tax rate would vary greatly according to how many axles the weight was spread over. For six-axle semis with a trailer, carrying 40 tons in intercity travel, the marginal-cost tax rate is not even double the actual tax rate, but for three-axle trucks carrying the same total weight on the same route, the marginal-cost tax is over $1.00 per mile. For comparison, the marginal-cost tax needed on a car to cover its road wear would be less than $0.001 per mile.

PARKING

So far in this chapter we have been thinking about the external costs of vehicles when they are moving. But cars also impose unpaid costs on society when they are not moving. Both public and private parking are heavily subsidized in the United States.

Most public parking facilities, especially in city centers, are subsidized as city councilors try, often desperately, to prevent the decline of the city center. Rarely do the revenues cover even the operating costs of public parking structures, leaving depreciation costs of the structures and interest costs on the opportunity cost of the land and capital involved to be covered elsewhere in the city budget.

Every city is different, but a close look at Ann Arbor (MI) may prove instructive. Ann Arbor maintains 4000 public parking spaces in structures and another 500 public spaces in lots. The total operating cost of all this is currently about $5.5 million per year—and a lot of maintenance has been deferred over the years. The

---

BOX 14.5 Should Government Vehicles Be Exempt?

Publicly owned vehicles are often exempted from road-user charges on the grounds that charging such fees would simply push money around from one government account to another (Small *et al.*, 1989). This is a bad idea, for two reasons.

One, it removes the incentive for the relevant government agency to consider social costs when it makes decisions about how and how much to use its vehicles. Two, it foregoes the opportunity for budget makers to know the true social cost of a government activity.

Consider, for an extreme example, fire-hydrant spaces. If the fire department were charged for these—presumably at the relevant parking-meter rates—it would of course raise the budgetary cost of fire prevention. But the city would also have enough increased revenue in its parking-meter budget to augment the fire department's budget accordingly. And the fire department would then have an incentive to seek ways in which it could substitute, say, longer hoses or stronger pumps for greater hydrant frequency.

---

total revenue is only about $4.5 million per year (*Ann Arbor Observer, 1996a*).[14] This means a subsidy of more than $1 million per year. The structure spaces cost about $12,000 each at replacement value; allowing for a 50-year life, charging a 5% real opportunity cost of capital, and considering the City's foregone revenues from the 3% property tax on structures, this means additional costs of $2.9 million.[15] The spaces, both structures and lots, reside on about 9 acres of prime downtown land, worth some $500,000 per acre, and the interest charges and the foregone property tax revenues on this land add to another $0.4 million.[16] All these various costs total to $8.8 million, which means a subsidy from the City of Ann Arbor of over $4 million per year.[17]

There are benefits from these parking spaces beyond just the revenues. For example, shopping and working downtown are made quicker and easier. Are Ann Arborites willing to pay $4.5 million per year for this easier and quicker downtown? There are a little over 100,000 people in Ann Arbor—the subsidy amounts to $45 per person per year.[18] Would a majority of Washtenaw County citizens vote for an annual per-capita tax of $45 in order to maintain the existing pricing of Ann Arbor's public parking structures (Q14.3)?

Americans also enjoy extensive privately subsidized parking in their roles both as producers and as consumers. The U.S. government estimates that the private subsidies to parking amount to some $300 *billion* per year (OTA, 1994). In per-gallon terms, that is around $3 per gallon of gasoline!

Over 90% of the Americans who drive to work park for free; where this free parking is provided by employers, its market value is roughly $50 billion per year (Kessler and Schroeer, 1995). Such employer-provided parking is effectively subsidized by both federal and state income tax codes because the cost is deductible for

---

BOX 14.6 Off-Street Parking Mandates in Zoning Ordinances

Traditionally, city zoning boards have required that every new building provide an adequate number of new off-street parking spaces; some zoning ordinances even prohibit charging a price for using these spaces. The table below offers a sampling of one consultant's recommended zoning requirements (taken from Shoup, 1995).

Land use	Minimum parking spaces
Barber shop	2 per barber
Beauty shop	3 per beautician
Bicycle repair	3 per 1000 square feet
Bowling alley	1 per employee plus 5 per alley
Heliport	5 per touchdown pad
Mausoleum	10 per interments per hour
Nunnery	0.10 per nun
Rectory	0.75 per cleric
Swimming pool	1 per 2500 gallons of water

The purpose is to prevent the new construction from further congesting the on-street parking in the area. But think what this does to the incentive to own a car and to drive it of the people who live or work in this new building. Their parking there is cheap, if not free—in the sense that the cost of the space is buried in the rent—and hence the effort to reduce the parking problem adds to the driving congestion (Shoup and Pickrell, 1978; Shoup, 1997). Minimum parking requirements inflate demand for parking, and this inflated demand then becomes an argument for even larger minimum parking requirements. Think about what would happen if such ordinances were simply abandoned, and the free market was left to determine the quantity and price of off-street parking (Q14.4).

---

employers but not counted as income to employees.[19] Rarely are employees given the option of cashing out their free-parking privilege even though that would cost employers little and would give employees an opportunity-cost incentive to make more socially correct transportation decisions (Shoup and Willson, 1992).

When Americans shop, they usually park for free (or get their parking fees rebated by the stores from which they purchase). Shopping centers typically provide so much parking space that it is filled for no more than 10 or 20 hours per *year* (Shoup, 1995). The land and capital costs of the parking facilities are, of course, paid by consumers in the form of higher prices of the goods and services they buy. But those higher prices are paid whether or not they drive and park, and hence there is no incentive to consider the parking costs when making decisions about mode and frequency of shopping.

FINAL THOUGHTS

Notice that none of these problems that we have been discussing in this chapter can be handled by higher gasoline taxes—except in the very indirect sense that less driving means less of each of the problems. A higher gasoline tax reduces driving whether or not it is at a rush-hour time on a congested road.

Notice also that driving with heavy weight on the axles and parking in big, uncongested shopping-mall spaces do not impose external costs on anyone. But they do end up increasing the taxes of others (to repair roads) or raising the prices others pay at the mall (to cover the costs of building and maintaining the parking areas). Cars in America not only generate external costs but also get many of their other costs subsidized. These subsidies are like external costs in that they lower the private marginal costs of driving.

ENDNOTES

[1]In urban areas, 19% of the land has been paved over for road surfaces (Tolley and Turton, 1995).

[2]Recall what is meant by "capitalized value of the marginal product." It is the present value of the future stream of foregone marginal products—i.e., this year's marginal product, plus next year's marginal product times $(1+i)^{-1}$, plus the following year's marginal product times $(1+i)^{-2}$, etc., with i being the appropriate discount rate.

[3]You might wonder why gasoline is wasted when people go slower. Partly because congestion often means idling, with no progress at all, but mostly because congestion means slow speeds, and American cars are tuned to run most fuel efficiently at high speeds. Maximum fuel efficiency was achieved at 35–40 MPH in the 1970s and 1980s, but it is now achieved at 50–55 MPH (Davis and McFarlin, 1996).

[4]Technically, I should say the optimal number of lanes is the same or smaller with marginal cost pricing, since the number of lanes is an integer, not a continuous variable.

[5]Singapore also limits the total number of cars that can be registered, and motorists have to bid for the right to own a car. Currently this right costs almost $50,000 (*Economist*, 1997b).

[6]The risk of traffic gridlock is so great in Bangkok that most gasoline stations sell the "Comfort 100," a red plastic bottle that serves as a portable urinal, with an optional cone-shaped funnel for female use (*Economist*, 1993).

[7]So hordes of low-wage workers wait at the start of the three-in-one lanes, selling their services as auto occupants—this is just one of the many ingenious ways of earning a living there (Porter, 1996). While this transfers income from the very rich to the very poor, it does little to reduce congestion.

[8]But the toll revenues should *not* be earmarked to expansion of the number of lanes on these roads. Remember, the optimal number of lanes is reduced, not expanded, by congestion tolls.

[9]Carpoolers use their own cars; vanpoolers ride to work in a van owned, insured, and licensed by a vanpool service. The private advantages of pooling are the reduced money costs of commuting, especially if congestion tolls are involved; the private disadvantages are the increased time costs collecting passengers at the start of the commute and distributing them at the end—carpooling could even increase the total time and mileage of vehicles (Lee, 1984; Kessler and Schroeer, 1994).

[10]There is the risk, evidenced in some cases, that HOV lanes will create new carpoolers out of people who used to be bus-riders (Leman *et al.,* 1997). This is not good for reducing congestion since full buses are better than full cars.

[11]Remember that earlier costs are essentially higher costs.

[12]The algebra gets cumbersome, but loosely the argument is as follows. If T is the life of the road, and each vehicle cuts this life by t, then T/t vehicles can pass over it before it needs repavement. If the total cost of replacing the road is x, then the average (and marginal) cost of each road user is x divided by T/t, or xt/T. If that cost is charged to each user, then the total revenue collected from these T/t vehicles will be xt/T times T/t, or exactly x.

[13]Actual capital expenditures on roads are, of course, not the correct measure of the total social cost of using our road capital. That is the interest and depreciation on the road stock, and, since everyone agrees that our roads are deteriorating and will soon require massive replacement expenditure, the correct figure is almost certainly much higher than the current actual capital expenditure.

[14]The pricing is curious. Street parking is metered at 60 cents per hour while the structures cost 70 cents per hour. This means that the downtown employees, who arrive first in the morning, park for the entire day at the curbside meters, forcing short-time visitors to use the more distant, multi-storied structures. (Flash: this anomaly is now corrected.) When you think about it, parking meters may be an idea whose time has gone—the entire rest of the world only has one-third as many parking meters as the United States. They cost $2000 each and are prone to vandalism (Vise, 1998). They are easily replaced, as in most of Europe, by a system of time-dated parking stickers that are affixed on the inside of the windshield. Only one well-armored machine per city block is needed to dispense these stickers.

[15]This amount ($2.9 million) counts $(1/50)(\$12,000)(4000)$ for depreciation, $(0.05)(\$12,000/2)$ (4000) for interest (assuming the capital to be now half-depreciated), and $(0.03)(\$12,000/2)(4000)$ for property tax (assuming the private sector would have built comparably valued structures on the land)(Niskanen and Hanke, 1977).

[16]This amount ($0.4 million) equals $(0.05+0.03)(9)(\$500,000)$, where 5% is the real interest rate, 3% is the property tax rate, there are 9 acres, and each is worth $500,000 per acre. We should recognize that downtown acres might be worth less than $500,000 an acre if there were no subsidized public parking facilities there, but the above will do for a rough calculation.

[17]All of these numbers ignore "deferred maintenance"—which means that major repairs are long overdue. Deferred maintenance is now estimated to be as high as $30 million (*Ann Arbor Observer*, 1996b; O'Connor, 1998).

[18]If the parking structure is not crowded, and your parking does not prevent anyone else's, you do *not* impose an external cost when you park—the space has already been built, and the marginal cost of your using it is (practically) zero. But the decision to overbuild parking facilities and provide them at low prices (i.e., below average total cost) does redistribute welfare from nonparkers to parkers and does encourage people to become drivers and parkers.

[19]With employer parking subsidies, everything over $165 per month is taxed as employee income. If the employer subsidizes an employee's vanpool, bus, or subway costs, on the other hand, everything over $65 per month is taxed as employee income. But concern for this differential is largely "academic" since very few employers subsidize employee vanpool, bus, or subway costs.

Appendix: The Theory of Highway Congestion

"Nobody goes there any more.
It's too crowded."

Yogi Berra

The speed at which one can drive on any highway depends upon the density of cars on the highway. If there are very few cars on the road, a fairly high speed may be maintained by all of them, and additional cars entering the road may not, at first, affect that speed. But at some point, as cars enter, the closer spacing of the cars requires reduced speeds—this is congestion. From then on, as more cars enter and become ever more densely packed, all cars must go ever more slowly to maintain any given level of safety.

Figure 14A.1 shows the typical relationship between average speed and density of vehicles. The top, left, flat portion of the curve represents the region in which density is so low that no congestion occurs. The downward portion of the curve represents ever increasing congestion. The point where the curve reaches the horizontal (density) axis indicates the extreme where the cars have become so tightly packed that they are unable to move at all.

The flow of traffic is the number of vehicles completing a trip per lane per hour. Speed is miles per hour (MPH), and density is vehicles per mile. So flow is simply speed times density. The relationship between speed and flow is shown in Figure 14A.2. Again, the upper flat portion indicates the absence of congestion at low flows of traffic. The average speed falls as flows increase. But notice that the fall in speed eventually exactly offsets the increase in density, and the flow is maximized (at F_{max}). Should density increase beyond this point, the speed falls off so much that the actual flow is reduced. The correct social goal is not to maximize density or to maximize speed, but to find the optimal combination of high flow and fast time.[1A]

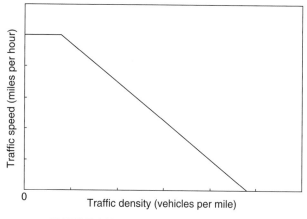

FIGURE 14A.1   Relation of Speed and Density

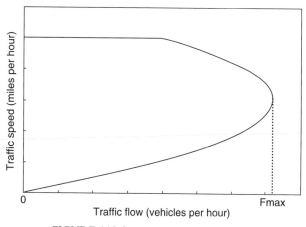

FIGURE 14A.2   Relation of Speed and Flow

The time taken to complete a 1-mile trip is the inverse of the average speed—hours per mile equals 1/MPH. So the average time cost per mile of each driver is the average price of the driver's time (wage rate) times the average time (hours per mile). This should ring a bell—if it does not, look back at the (P_t/MPH) term in Equation [2.3]. This average cost is constant if there is no congestion, but once speed is being reduced by an increased flow of traffic, the average cost begins to rise. When average cost is rising, as you know, marginal cost (MC) is above average cost (AC). Figure 14A.3 shows the relationship of MC and AC to traffic flow.[2A]

Think why MC is above AC in the presence of traffic congestion. When an additional car moves onto the road, its driver must "pay" in the driver's own time the AC per mile of the trip—the driver's wage rate times the hours per mile of the trip. But when this driver enters the roadway, all other traffic is slowed slightly

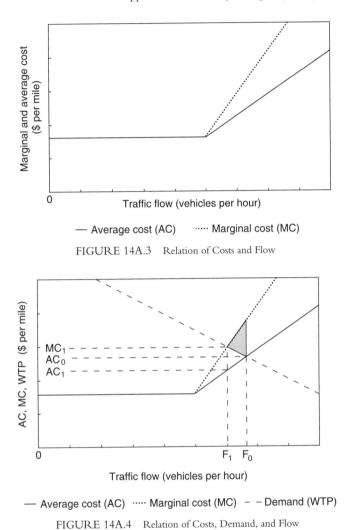

FIGURE 14A.3   Relation of Costs and Flow

FIGURE 14A.4   Relation of Costs, Demand, and Flow

from the increased congestion the new car causes. The new driver adds time costs to all existing traffic. This is the externality of congested driving. The excess of MC over AC measures the external cost to all other drivers of the marginal driver's entrance onto the road.

A Pigovian tax—here a highway toll—is called for. The tax should equal the difference between the MC and the AC of driving. But the gap between MC and AC is different depending upon the flow of traffic. At which MC–AC gap should the toll be fixed? This depends upon demand for the road.

In Figure 14A.4, the demand curve for the highway is shown, superimposed upon the earlier MC and AC curves. Highway demand is just like demand for anything else, except that here the driver may pay two different kinds of price for

---

BOX 14A.1 A Numerical Example of an Optimal Toll

Skip this box if mathematics is not your bag, but for those who would like to see how congestion tolls can be set in practice, read on. First, let us put all the preceding into algebra: S is speed, D is density, and F is flow. The speed–density relationship when there is congestion can be approximated as

$$S = a - bD, \qquad\qquad [14A.1]$$

where a and b are positive parameters estimated from highway observation. The flow–speed–density identity is

$$F = SD, \qquad\qquad [14A.2]$$

You can now derive the speed–flow relationship (like Figure 14A.2) and the marginal cost and average cost curves (like Figure 14A.3) if you can solve a quadratic equation, take a derivative, and tolerate an immense pile of algebra.[3A] The correct toll, for any flow, is the difference between MC and AC at that flow. The next table gives the resulting optimal tolls for a road where $a = 65$ MPH, $b = 0.35$, $F_{max} = 3018$ cars per mile per hour (i.e., almost 1 car per second), and the average value of time (P_t) of drivers is \$4 per hour.

Flow (F) (cars/hour)	Optimal toll (\$/mile)	Density (D) (cars/mile)	Speed (S) (MPH)
1000	0.01	17	59
2000	0.03	39	51
2500	0.06	54	46
2900	0.21	75	39
3000	0.69	86	35

Note: When there are 86 cars per mile, this means less than 15 yards between cars on average.

---

driving—there is always a time cost, and there may be a money cost as well if a toll is charged. Time and money are easily added together by use of the driver's relevant wage rate.

Consider first the highway without a toll. Drivers pay for the use of the road in time only. When deciding whether to use this road at this time, each driver asks himself or herself whether his or her willingness-to-pay for the trip is greater than the average cost of making it. As a result, F_0 drivers will choose to make the congested trip, and the average cost of each is AC_0. Drivers whose WTP is less than AC_0 will choose other roads, other times, other modes of transport, other jobs, or carpooling.

The highway is overused. Between F_1 and F_0, there are drivers whose WTP is less than the MC of their road use. The deadweight loss due to the excessive con-

---

BOX 14A.2 The Paradox of High-Occupancy Vehicle Lanes
High-occupancy vehicle lanes pose an interesting paradox. If there are fewer cars, and hence less congestion, in the HOV lane, the average time of all travelers could be reduced by putting more cars into the HOV lane. The average commuting time of any given number of commuters is *minimized* by having the ordinary lanes and the HOV lane all with the *same* number of cars and the *same* average speed.[4A] But nobody would go to any bother to gather partner-riders in order to qualify for the HOV lane if it moved no faster. First-best efficiency requires all lanes to move at the same speed, so an HOV lane is second-best. But the *average* commuting time of all commuters can be improved if enough people switch to the new HOV lane.

---

gestion of the road is the shaded area in Figure 14A.4. In order to reduce the highway traffic, a toll can be levied equal to the gap between MC and AC at F_1, a toll per mile of (MC$_1$ minus AC$_1$). This raises the cost of the highway use from the AC curve to a curve (not drawn) exactly (MC$_1$ − AC$_1$) higher, and it discourages $(F_0 − F_1)$ drivers from using the highway.

Who gains and who loses from this toll? Overall there is a social gain, for the deadweight loss of use at F_0 is removed. But every driver loses in the process: $(F_0 − F_1)$ drivers are induced to leave the road and are thereby made worse off. Those F_1 drivers who continue to use the road now pay in money and time a price of MC$_1$, where before they paid in time only, a lower price of AC$_0$. If all drivers lose, who gains? Whoever gets the toll revenue, an amount equal to the rectangle, (MC$_1$ − AC$_1$) times F_1. No wonder drivers resist tolls—while it makes society better off, it leaves all drivers worse off.[5A] To make tolls palatable to drivers, it is necessary to find a way to pass a significant portion of the toll revenue back to them.[6A]

One final question before leaving this theoretical appendix: can high-occupancy vehicle lanes serve as an efficient substitute for tolls? Opening up a new HOV lane means that drivers now have an option of going rapidly if they are willing to muster up enough passengers for the faster HOV-lane trip. Some will choose to do that. This will shift the demand curve for the original non-HOV lane(s) to the left (in Figure 14A.4), but drivers will still choose to enter the non-HOV lane(s) as long as their WTP exceeds the AC of the lane. Excessive congestion will still occur there since the optimal flow occurs where WTP equals MC, not where it equals AC, and WTP equals MC at a flow that is smaller than the flow where WTP equals AC. The new HOV lane will reduce congestion, but not optimally.[7A]

ENDNOTES

[1A]Traffic engineers mistakenly think that the optimal speed of traffic is that which permits the maximum vehicle flow (F_{max} in Figure 14A.2). For urban interstates, highway engineers estimate that this "optimal" speed is about 40 MPH (May, 1990). Make sure you understand their error (Q14A.1).

[2A]Figure 14A.3 is drawn, for simplicity, with straight-line MC and AC curves in the region where congestion occurs.

[3A]Find the basic speed–flow relation: $S^2 - aS + bF = 0$. Solve this quadratic equation for S in terms of F; time per driver per mile is the inverse of this speed. Multiply that expression by P_t (the average wage rate of the drivers) to get the AC of drivers; then multiply that by F to get the total cost of all drivers. Take the derivative of that with respect to F to get the MC of drivers. The optimal toll is (MC - AC).

[4A]If this statement is not obvious to you, and you are willing to do a little algebra and calculus, think of N people each driving alone to work on a highway of two lanes. There is congestion, and the average speed in each lane is $(a - bX)$, where a and b are positive parameters and X is the number of cars in the lane. Initially, each driver will seek the faster lane, so there will end up being $N/2$ cars in each lane, and the average speed in each lane will be $(a - bN/2)$. Now make one of the lanes an HOV lane and assume for simplicity that each car in the new HOV lane has exactly three people. Y people switch to the HOV lane, so that the average speed in the HOV lane is $(a - bY/3)$ and the average speed in the other lane is $(a - b(N-Y))$. The overall average speed, you can show, is maximized when 3/4 of the drivers switch to the HOV lane, so that there are $N/4$ cars in each lane, and each lane is moving at the same speed. But you can also show that even if only 1/3 of the drivers switch to the HOV lane, the average commuting speed is improved (Q14A.2).

[5A]This statement is not quite accurate. We have been assuming that all drivers value their time at the same wage rate. In fact, there are low-wage drivers and high-wage drivers. If a driver has a very high value of time, he or she may be made better off by the toll since it speeds the trip up, possibly saving enough time to be worth the toll.

[6A]Think about how you might do that. One way you must *not* do it is to have commuters save up their toll receipts and get reimbursed later from the toll revenues (if that is not clear, look again at Box 3.2).

[7A]What if the HOV lane is not a new lane but simply a conversion of an existing lane? Then the demand curve for the ordinary lanes that remain is shifted to the right for each remaining lane, but it is also shifted to the left by the choice of some drivers to use the HOV lane. Which effect dominates is not clear. So, whether congestion in the remaining ordinary lanes is increased or decreased is not clear.

CHAPTER 15

Water Pollution

"Water, taken in moderation,
cannot hurt anybody."

Mark Twain

Though much less so than air pollution, the automobile also causes water pollution, principally during the transportation and storage of petroleum and the disposal of its waste products. Here, we will examine three ways in which the automobile contributes to water pollution: through groundwater contamination, through stormwater treatment costs, and through ocean oil spills.

OIL AND BATTERIES

The disposal of automotive by-products, whether in proper landfills or not, can lead to chemical leaching into the underlying groundwater. Most states now ban the disposal of lead-acid batteries and waste oil in general landfills because of their toxic components. Such bans, however, are hard to enforce at the household level, especially when an alternative disposal process is lacking or is costly in terms of the disposer's time.

The EPA estimates that only about one-third of all waste oil is being collected and recycled, and most of that through subsidized drop-off locations (Merrill, 1996). But budgets are usually tight and subsidies are usually small. Of course, it is

173

possible to stimulate proper disposal without subsidy. Germany, for example, mandates a deposit on new oil, which is refunded when the waste oil is returned to an authorized collector and reprocessor (Bohm, 1981). California taxes new oil at $0.04 per quart and applies the revenues to drop-off infrastructure and education (Merrill, 1996).

Lead is highly toxic, especially to growing children. Now that leaded gasoline has been phased out, car batteries are the major source of waste lead. Old car batteries are now about 85% recycled, but the rest ends up in landfills (where the lead can leach into the groundwater) or in municipal incinerators (where the lead can get emitted into the air).

LEAKING UNDERGROUND STORAGE TANKS

Leaking underground storage tanks (called LUSTs, honest) for oil and petroleum are considered the most serious source of groundwater pollution in the United States. There are over 1 million underground storage tanks in the United States, roughly one-fourth of which have leaked contaminants into the surrounding soil and groundwater. Prevention is the main policy, through leak-detection systems, regular inspection, and protection against corrosion, overflow, and spill. The cure, when leaks are detected, is removal of the tanks and remediation of the area, usually by hauling the contaminated earth to a landfill and by pumping out, treating, and replacing any affected groundwater. Legally, the remediation is supposed to be complete at every detected site, but this is almost always too expensive. Only gradually are benefits and costs being compared—involving the

---

BOX 15.1 Recycling Lead

The conventional view has long been that greater recycling of old car batteries should be encouraged, perhaps even mandated. Increasing lead battery recycling from 85 to 95% would mean 100 tons per year fewer airborne lead emissions from primary lead smelters and 450 tons per year fewer airborne lead emissions from municipal waste incinerators, while increasing the airborne lead emissions of secondary smelters (which do the recycling) by only 60 tons per year.

But wait a moment. America's 2 primary lead smelters are located in Montana and Missouri, far from most of America's children. The 50-odd secondary smelters are mostly located in the eastern United States and California and Texas, in much more densely populated areas. By considering the density of the affected population as well as the amount of lead, an EPA study estimated that *more* children would be damaged with the higher battery recycling rate. As a result, the EPA decided not to move forward on this front. Indeed, it might have been useful to think about what the effect of *reducing* battery recycling *below* 85% would have done (Walker and Wiener, 1995).

proximity of the leaking tank to groundwater and the number of people reliant on that groundwater—and the possibility that it is best to do little or nothing about some old leaks is being suggested (Marsh, 1996; EPA, 1995c; Carrington-Crouch, 1996).

Owners of underground petroleum storage tanks must now carry insurance against future leaks. In order to provide funds for the federal government to help correct old leaks where the tank owner is unknown or financially unable to respond, a tax of $0.001 per gallon is levied on all motor fuel. Much of the responsibility for cleanups has been delegated to the states, who have also levied taxes on the tanks themselves and/or on the petroleum flow—typically about one-half cent per gallon. The revenues collected are earmarked to the cleanup of tank leaks and so far have been adequate for that job. But this is not a good example of a Pigovian tax on an externality—such a tax should be based on the expected future damage done by tank leakage, not the cost of the corrective action taken to alleviate that damage (Boyd and Kunreuther, 1995).[1]

Since the introduction of costly controls and liabilities, the number of underground storage tanks in the United States has been reduced by about half, despite the fact that Americans are driving more and buying more gasoline every year. How so? More gasoline is being stored in above-ground storage tanks (ASTs), where leaks are easier to spot and control, but which are more prone to fire, explosion, and vapor emissions. Also, the number of gasoline stations has declined,

---

BOX 15.2 Benefit–Cost Analysis of LUST Policies

Since the LUST program is expensive, it would be reassuring to know that its benefits exceed its costs. The EPA undertook two such analyses, one of the quicker leak detection aspects and one of the complete cleanup aspects (EPA, 1988).

Leak detection. Quicker leak detection involves upgrading, repairing, replacing, and retrofitting old tanks as well as greater monitoring for leaks. These costs were estimated to run a little over $1.0 billion per year. The benefits involve reduced vapor emissions, reduced damage to groundwater, reduced losses of petroleum, and reduced cancer incidence for those who drink well-water. These benefits, not including the lives saved from cancer, run around $0.2 billion per year. Finally, there are estimated to be fewer than *four* cancer cases avoided each year—a net cost of at least $200 million per life saved!

Leak cleanup. Cleanup costs are expected to be about $2 billion per year. What are the benefits of immediate and complete cleanup? The EPA *assumed* that the post-detection damages avoided were "at least as high as the cost" of cleanup and therefore that the benefit–cost result was favorable! Is that assumption reasonable? Of course not. It might be acceptable in an ideal world where sites were cleaned up only if the damages avoided exceeded the cleanup costs, but the EPA requires all leaks to be cleaned, whatever the damages avoided and whatever the cleanup costs. Effectively, the EPA has not yet done a benefit–cost analysis on the LUST cleanup regulation.

with stations having become much larger on average. With fewer, larger gas stations, there are lower LUST costs per gallon, but it also means that we must drive further on average to refuel our cars—especially in rural areas—and that there are a growing number of abandoned underground tanks whose leaks are more likely to go undetected.

STORMWATER RUNOFF

Waste oil and other pollutants also find their way into groundwater through what is called "nonpoint" pollution, the steady minute flow from engines to roadbeds—for oil, about 1 quart per vehicle per year (Corrales *et al.*, 1996). The oil and other pollutants are periodically flushed by rain through storm drains into rivers and groundwaters.

The only practical way to stop this is by treating stormwater runoff just like sewage—practical but expensive. Moreover, the more an area is paved, the greater will be the stormwater runoff from any given storm, and hence the larger must be the sewage treatment facility, or the larger must be the stormwater holding ponds, or the more frequent will be the overflow of untreated pollution.[2] Each has costs, and none of these costs are borne directly by the vehicles that created the stormwater problem.

Since urban agriculture—the fertilizers and pesticides poured onto suburban lawns—also causes stormwater pollution, it is not easy to divide the external costs up between the two sources. But estimates of the vehicle part of the added sewage treatment costs run around $2 billion per year, about 2 cents per gallon of gasoline (OTA, 1994).

OIL SPILLS

As the media definitely lets us know, oil spills happen. Such spills are not only expensive to contain and clean up, but there is inevitably irremediable damage to human beings, both as consumers and as producers, and to the other littoral flora and fauna. On average during the 1980s, tankers spilled 9000 tons of crude oil per year into U.S. coastal waters; in March 1989, the Exxon Valdez itself spilled 34,000 tons and cost more than $2 billion to clean up (Hopkins, 1992).[3]

Left to themselves, oil tanker companies would not take sufficient care to prevent oil spills and would not do enough to clean up oil spills that they caused. Optimal oil spill damage is somewhere between an unattainable zero and what an unregulated oil shipping market would cause. There are three ways that U.S. policy might approach deterrence of oil spills: (1) technological specification of oil tanker structure and procedure; (2) Pigovian taxation of the externality; and (3) legal liability of oil-spilling companies for all damages the spills and their cleanups cost. In "theory," any of the three approaches could succeed in achieving the optimal spillage and damage; in fact, especially in an uncertain world, some mix of policies may be appropriate (Kolstad *et al.,* 1990). In the United States, all three policies are pursued. Let us look at each, briefly.

If we knew exactly what oil spill safeguards were optimally applied, we could mandate them. But in reality, technical "fixes" are usually preferred to behavioral requirements for reasons of political pressure, regulatory ignorance, or administrative convenience—even though there is growing evidence that most oil spills are really caused by human error (Brulle, 1982; Goodstein, 1992; Wells *et al.,* 1993). Double-hulling of oil tankers, for example, is now required for all new tankers in U.S. waters. Existing tankers, however, are not required to be retrofitted, which incidentally encourages a slower replacement of old tankers. Moreover, double-hulling tankers of any given dimensions both makes them heavier, and hence more likely to sink, and leaves them with smaller oil capacity, and hence necessitating more trips to move any given volume of oil (Caswell, 1993). In short, technological specification is likely to end up specifying the wrong kind of safeguards, the wrong degree of safeguarding, or safeguarding for the wrong mix of activities.

The correct Pigovian tax would be set equal to the marginal expected oil spill damage, where the damage includes both the cost of cleanup and the cost to society of damage that remains after the cleanup (Kohn, 1993). Such a tax would have to be levied on the ex ante expected oil spilled—not just the amount of oil transported—and hence would require detailed knowledge of the efficacy of the oil spill safeguards taken by each tanker. Under an optimal Pigovian tax policy, there is no reason for thinking that the tax revenue collected is the optimal amount for the government to spend on oil spill cleanup. Possibly, much of the tax revenue should go into the general fund to be used for other purposes, and possibly, more should be spent on cleanup than the tax collects. The U.S. Congress, however, has placed a 5-cent-per-barrel tax on both domestic and imported oil, with the revenue earmarked to an oil spill response and cleanup fund. Note that the tax does not vary from ship to ship and hence does not depend at all on the safeguarding or the location of the ship.

Legal liability for damage would internalize the externalities—provided that all spills were detected, all costs were extracted from the offender by the courts, and the offenders were uninsured. None of these three provisos is likely to be attained in fact: much oil leakage will go undetected; some costs will go unmeasured or uncollected, and most of the costs will be insured. As a result, the private oil spill costs expected by the tanker companies will be less than the full social costs, and their safeguards will accordingly be less than optimal.

If one depends upon legal liability to reduce optimally the number and size of oil spills, then it is essential that full costs be levied against those who cause oil spills. Just what are those "full" costs? In principle, we should expand the cleanup operation as long as the benefit of additional cleanup exceeds the marginal cost of that cleanup, and the oil spiller should then be assessed the total cleanup costs plus the total unabated damages (Polinsky and Shavell, 1994). Notice that this leads to a simple action rule. All the U.S. government needs to do is make any oil spiller fully liable for all unabated damages, and the oil spiller will have an incentive to do the optimal amount of cleanup. Estimation of the monetary value of the unabated damages is, of course, not easy.[4]

Since the full costs of oil spills may be huge, the Oil Pollution Act of 1990 imposed unlimited liability on companies whose tankers spill oil in American waters. This seemingly sensible action, however, raises some indirect problems. It makes oil spill insurance much more expensive and encourages the formation of "one-ship" companies—with tankers that are undersized, underinsured, and too little safeguarded.[5]

Two final things to note. First, while it is important that the potential oil spiller expects to pay for any damages, it is *not* important that the victims of the oil spills be compensated, although concerns for fairness may urge that some of the collected damage money should go to them. Why not all? Consider the animals that were damaged by the Exxon Valdez spill. One of the costs charged to Exxon was for the deaths and damages to sea otters, and those charges were earmarked for otter rescue centers, which treated and released some 200 otters—at a cost of $90,000 per otter (Keeble, 1991). It is arguable that a better use for that money could have been found.[6]

Second, we should *not* do not everything to clean up an oil spill—just the optimal amount of things.[7] A benefit–cost analysis is essential. But in the United States such a B/C analysis is explicitly not done. Instead, when

> a major oil spill occurs . . . coordinated teams . . . help contain the spill, clean it up, and assure that damage to human health and the environment is minimized. . . . [When] the cleanup activities have ceased, there are still pools of oil left in some areas where it is assumed that the harm caused to the ecosystem by the oil is not greater than the benefits to be gained from further cleanup. (EPA, 1993b)

Note the critical word in this quote is "minimized," when it should be "optimized."[8]

Oil spills and other environmental problems also arise from the operation of offshore drilling platforms on the outer continental shelf (OCS) surrounding the United States, although platforms and their attendant pipelines have better spill records than tankers (Grigalunas and Opaluch, 1990). Platform safeguards against oil spills are handled in much the same way as tankers—through technical requirements and legal liability—but there are two additional criteria of interest.

First, the Minerals Management Service of the Department of the Interior undertakes a benefit–cost analysis of OCS drilling in order to ensure that the national benefit of the expected oil exceeds the costs, including any expected environmental costs. If the mandated technical safeguards were optimal and the liability were fully effective, the oil company's bid for the OCS drilling right would in itself be proof that the social benefit–cost test was passed, except for one thing—one of the national benefits of OCS oil is reduced tanker oil spill costs since more American oil means less imported oil, and the private drilling company would not count this external benefit in its bid calculation.

BOX 15.3 Disposal of Deepwater Oil-Drilling Platforms

Once the useful life of an oil-drilling platform is over, it must be disposed of. For those near shore and in shallow waters, it is clear that they must be taken to land for dismantling. But for large, deepwater platforms, it is not so clear.

In the North Sea, the oil companies claim that the safest and most environmentally sound method of disposal is to sink some of the platforms—in water so deep that few flora or fauna would be affected and little contamination would surface. The oil companies also stress the danger that a towed platform might break up as it neared shore, causing much worse damage than it ever could in deep water. It also happens that deepwater disposal is much cheaper than towing, dismantling, and recycling (*Economist*, 1996c).

This raises many issues, but one stands out. Suppose deepwater disposal is the correct social (as well as private) choice. Insisting on land disposal would unnecessarily raise the cost of petroleum products and excessively reduce driving. On the other hand, suppose driving is currently excessive from a social viewpoint, but higher gasoline taxes are not politically feasible. Should one push for regulations—even those we know to be unnecessary—just to drive up the real costs of gasoline (Q15.2)?

And second, the government benefit–cost analysis is done not only for the nation as a whole but also for the region in which the drilling occurs. This means, in effect, that there must be plans to fully compensate regional victims of any oil spills because otherwise there would be inadequate regional benefit to offset the expected oil spill cost. But compensating victims discourages potential victims from locating elsewhere, and society has a right to expect potential victims to "take care" to reduce the real costs of any offshore platform leaks.

FINAL THOUGHTS

What does all this actual and potential water pollution by cars and their fuels cost? Few efforts have been made to estimate these external damages, but one study guessed that the total contribution of motor vehicles to U.S. water pollution problems is around $30 billion per year, or around $0.30 per gallon (Litman, 1995).

ENDNOTES

[1]Petroleum is also taxed under the Comprehensive Environmental Response, Compensation, and Liability Act of 1980 (better known as CERCLA or Superfund), the very expensive attempt to clean up completely all of America's existing hazardous waste sites. Past petroleum tank leaks were explicitly exempted from Superfund concern, so presumably this tax seeks to gather revenues for the federally

funded Superfund cleanups of hazardous petrochemical waste products. This tax is estimated by the EPA to add less than $1/10^{th}$ of 1 cent to the price of a gallon of gasoline (Hird, 1994). This also is not a proper Pigovian tax, being linked to past, not current, damages.

[2]Stormwater holding ponds are just that, ponds that collect water at times of heavy rainfall and then discharge it to the treatment plant during dry periods. The cost advantage is that the ponds are cheaper than a treatment plant large enough to handle the heaviest rainfalls.

[3]The world's largest "spill" ever was the Iraqi discharge in 1991 of more than half a million tons of Kuwaiti crude oil into the Persian Gulf.

[4]How would an economist go about estimating the dollar value, for example, of a dead otter? Our methodology for valuing human lives offers no help. This is not just an academic question: the National Oceanic and Atmospheric Administration (NOAA) was required by the Oil Pollution Act of 1990 to promulgate natural resource damage assessment rules for oil spills. The courts have suggested that "restoration costs" are a basis for damage assessment. Since we cannot restore a dead otter, this presumably means restoring the size and health of the otter population. One final puzzle arises. Suppose the otters are not dead, but potential tourists think the oil spill has killed them, so they choose other (than otter-watching) vacations, and the profits of local tour operators go down. Are these lost profits a damage for which the oil spiller should be liable (Q15.1)?

[5]One-ship company tankers will be undersized in order to reduce the amount of assets that can be seized in a court judgment. By failing to take advantage of economies of scale, these small tankers may raise both the transport costs of oil and the probability of an oil spill. They will be underinsured and too little safeguarded because bankruptcy will let the firm avoid most of any oil spill liability. All this is not just a fanciful theory. Within a year of the Oil Pollution Act of 1990, nearly half of the oceangoing tankers serving the United States were owned by single-ship companies, and many large shippers were transferring oil to small, independently owned ferry ships before entering U.S. waters (Sullivan, 1990; Ketkar, 1995).

[6]You may be saying, OK for otter victims, but how about compensating people victims? In order to avoid thinking about "nasty" Exxon, let us suppose that oil spills are really an "act of God" and totally ruin a particular region's fishing in half the years. Fishermen catch $4 worth of fish in the good years and nothing in the bad, for an average income of $2. Alternatively, they could fish elsewhere and catch $3 worth of fish every year. From a social viewpoint, they should go elsewhere, since $3 worth of fish per year is better than $2 worth. If, however, we give the fishermen $4 in compensation in the oil spill years, then they will get $4 in every year, whether it is good or bad, and they will not go to the $3 fishing grounds. As a society, we lose by this decision: we end up each year with $2 worth of fish on average when we could have had $3 worth of fish. The lesson is that we must not distort the incentive for the victim to "take care" (see Chapter 10)—in this case, taking care to avoid the potential external cost.

[7]Indeed, the optimal amount may sometimes be zero. It is respectably argued that often nothing should be spent on cleanup, claiming that with existing cleanup technology more damage is done by attempting to remove the spilled oil than would be done by just leaving it (Foster *et al.*, 1990). Certainly, the motivation behind much of the Exxon cleanup was the creation of local jobs and fortunes, not the accelerated recovery of the ecological system.

[8]The second sentence in the preceding quote is offered as a puzzle for the reader. To me, "the harm caused to the ecosystem by the oil" is always exactly equal to "the benefits to be gained from further cleanup" regardless of how much cleanup is done!

CHAPTER 16

Potpourri

"Fillet of a fenny snake,
In the cauldron boil and bake;
Eye of newt, and toe of frog,
Wool of bat, and tongue of dog;
Adder's fork, and blind-worm's sting,
Lizard's leg, and howlet's wing;
For a charm of pow'rful trouble.
Like a hell-broth boil and bubble."

William Shakespeare
Macbeth

As we near the end of this journey through automotive externalities, a brief, final listing of a few other unpaid costs that accompany auto use is appropriate. The chapter is called "potpourri," implying a mixed bag, and to some extent it is that. But there is a connection between them. They accompany auto use, but they are far from a necessary concomitant of auto use.

With all the earlier externalities that we have been discussing, the external cost is an almost inevitable by-product of auto use. No matter what (internal combustion engine) car you drive, there is a need for imported fuel and there is at least some air pollution and global warming. No matter how soberly, carefully, or slowly you drive, there is always a risk of injuring or killing someone else. Cars congest, need roads, and have to be parked somewhere. They need oil, and it can spill, and it has to be disposed of. We have talked about how policies can reduce these externalities, but they can never be mitigated completely as long as our present cars are driven. In almost every case, part of an optimal mitigation involves less driving.

In this chapter, however, we turn to unpaid costs that are much more loosely associated with auto use. So loosely, in fact, that for each problem the optimal policy is almost completely independent of auto use. The correct Pigovian tax on an activity depends upon the marginal external costs caused by that activity. For each of the following problems, driving is really not the activity that basically causes the problem.

The list includes: (1) noise, (2) roadside litter, (3) police, court, and incarceration costs, (4) disposal of junked automobiles, and (5) urban sprawl.

NOISE

When you ask the person-in-the-street about auto externalities (not exactly using that term, of course), noise usually appears high on the list. But it is far from the top of the policy list in Washington, and even anticar activists do not holler much about it. The EPA used to worry about vehicle noise, but the Reagan administration silenced that. Indeed, outside of some workplaces, where extremely high noise levels have been reliably documented to cause serious stress and hearing loss, noise no longer seems to concern anyone in Washington.

With road noise, as with road wear and tear, the chief culprit is trucks, not cars. A truck typically emits a much higher sound level than does a car. Truck engines are larger, they are diesel, and they are run at higher engine speeds. Auto noise would probably bother very few people were it not for the addition of trucks and other large commercial vehicles (Rosenthal, 1975). One government study estimated that large trucks on urban roads with moderate traffic caused 6–12 cents per *mile* in noise damages (FHA, 1982).

The two possible exceptions to the argument that road noise is not the fault of the car are the horn and the theft alarm. Let us look briefly at each.

The horn is, in certain circumstances, a very cheap and effective piece of safety equipment. The problem is its excessive and extraneous use for reasons other than safety. Efforts to reduce horn noise follow two paths, neither satisfactory. One path is legislation against unnecessary noise; but when horns are going off most obnoxiously, police are usually too busy to pay attention to them, and anyway they have difficulty identifying the offending vehicles. The other path is mandating quieter horns, but this undermines the safety value of the horn.[1]

The economist is tempted to derive some sort of tax on horn use to reduce noise pollution, but recall that the horn, when properly used, provides an external *benefit*—alerting other drivers, bicyclists, or pedestrians of impending crisis—so that horn use should sometimes be subsidized rather than taxed. Sorting all that out in a tax/subsidy scheme at reasonable cost is surely impossible.

The auto theft alarm is similar to the horn in that it can generate both positive and negative externalities. The noise of false alarms provides an external cost, but the general disincentive to auto theft protects others' cars as well as the car of the alarm purchaser.

If noise bothers you, better buy earplugs.

ROADSIDE LITTER

Wherever in the world standards of living have risen high enough to proliferate the one-way container, roadside litter abounds. In principle, such litter is a people problem, and only very secondarily a car problem, and the ideal policy response is a hefty fine for littering. The amount of the fine would, in Pigovian fashion, be related to estimates of the eyesore damage and pickup costs of such litter.[2] Unfortunately, while most states do advertise high fines for highway littering, few litterbugs are apprehended and fined in fact. Highway patrols seem to have more pressing things to do than to ticket litterbugs. The expected *private* cost of highway littering is close to zero.

How much cost does highway littering impose on society? A lower-bound estimate would be the amount that states and cities spend on cleaning up their roadsides. Why is this a lower-bound estimate? It is a lower-bound estimate if the relevant governments have done, at least implicitly, their benefit–cost tests and do more cleanup up to the point where the marginal eyesore benefit equals the marginal cleanup cost and the total eyesore benefit of cleanup exceeds the total pickup cost of the litter.

An indirect estimate of the cost is available in states that have passed laws requiring mandatory deposits on soft-drink and beer containers. The major benefit of such laws is a drastic reduction in beverage container litter (and also a reduction in the beverage containers headed directly for the landfill), and beverage containers account for an overwhelming portion of highway litter (Porter, 1978). But the costs of mandatory deposits are high. In Michigan, the annual costs have been estimated to be: (1) consumer inconvenience costs of returning containers of $6–12 per person; (2) increased resource costs of producing and recollecting returnable containers of $5–30 per person; and (3) foregone consumer surplus as a result of the reduced consumption due to higher prices and greater inconvenience of $1–3 per person (Porter, 1983).

The total cost, therefore, is something between $12 and $45 per Michigan resident. Though quite possibly incorrectly, one might be willing to assume that the median Michigan voter valued the benefits of litter reduction at least as highly as the costs of the mandatory deposits imposed in order to achieve the litter reduction. Less than a dozen states, however, have embraced mandatory deposits on beverage containers. Nevertheless, all the preceding suggests that it is not impossible to accuse automobiles, or rather their occupants, of doing something like $1 billion per year of litter damage to the roadside environment.

Does this urge a penny a gallon gasoline tax because of roadside litter? Hardly. Taxing all drivers' miles, or gallons, because some drivers litter would be a little like attaching the average speeding fine to the annual cost of the drivers licenses of every driver and then doing away with highway patrols. That would be so imperfect a Pigovian tax as to be a travesty.

Perhaps our best course is to hope that America will grow up to its affluence.

BOX 16.1 Highway Salt as a Deicing Material
We have long used salt for deicing roads, especially in Michigan, which sits on a bed of geologic salt. As a result, salt is cheap, in a private cost sense, but its external costs have been estimated to be nearly $1000 per ton used in additional costs of repair and maintenance of roads and bridges, in vehicle corrosion costs, and in aesthetic costs through roadside flora damage (Vitaliano, 1992). A substitute deicing material, calcium magnesium acetate (CMA), is available to city and state highway agencies, but at much higher price (roughly $700 per ton versus $60 per ton).

Why do public agencies not consider *social* cost when making their deicer choices? Until recently, the federal government subsidized the repair of bridges and roads but neither taxed the use of salt nor subsidized the use of CMA. How did this affect the state and local highway agencies' deicer choices (Q16.1)?

POLICE, COURT, AND INCARCERATION COSTS

Depending on exactly how you calculate it, you find that the total cost of motor vehicle registration, driver licensing, highway police, and highway-related courtroom and jailhouse activity runs some $20–70 billion per year in the United States, and only a small percentage of this cost is covered by fines and fees (Hart, 1986; OTA, 1994). The deficit is covered from general funds, which means from taxes on law-abiding drivers and nondrivers.

This sounds unfair, but it is not easy to correct. Consider the following simple example. Speed sometimes kills, some people speed, and when they speed they raise the probability of killing someone. The correct Pigovian tax on speeders depends on the expected increase in highway deaths due to speeding. More precisely, the expected speeding fine—that is, the probability of being caught times the fine for speeding—should equal the expected excess deaths times the societal value of life.[3] Recall the argument in Chapter 11. Raising the probability of being caught requires increased highway patrol resources, but raising the speeding fine requires no resources at all—in fact it augments the relevant government's budget revenues. So, in theory, fines should be very, very high, and there should be very, very few patrol cars. However, there are political and philosophical limits to how high speeding fines can be set. Given this maximum fine if caught, there may be *no* number of patrol cars that can raise enough revenue to cover their costs. Few patrols will catch too few speeders, and many patrols will cost too much.

That was a long paragraph, but you get the idea. It is easier to say that speeders should pay their way than it is to achieve it. Increasing the revenues from speeding fines in order to cover the enforcement costs requires greater highway patrol resources, which in turn further raises the speeding revenue needed to cover the enforcement costs.[4] It may be unfair to run a deficit in highway police, court, and incarceration costs, but it may be impossible to correct the problem.

In any case, this is a general law enforcement problem that greatly transcends the automobile.

DISPOSAL OF JUNKED AUTOMOBILES

Not too many years ago, a major crusade of the First Lady of the United States (1960s, Lady Bird Johnson) was to stop the eyesore of discarded motor vehicles littering the countryside. For decades, the price of new raw materials had been declining and the wage rates of potential recyclers rising, so there was no profit in recycling autos once their mobile life had ended. Some European countries (and New Mexico) initiated mandatory deposits on new automobiles, which were refunded when an auto hulk was properly turned over to an authorized junk dealer (Bohm, 1981).

Today, however, only 5% of defunct automobiles are abandoned, and of those that are properly disposed of, around 80% of the vehicle (by weight) is recovered for recycling or reuse (Keoleian et al., 1996; Bigness, 1995). This dramatic change in junked car disposal over the last three decades has comes about from a variety of sources, such as the development and proliferation of dismantlers, shredders, and steel minimills that have increased the efficiency of the recycling and reduced the transport distances involved. Nevertheless, 100% of 5% of the junked cars and 20% of the other 95% still impose external costs in the form of street and highway cleanup costs, "eyesore" damage, and the (at least partly) unpaid costs of landfill space usage.

One study guesses that the subsidy to the disposal of automotive waste products amounts to some $4 billion per year (Lee, 1993). But there is nothing special here about motor vehicles—in the United States, we subsidize the disposal of almost all waste products in the sense there are few direct charges for waste disposal.[5] Taxing gasoline or cars would be very second-best ways of correcting the market failures of our solid waste disposal system. The goal, remember, is not to recycle everything in the car, just those things that make economic sense to recycle. If waste disposal were priced correctly, the optimal fraction of the car would get recycled.

There is also a little-noticed trade-off going on. Automakers have been achieving CAFE standards partly by replacing metal parts with lighter plastic parts. But the plastic, called "fluff" by the auto recyclers, is at this time not recyclable. Higher CAFE requirements have been reducing the recyclability of the auto, adding to the landfill cost of its disposal.

URBAN SPRAWL

The automobile has made it possible for people to live further from their workplaces and in larger and less-dense housing plots. This urban sprawl, as it is called, is considered by many to be a blight on American cities. It separates the rich even

---

BOX 16.2 Disposing of Old Tires

Americans dispose of, on average, about one old tire per person per year. Until World War II, worn-out pure-rubber tires were melted down and reused. But in the last half-century, since the introduction of steel belts and synthetic rubber, reuse has been too costly, and old tires have been mostly landfilled, although some were stockpiled or littered to avoid landfill fees. But tires neither compact well nor degrade rapidly in landfills, so most states now either ban tires from their landfills or require them to be shredded first. Continued surface disposal is even less desirable, as it constitutes a fire hazard and a breeding site for rats and insects.

As a result, tire brokers have sought new and cheaper ways of getting rid of old tires. Some of the ways are: retreading old tires, which has seen decades of decline because real new tire prices have been falling, retreading steel-belted radial tires is expensive, and tire disposal has been essentially costless; incineration, since tires have even more fuel value per pound than coal; and rubberized asphalt roads, which cost nearly twice as much initially but provide a more comfortable ride, reduce noise, are temperature-resistant, and last two to four times as long (McPhee, 1993; McAdams, 1993; Serumgard and Blumenthal, 1993; Brodsky, 1993; Rhyner *et al.*, 1995).[6]

Why are we not riding on more of these smooth roads? Three reasons exist. One, state highway departments usually fix their road specifications in terms of materials, not longevity, so road contractors cannot use new improved materials. Two, fearing "sweetheart" contracts to politically favored road-builders, the federal government requires states to accept the lowest bid, regardless of longevity, so more durable but more expensive materials cannot win contracts. Three, by law, road-builders are not required to guarantee the quality or durability of the roads they build (Dance, 1991).

But none of this hits the problem of the billions of old tires that have just been piling up in tire junkyards over the past half-century. They are undesirable for recycling because tire shredders are damaged by their accumulated rocks, dirt, and water (Verde, 1996). Several states have enacted small taxes, per tire or per vehicle, with revenues earmarked either to the disposal of old tire stockpiles or to increased research into better future use of old tires (EPA, 1993a).

---

further from the poor, and leaves the inner cities with declining property tax bases with which to finance basic urban services. Less-dense and more-distant housing increases the costs of providing basic urban services, usually by much more than the developer pays to the sprawled municipality. Finally, the sprawl eats away at the woods, open spaces, and wetlands between each city and its neighbor cities.

While all of these sprawl costs have obviously been made possible by the automobile, it is not at all obvious that they are best attacked by raising the cost of driving.[7] For each of the sprawl problems mentioned in the preceding paragraph, there are more direct and hence better policy approaches than through the automobile. The sprawl issue is mentioned here only because higher driving costs do induce people to live closer to their workplaces.

FINAL THOUGHTS

We could lengthen the preceding list—illegitimate babies are conceived in cars (or used to be), bank robbers make getaways in cars, car traffic induces roadside billboards that block views of natural beauty, etc. But the five already discussed are enough. Indeed, if each of these peripheral problems is much better handled through other-than-automotive policies, why do I bother to bring them up at all? Because they are major parts of a long list of evils that are often attributed to the automobile—as if a scoundrel were further condemned by his or her dislike of broccoli. When thinking economically about cars and drivers, think about *what really causes the external costs*, and tax or regulate *that*. Don't even think about broccoli.

ENDNOTES

[1]Indeed, as cars have become better insulated from exterior noise, it has become necessary for ambulances, police cars, and fire trucks to install ever louder sirens in order to penetrate the nearby drivers' ears. These sirens serve a useful social purpose, to warn everyone that a public vehicle is approaching at high speed. The externality resides in the excessive soundproofing of the cars, not the excessive noise of the sirens.

[2]I use the word "eyesore" as a catchall for all the damages that litter causes before it is picked up—not only aesthetic displeasure but also cut feet, farm equipment damage, wildlife death, etc.

[3]More precisely yet, both the probability of being caught speeding and the excess deaths should be measured as rates per mile. The fine should also include a share of the cost of the highway patrols needed to prevent speeding.

[4]There are doubly diminishing returns operating here. A, say, 10% increase in patrol cars would probably not increase the number of speeders caught by 10%, even if the total number of speeders remained constant. But the increased number of patrols will also induce a reduction in the number of speeders.

[5]The fact that you pay for the city's refuse collection and landfill through property taxes is, you should by now realize, completely irrelevant. When you throw something in your trash can, society incurs extra costs collecting, recycling, burying, and/or burning it, but you pay nothing extra on the margin—except in a few thousand American cities with pay-by-the-bag pricing (Canterbury, 1997).

[6]Something that costs twice as much and lasts twice as long is more expensive in a present-value sense. For proof, compare the present values of roads that need to be replaced every T years at a cost of X for replacement with roads that need to be replaced every $2T$ years at a cost of $2X$ for replacement, and convince yourself that

$$X\{1 + (1+i)^{-T} + (1+i)^{-2T} + (1+i)^{-3T} + \cdots \} <$$

$$2X\{1 + (1+i)^{-2T} + (1+i)^{-4T} + (1+i)^{-6T} + \cdots \}$$

for any positive values of X, T, or i (with i being the discount rate). But if the road costs twice as much and lasts *three* times as long, it will almost certainly be cheaper in the long run in a present-value sense. Try to prove this (for any reasonably low interest rate) (Q16.2).

[7]In New Jersey, for example, higher gasoline taxes have been suggested as part of a plan for the government to buy up peripheral city land to prevent development there, using the revenue raised by the new taxes (Preston, 1998).

Where Next ?

CHAPTER 17

Where Should We Go from Here?

*"The freedom that the automobile
has given the average American
is a good thing,
even though it may take him a long time
to learn how to use it."*

Elmer Davis
America as Americans See It

People tend to give an extreme response to the question of where we should go from here. Some say that we should do nothing, or that we can do nothing, given the country's history, culture, politics, psychology, etc. Others go to the other extreme, talking of revitalized mass transit systems, restructured cities, denser housing, mandated carpooling, bicycle paths, travelator networks, etc. I don't think we can afford to do nothing, and I don't think a restructuring of America is feasible or sensible. Instead, I am going to suggest something in between. We will first review what American automotive policy has done over the past three decades and then think about where we might go over the next decade.

WHAT'S WRONG WITH CURRENT POLICY?

Throughout this book, we have taken up automotive policies one at a time. We started with the security problem posed by gasoline use and looked at policies to enhance fuel efficiency. Then we turned to the air pollution policy and looked at policies to reduce automotive emissions, and so forth. Problem, policy; problem, policy; problem, policy; etc. In fact, the U.S. government has also approached each of these goals in this way, one at a time, largely ignoring possible interactions among the various policies and possible impacts of particular policies on other automotive policies and problems.

These interactions ought not to be ignored. For the most part, the policies are not complementary. They conflict with each other; they involve trade-offs. The more policy has achieved toward one goal, the more another goal has been undermined.

The conflicts between the goals should be, at this point, obvious. Greater fuel economy is largely achieved by making cars smaller and lighter. But the weight of a vehicle, as we have seen, is positively related to crash survivability—lighter, more fuel-efficient cars are less safe, especially in their crashes with light trucks. The converse of this is that safer cars mean heavier cars, and heavier cars get lower miles per gallon. CAFE standards have induced many drivers to switch to light trucks, but these, despite being heavier, are inherently less safe than cars (in single-vehicle crashes) because they are higher and have a smaller turn radius, which means that they spin, flip, and roll much more easily.

Fuel economy and air pollution emissions also involve conflicts, albeit lesser conflicts. Since the EPA fixes emissions per mile, cars with greater fuel economy are permitted to have higher emissions per gallon. An automobile that is tuned for maximum fuel efficiency is not tuned for lowest emissions, and vice versa. Emissions equipment, such as the catalytic converter, also adds weight to the car, which reduces fuel economy. Air pollution policy is even, in a small way, in conflict with safety features—the catalytic converter can start fires.

Policies that make cars safer, cheaper, faster, or more convenient increase the amount of driving done, and this leads to greater gasoline consumption, greater air pollution, more highway accidents, more congestion, etc. Policies that make new cars more expensive or more inconvenient induce people to keep their old cars longer or to buy trucks, and old cars and trucks are the worst on the road in terms of fuel efficiency, emissions, and safety equipment.

Even the separate policies, as we have seen, regularly target the wrong objectives. CAFE targets miles per gallon, though it is intended to affect gallons. As a result, while the fuel efficiency of U.S. cars has risen dramatically, we consume about 1 million more barrels of oil per day than we did before the first OPEC price shock. The EPA targets auto emissions per mile everywhere, though it ought to be concerned with emissions in areas with inadequately clean air. As a result, half of all Americans are spending more money than necessary to keep their air clean, and the other half still live in areas where the ambient air quality is deemed by the EPA to be unhealthy. The NHTSA targets safety equipment (and through recalls, defects affecting safety), though it is intended to affect safety itself. As a result, while the NHTSA has brought down highway deaths per VMT dramatically in recent decades, it has not much reduced total highway deaths. The highway death rate came down more in the *year* following the OPEC price hike of 1973 than in the entire two decades of NHTSA policies.

More generally, for almost every externality we have examined, the external costs can be logically divided into two components that are multiplied together: external cost per gallon times number of gallons (or external cost per mile times number of miles). Cost-effective policies should work on both of these components. But our actual policies almost always work only on one component, external cost per gallon (or per mile), and completely ignore the other component, number of gallons (or miles).

Even for the component that policy does address, external cost per gallon (or per mile), policies rarely try to use market-oriented incentives to induce people to change. Instead, changes are simply mandated. What is wrong with this command-and-control approach? Almost everything. Basically, the mandated change is, by definition, unwanted by consumers, so consumers have every incentive to avoid or evade the mandate. Manufacturers, trying to please consumers, also have an incentive to resist the change or find sneaky ways around the mandate.

A seriously enforced mandate that firms "do at least x" is in essence a two-tiered tax system. The tax is very high on firms that fall short of doing x, but there is a zero incentive for achieving more than x. A mandated minimum change is, in effect, a mandated maximum change.

Since it is harder to mandate behavior, there is a tendency to set CAC mandates in terms of physical equipment—a "technical fix." But, once a particular technical "fix" is mandated, there is no incentive for anyone to maintain the mandated equipment or to search for alternative means of achieving the same goal at lower cost.

To justify a technical mandate in one car, the same change must be mandated for all cars—the "one-size-fits-all" approach to regulation. This foregoes all kinds of possible cost-effective substitutions between models. And "grandfathering" existing cars, which means not requiring any retrofits at all when new equipment is mandated on new models, foregoes all opportunity to meet externality abatement through changing the number of old cars, the configuration of old cars, or the behavior of the drivers of old cars.[1]

WHAT HIGHER GASOLINE TAXATION CAN DO

Higher gasoline taxes achieve almost all the same objectives with none of these drawbacks. By raising gasoline prices, gasoline taxes induce drivers to drive less *and* to buy more fuel-efficient cars. But note, such taxes do not force anyone to do anything that they do not want to do. All reactions to the taxes are voluntary responses to these taxes, and hence they are, by definition, desired. And almost every one of the externality problems we have been discussing throughout this book is greatly ameliorated simply by reduced driving.

Focus first on reduced driving by itself, without any other adjustments by car owners and drivers. Less gasoline means fewer gasoline imports and fewer oil spills.

Less gasoline and less driving means less air pollution, both locally and globally. Fewer miles means fewer highway accidents, less congestion, fewer parking problems, less pressure to expand congested road systems, less wear and tear on the highways, and less vehicle-caused leakage into the groundwater.

Higher gasoline prices also induce car owners to make other adjustments beyond just the amount of driving. They will want more fuel-efficient cars and will gradually adjust to them. If the higher gasoline taxes are emissions-based, as they should be, people will want more emissions-efficient cars as well. As a serendipitous by-product, higher and emissions-based gasoline taxes will make mandated CAFE and air pollution emissions standards redundant. Since congestion is an especially big gas eater, drivers will want to avoid congested roads and times; gasoline taxes are hardly a full substitute for congestion tolls, but they do work in the right direction—less driving means less congestion.

How big should gasoline taxes be? Many have tried to quantify the external costs and hidden subsidies of driving, and they typically get estimates of at least $2 per gallon, and figures like $5 or $10 per gallon are not unheard of (Hansson, 1990; Gordon, 1991; Moffet, 1991; MacKenzie et al., 1992; Miller and Moffet, 1993; Lee, 1993; OTA, 1994; Litman, 1995; Carson, 1996). It has not been the purpose of this book to add another detailed numerical estimate, but I—and I hope you, too—believe that at least $1 per gallon is certainly in the right ballpark. If even 1/20th of the EPA's estimated 180,000 annual air pollution deaths are attributed to the automobile, that's $0.27 per gallon (i.e., 9000 times $3 million per life, divided by 100 billion gallons).[2] Then the 20,000 annual nondriver highway deaths mean another $0.60 per gallon (i.e., 20,000 times $3 million per life, divided by 100 billion gallons). We are nearing $1.00 per gallon before we even get to issues of energy security, global warming, highway injury, driver death, congestion, road maintenance, parking, and water pollution.

Knowing how big the taxes ought ultimately to be is now quite unnecessary, since no one would want to move quickly to such high levels of taxation. Figure 17.1 warns us that sudden, big, unexpected gasoline price increases can single-handedly cause negative growth in GDP. Phasing higher gasoline taxes in steadily over time is not just a ploy to make big changes more politically palatable. If a large increase is phased in gradually but announced initially, it can achieve the same effect as a once-and-for-all large increase without macroeconomic disruption or massive income redistribution.

Consider an emissions-based gasoline tax increase each year for the next 10 years that averages a real 10 cents per gallon. This represents a slightly under 5% per annum real increase in gasoline prices over that period and would nearly double the real retail price of gasoline by the end of the 10 years. An early commitment to this path would induce people to begin immediately to plan their adjustments, and it would give people time to gradually phase in their adjustments. If the long-run price elasticity of demand for gasoline is one and if nothing else changed to affect our demand for gasoline, the near doubling of the real price of gasoline would eventually nearly halve our gasoline consumption.

BOX 17.1 The Macroeconomics of Gasoline Tax Increases
Periodically, there surfaces a study showing that a, say, 10-cent-a-gallon increase in the gasoline tax will reduce the national output (GNP or GDP) by $10 billion, increase unemployment by 80,000 people, and raise the Consumer Price Index (CPI) by 0.3%.[3] These figures are supposed to be shocking, but they shouldn't be.

In 1987, the average federal and state gasoline taxes were about 30 cents per gallon, and gasoline tax receipts about $30 billion. A tax increase of 10 cents a gallon ought to garner another $10 billion. If no other tax is cut, if the government just sits on the increased tax revenue, and if consumers make no adjustments to the change in relative prices, then GNP will indeed go down by $10 billion.

Divide the 1987 GNP, $4.5 trillion, by the 1987 employment level, 114 million, and get $40,000 per job. This suggests that a decline in GNP of $10 billion might be expected to reduce employment by 250,000 jobs—the forecast of increased unemployment in the first paragraph of this box is at first glance surprisingly low.[4]

Finally, in 1987, consumers spent about $100 billion on gasoline out of a total consumer expenditure of $2600 billion—that's 3.8%. If 3.8% of your expenditures go up 10% in price, if no other prices change, and if you do not change your expenditure pattern, then the average price you pay for all purchases goes up by 0.38%.[5]

But suppose the government starts to spend the new tax revenue or to cut other taxes. Now all these macroeconomic disasters begin to become undone. If the government spent the entire new tax revenue, or if it cut taxes elsewhere in the economy by that amount, then we should expect the GNP to go back up by the $10 billion and employment to go back up by the 80,000.[6] And the 0.3% CPI increase, even if it is not reversed, is less than a typical month's increase in the CPI over the past half-century—it will quickly become insignificant from a macroeconomic viewpoint.

Higher gasoline taxes will have significant microeconomic impacts—particularly on gasoline consumption and vehicle use. If introduced gradually, and offset by increased government spending or reduced taxes elsewhere in the economy, higher gas taxes need *not* have significant macroeconomic impact. Figure 17.1 shows the trends of real gasoline prices and GDP in the United States over the past third of a century. Even big, sudden, unexpected rises in the gas price caused only minor dips in real GDP—only in 1982 did GDP fall by more than 1%, and in that year the gas price had risen by nearly 1 dollar a gallon over the previous 3 years.

Halving our gasoline consumption would not mean halving our driving miles. Two powerful forces are operating to offset the increased price of gasoline. One, many people would gradually move to more fuel-efficient vehicles—look once more at Equation [2.3]—and this would reduce the cost of driving miles. Two, reduced driving would mean reduced congestion, raising the average speed and fuel efficiency of auto travel—Equation [2.3] again—and these would further reduce the cost of driving miles. While doubling the price of gasoline might mean halving our gasoline consumption, it would not mean halving our driving.

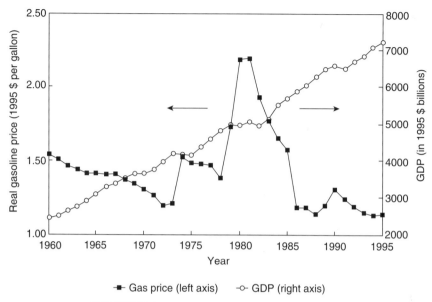

-■- Gas price (left axis)   -o- GDP (right axis)

FIGURE 17.1   Macroeconomic Impact of Gasoline Prices

How painful would this drastic reduction in our driving be? Raising the gaso-line tax by $1.00 per gallon—by the end of the 10-year path of 10-cent rises—means about $78 billion in foregone consumer surplus per year.[7] That is around $300 per person per year in the United States.

At first glance, $300 is a surprisingly low figure. But remember, people do not give up their most valued driving, but rather their *least* valued driving. No one will stop commuting, become unemployed, or starve to death. Most of the reduc-tion will show up as fewer shopping trips for odds and ends and as more carpools to soccer games or the bowling alley.

What is more, more than half of that $300 per person per year is a transfer, through the gasoline taxes, from ourselves to ourselves. That is, from ourselves as drivers to ourselves as citizens—we can use the additional gasoline tax revenue for new government spending that we desire or, more probably, for reductions in other taxes. Since gasoline taxes are regressive, any reductions in other taxes should be either reductions in regressive taxes or reductions that make the rest of the tax system more progressive. Politically, the imposition of higher gasoline taxation would probably not be feasible if the commitment to it were not accompanied by a commitment to simultaneously lower other taxes.

This leaves something like $130 per person per year in *real* deadweight loss—the WTP dollar measure of the loss of welfare because we would be foregoing many of our former driving pleasures. For this $130, we would be getting half as much automotive air pollution, half as much highway death, etc. Would you give

---

BOX 17.2 Are Potholes the Same as Gasoline Taxes?

Most states pay for highway work largely from gasoline tax revenues. So states with low gasoline taxes have low expenditures on road construction and maintenance. Michigan, for example, ranks 45th among the states in its gasoline tax rate and 45th in its road and bridge investment (Blumenstein, 1997).[8] One student asked me—not jokingly, I think—whether the resulting proliferation of potholes does not have exactly the same effect of discouraging driving as would higher gasoline taxes.

The answer is that potholes certainly do discourage driving, by decreasing the smoothness of driving and increasing the maintenance costs of cars. But potholes are *not* a cost-effective way of discouraging driving. How about heavy road congestion, long queues for drivers license applications, 10 MPH speed limits on Interstates, requiring cars to burn Chanel No. 5 as a fuel, or mandating that all cars drive at all times in reverse gear? All of these would also discourage driving, but they also would not be cost-effective. The gasoline tax is unique in that it discourages driving without wasting real resources. What the driver pays becomes the government's revenue. With all other policies to discourage driving, what the driver pays is a deadweight loss that represents no gain to anyone else.

---

up $130 per year to cut the number of highway deaths by nearly 20,000 per year? That's barely a half-penny per life—and one of those lives, as they say, may be your own. Even if the higher gasoline tax did no good for anything except highway deaths, it would save lives at a cost of less than $2 million per life. Given the widely accepted range for cost of expected lives saved as $1–5 million, this sounds like a good deal, especially when we remember that a large fraction of these lives are young lives.

Why stop at higher taxes for just gasoline? Many of the arguments in the preceding chapters are arguments for broader energy taxes, not just for gasoline taxes. All fossil fuel use increases our dependence on foreign oil sources, at the margin and through substitutions, and all fossil fuel use increases air pollution, both local and global, in varying degrees depending upon which type of fossil fuel is used and which pollution safeguards are applied. But gasoline taxes are special, and should be higher, because gasoline use also means highway construction, congestion, and calamity. There are, indeed, good arguments for energy taxes—BTU taxes or carbon taxes—but it remains true that gasoline generates greater external costs than other fossil fuels. Accordingly, gasoline taxes need to be higher than energy taxes in general.

Cars are costly. Cars kill. Isn't it time that we woke up to that fact? Like alcohol and smoking, when used in immoderate doses, driving imposes costs on drivers themselves. Worse, like secondhand smoke and alcoholic abuse of others, "secondhand" driving imposes high costs on the rest of society. There is nothing like taxation to bring drivers' own self-interest into line with social realities.

WHAT'S WRONG WITH GASOLINE TAXATION?

Why don't we leap at the opportunity to solve so many of our auto troubles by shifting a little from, say, income taxation or social security taxation to gasoline taxation? Many countries have, and many are continuing to do so. Great Britain, for example, has been increasing fuel prices by 5% per year in real terms and is committed to continue this rate of increase (*Economist,* 1996b). But in the United States, we traditionally scream at the thought of even a nickel increase in gasoline taxes. Why? Some reasons:

1. The gasoline tax is seen as "discriminatory" (AAA, undated). Noneconomists often fail to recognize that Pigovian taxes are a good way to diminish external costs. They see the excise tax on gasoline as a capricious tax, like that on long-distance telephone calls.

2. Additional gas taxation is suspected of being a devious and underhanded addition to total taxation. Tax cuts elsewhere either are not expected or are intentionally ignored. Americans have made it abundantly clear in recent years that we do not want higher overall taxation. New gasoline taxes must be accompanied by tax cuts elsewhere.

3. The gas tax is seen, correctly for the upper half of the income distribution, as regressive. If all other taxes were cut proportionately, the new gas taxes would most heavily burden the middle of the American income distribution. This means that the tax cuts elsewhere have to be chosen carefully to offset that increased regressivity.

4. It seems unfair that drivers in the large western states should "bear a disproportionate brunt of any increase" (AAA, undated). But Pigovian taxes are not supposed to be "fair," they are supposed to correct externalities. If drivers in western states generated twice as much negative externality as eastern drivers, then they should be taxed twice as much. But with more correct Pigovian gasoline taxation, the average resident of Wyoming would *not* "pay more than twice as much as a resident of the District of Columbia" (AAA, undated). Gasoline tax *rate* increases would be much higher in air-quality nonattainment areas, like the District of Columbia, than in attainment areas, like Wyoming.

5. Gasoline taxes are seen as too crude an instrument to get at the many varied aspects of auto externalities. They are. Even if the gasoline taxes were emissions-based, they do not in themselves address the problem of high-risk driving; they inadequately deter dangerous driving by the very young, the very old, the alcohol impaired, and the accelerator challenged; they do not correctly attack highway congestion; they do not directly touch parking and zoning and sprawl problems; and they do nothing about possible groundwater problems caused by *past* gasoline use. Higher gasoline taxes are a start on almost all the car problems, but the finish requires a number of other changes. That fact does not diminish the usefulness of higher gas taxes.

6. Higher gasoline taxes not only raise the price of car driving, but they also raise the cost of bus travel and truck transport. Some people worry about making poor people's bus travel more costly or making all of our trucked goods more expensive. They shouldn't worry. Buses and trucks cause external costs, just like cars—trucks, as we have seen, are in many ways worse than cars—and those external costs also need internalizing. Moreover, fuel costs are a small part of total bus or truck transport costs, and higher fuel taxes are unlikely to push these costs up much. If car drivers paid for their own externalities, bus systems would experience such demand growth that their fares might go down, not up.

In short, the arguments against higher gasoline taxes—if these taxes are carefully tailored, cautiously phased, and properly accompanied by tax cuts elsewhere—are not at all convincing. They are founded in ignorance, and that ignorance is encouraged by those who profit from heavy driving. But it will not be the first time that bad arguments have won a debate. So, we go on to one final chapter, where we assume that higher gasoline taxation is a political nonstarter, stop thinking about why we cannot do what we should do, and start asking what we *can* do.

ENDNOTES

[1] To balance fairness and equity, the government might want to subsidize retrofits, but it should not completely ignore them.

[2] This $0.27 per gallon is, of course, an average over the United States. Where the air is sufficiently clean, the correct tax is zero, and where it is very dirty, the correct tax is very high. In Southern California, for example, the correct air pollution tax has been estimated to be around $1 per gallon (Cameron, 1991 and 1994).

[3] These are the actual forecasts of one such study by Mark French (1987) of Wharton Econometric Forecasting Associates (the dollar figures are here left in that study's 1987 prices—putting them into 1995 dollars would raise each by about one-third). The report, incidentally, was prepared for, and financed by, the American Automobile Association (AAA).

[4] The explanation resides in the high capital-to-labor ratios in automaking and petroleum, which means high value added per worker in these industries.

[5] A 10-cent-per-gallon tax increase in 1987 would have meant about a 10% gasoline price increase.

[6] Indeed, we might expect employment to go up more than 80,000 since the government would presumably spend the money on less capital-intensive products than vehicles and petroleum.

[7] Work it out (look again at the gas tax calculations toward the end of Chapter 6 for the method) (Q17.1).

[8] Those of you who snickered (in Chapter 5) about foreign governments using stiff inspections in order to artificially obsolete older vehicles and boost sales of new ones should ask if it is entirely a coincidence that America's automobile capital has also become its pothole capital.

CHAPTER 18

Where Can We Go from Here?

*"The church is near
but the road is icy;
the bar is far away
but I will walk carefully."*

Russian Proverb

Assume new carbon taxation of any kind is out. What can we do? Remember the basic problem—too much gasoline consumed, too much pollution produced, too many people dead on highways, too much congestion. . . . There are lots of things that we might try. Let's explore some.

MORE OF THE SAME?

As more people drive more cars more miles, we could continue with more of the same policies as before. Higher fuel efficiency (CAFE) standards, tighter emission controls, more safety equipment, etc. All these things are currently at the forefront of auto policy. Most environmental groups are lobbying heavily for higher CAFE standards, especially for "light trucks." The EPA has already announced that it intends to strengthen its auto and truck emission standards because if they do not, "emissions increases due to increases in vehicle miles traveled will likely overtake emissions reduction" (EPA, 1998). Mandatory side and ceiling air bags are being discussed.

But more of the same is not just more of the same. Most current standards are, as we have seen again and again, not cost-effective, and the costs get ever higher per unit of whatever is achieved.

What more of the same would do is push up the prices of new cars even faster. This probably would slow the growth of American cars per capita, but it would do little to slow the growth of American miles per car. What stricter standards achieve per mile would be largely, or maybe even more than, offset by increased miles driven.

RELIANCE ON TECHNOLOGY

The latest Department of Energy Comprehensive National Energy Strategy states five major energy goals: (1) "improve the efficiency of the energy system"; (2) "ensure against energy interruptions"; (3) "promote energy production and use in ways that respect health and environmental values"; (4) "expand future energy choices"; and (5) "cooperate internationally on global issues" (DOE, 1998). The achievement of goals (1), (3), and (4)—the economic efficiency goals—is almost entirely entrusted to "continued progress in science and technology."[1] Not only is there not a word about reducing American demands for energy, there is even a belief that technology and science can "provide future generations with a robust portfolio of clean and reasonably priced energy sources" so that Americans can continue to expand their energy-intensive consumption.

One does not have to be too cynical to see the reason for this belief in technology—it makes near-term politically unpopular changes unnecessary—and government finds an eager partner in business, for belief in new technology also postpones the need for any immediate profit-lowering changes in the petroleum or automobile industries. Thus was formed the Partnership for a New Generation of Vehicles (PNGV), a 10-year partnership of the federal government and major automakers to develop the technology for a new generation of "attractive, affordable vehicles that can achieve three times the fuel efficiency of 1994 models while meeting all applicable safety and environmental standards" (DOE, 1998).

Can it work? It is working. Hardly an auto show goes by without some major American, Japanese, and European automakers unveiling yet another variant of an electric, hybrid, or fuel-cell vehicle. Some are even marketed to the public, either at a very high (cost-covering) price so consumers don't want to buy many or at a very low price (subsidized by the producers themselves) so producers don't want to sell many.

If consumers don't want them because gasoline is cheap and producers don't want to make them because consumers don't want them, it is not surprising that the Partnership for a New Generation of Vehicles has become largely a public-relations campaign, accompanied of course by the industry's loud pledges of a "good faith effort" and reassurances that "we're deadly serious about it" (Johnston, 1997; Blumenstein, 1998). Meanwhile, *Automotive News*, the industry's inside information on what is going on in Detroit, reports that

> much progress is being made in automotive technology, but most advances are being adapted to increase acceleration and performance. . . , not to boost efficiency or lighten vehicles. (Stoffer, 1997)

There is one additional problem with the technology route. Usually, technical change is induced—as the price of something goes up, firms are induced to undertake research to find ways to economize on its use. Most of our history can be encapsulated as an upward ratcheting of rising real wage rates, the discovery of productive labor-saving inventions, further rises in real wage rates, etc. Research without rising energy prices lacks market guidance. For example, we really don't know if electric car battery research should be emphasized or if fuel-cell cars will obsolete electric cars before battery prices become competitive. Automakers have little interest in guessing since they have no immediate intention of trying to sell either. Market-stimulated research keeps producers' eyes on the bottom line; public-relations or government-subsidized research wanders and wastes. Producing the best and cheapest non-internal-combustion-engine car will only become a goal when gasoline prices rise enough to make consumers demand it.

IF NOT TAXES, HOW ABOUT SUBSIDIES?

New subsidies are much more acceptable than new taxes. Is there some way for the government to subsidize cars and drivers so as to reduce the external costs they generate? There are many, one of which is already being undertaken—federal subsidy of research under the Partnership for a New Generation of Vehicles. Moreover, President Clinton is currently proposing a system of subsidies to encourage the purchase of radically more fuel-efficient vehicles. Although the proposal is not yet precise, it essentially sets a base fuel efficiency (MPG) and then offers a tax credit of $3000 to consumers who purchase vehicles with twice that base MPG, and a tax credit of $4000 for three times the base MPG (Stoffer, 1998a).[2] Since, presumably, nobody would be buying such cars whose income tax bill was less than $4000, this tax credit is essentially a cash subsidy.[3]

This subsidy, as we have often seen, does nothing to discourage driving—indeed, by itself, it may encourage the ownership of more cars and the driving of more miles. Could subsidies be used to directly attack the auto-commuting problem? Sure—we do it already by subsidizing alternative commuter systems, namely intracity buses.

There has been little discussion of buses and bus subsidies in this book, as you have probably noticed. When one discovers that some activity produces external costs, the first-best response is to tax that activity. Ideally, driving should be taxed and busing should also be taxed, albeit at a lesser rate (per passenger), because both generate pollution, congestion, carnage, etc. Subsidizing a substitute activity is a second-best response. But we are talking second-best responses in this chapter. So let's talk bus subsidies—and building HOV and HOT lanes, building bicycle paths, requiring cash-back of employer-provided parking, etc. As second-best policies, all of these, and more, make sense in theory. But in reality, none are able to significantly dent the car-commuting problem. Someone once estimated (perhaps seriously) that you could double the commuters from New Jersey to Manhattan who rode buses only if you cut the bus fare to *minus* $10—nothing is too much!

Perhaps the only subsidy that could really dent the American overdriving problem is a direct subsidy to *not* driving. How could this be done? By, for example, a tax credit of (say) 5 cents for each mile under (say) 8000 miles a car was driven each year. But recall that the symmetry of tax and subsidy ends when entry and exit are considered. A mileage or gasoline tax discourages car driving *and* car ownership. This subsidy discourages miles per car but actually encourages car ownership. Some people would buy cars, presumably old "zombie" cars, in order to *not* drive them. Maybe there is a combination of taxing car ownership and subsidizing not driving that would work, but it is getting complicated and would invite unforeseeable circumventions.

HOW ABOUT RATIONING GASOLINE?

Rationing miles or gallons will certainly reduce driving, provided only that the ration limit on driving is not so generous as to exceed the amount people want to drive. But what kind of rationing? Consider these three methods of rationing gasoline:

1. The government freezes the number of gasoline refineries and sets and gradually reduces the amount of gasoline each can produce. Price controls on gasoline are also needed since excess demand is quickly going to appear. Gas stations are essentially allocating on a "first come, first serve" basis (although favoritism for "good old customers" may also play a role). Gas stations will regularly run out of gasoline and get no more until the time arrives for their next allotment. Queues will arise, probably black markets, and perhaps even tanker-truck hijackings.[4]

2. Many of these problems can be overcome by passing out nontransferable ration coupons for gasoline. Each car owner gets coupons for so many gallons per week and must pay cash *and* coupon for each gallon he or she buys. The queuing problem is gone since the number of coupons issued would equal the amount of gasoline produced.[5] This is essentially the system the United States used during World War II, and it basically worked. But things were a little different then than now. The United States was committed to a major war on two distant and wide

---

BOX 18.1 Subsidizing Bicycles

The two major disadvantages of buses—fixed routes and fixed times—are both overcome by bicycles. There are (a few) people who think the bike, not the bus, is the intracity vehicle of the future. The principle advantages of the bike are its cheapness and its ease of parking. But these advantages do not sparkle as long as we keep gasoline so cheap and provide so much cheap parking for cars.

Efforts to encourage people to switch from automobiles to bicycles have almost all failed. For example, consider the Aarhus (Denmark) bicycle-and-bus promotion effort. In return for a resident's promise to use bike and bus "as much as possible," the City offered $2000 per year worth of free new bicycles, bus tickets, rain gear, child seats, bike repair service, etc. Only 200 of the city's 275,000 residents took up the offer (Bunde, 1997).

---

fronts, and its citizens were nearly unanimously committed to that war effort. Patriotism greatly smoothes the rationing route. Furthermore, suburbia was in its infancy and per capita car ownership was barely one-fourth of what it is today, so that relatively few people relied on extensive driving for their livelihoods.

3. The ration coupons of World War II were non-transferable on the grounds that each car's allocation was just sufficient for "necessary" driving. If coupon sales were allowed, it would be admitting that some people needed less driving than the coupons allowed and that others were doing more driving than they needed to. Since none of this belief is relevant today, there is no reason why ration coupons should not be marketable, especially if they were issued to each U.S. legal resident, whether or not they drove or owned a car.[6] Those who could economize on their gasoline use could sell their extra coupons—in effect getting a subsidy for not driving. Those who wanted more gasoline than their coupon allocation allowed could buy extra coupons—in effect paying a tax on their excess driving (very Pigovian).[7] And very sneaky—just like a tax in its results but without using the "T" word. Maybe this is what President Clinton had in mind when he said he is thinking of "a far-reaching proposal that provides flexible market-based and cost-effective ways to achieve meaningful reductions" (Clinton, 1997).[8]

"EDUCATING" CHANGE

That people can be "educated" to change their tastes is attested to by the dramatic change in American smoking habits in the last half-century. Over this period, many people became educated, or persuaded, to give up, or not start, smoking. Maybe the same could be done with driving—making people realize that each mile of driving, like each puff on a cigarette, endangers one's own as well as others' health and welfare. But smoking primarily endangers one's own health; driving reduces the health and well-being of others, and does so in many diverse and not easily observed ways. It is unfortunate that we cannot just show that driving causes cancer in laboratory animals. Then education would be easier.

Economists are uncomfortable talking about changing tastes. Recall why. The basic economic model of consumer behavior assumes that consumers know what they want, know what products are out there to buy, know how each of those products affects their own well-being, and rationally go about maximizing their welfare. We know these assumptions are extreme, and never more than partly accurate, but we believe this model is the best tractable way of making predictions about consumer behavior and assessing the impact of policy changes on consumer welfare. So we are uncomfortable when people start talking about changing consumers' wants through "education."

But it is more than this. Economic theory takes as the objective of the entire economic system the maximizing of the welfare of consumers. Remember "consumer sovereignty." A well-working market system is supposed to adapt to produce what consumers want. If what consumers want can be manipulated easily, then maximizing consumer welfare means shooting at a possibly shifting and shiftable target.

A final caution about "education." There may be a small difference between educating consumers to want to drive less and declaring consumers to be reeducated and forcibly restricting their driving. There is an old story about a radical orator promising an audience of poor people that "comes the revolution, everyone will have strawberries and cream." One of the listeners complains, "But I don't like strawberries and cream." And the speaker responds, "Comes the revolution, everybody will have strawberries and cream, *and like it*." I want people to drive less, but I do not want to make them drive less, I want to make them *want* to drive less.

FINAL FINAL THOUGHTS

We have come to the end of a long road together. We have seen the many ways that cars and drivers impose external costs and collect subsidies, and we have seen that our federal and state governments have recognized and attempted to ameliorate many of these auto problems. The problem is that the resulting policies selected have been largely ineffective and at a high cost. Now, with the Kyoto agreements and the continued failure of many cities to attain acceptable air quality, it looks as if these same governments intend to intensify their previously failed efforts to control the automobile. Am I too cynical when I am reminded of Arthur Kasspe's assertion, "If you think the problem is bad now, just wait until we've solved it."

BOX 18.2 Ending on an Up Note

"Next, Maybe GM Will Hand Out a Bicycle to Each of Its Employees." That is the headline of a recent *Wall Street Journal* article (Christian, 1997). They are joking, of course, but it is true that General Motors does provide bus shuttles from distant suburbs to its downtown Detroit headquarters. This from the company that regularly bought up intracity rail lines in the 1920s and 1930s in order to shut them down, thereby making the world safe for car commuting.

Is GM embarrassed about undermining car commuting? Apparently not. Peter Rowe, GM executive, says, "the whole purpose of bringing people downtown is to make their work as fun and as stress-free as possible. We think mass transit is a good way to accomplish that" (*ibid.*). Of course, it does not hurt that GM saves $200 per month in parking costs on each employee who opts for the bus. So far, more than one-third have.

What does GM plan to do with the parking lot next to its headquarters? From Rowe again: "We think a park will look a lot more attractive" (*ibid.*).

ENDNOTES

[1]Notice that officialdom still worries that OPEC (or others?) may cut us off from oil, goal (2).

[2]This tax credit is a reduction in the federal income tax owed, not a deduction from the income on which tax is paid. Notice the difference. With an income of $40,000 and a tax rate of 25%, a credit of $4000 reduces tax paid from $10,000 to $6000, while a deduction of $4000 reduces tax paid only from $10,000 to $9000 (i.e., from 25% of $40,000 to 25% of $36,000).

[3]Along with the "gas guzzler" tax (discussed briefly in Chapter 4), this is very close to the "feebate" system (also discussed briefly in Chapter 4), whereby low-MPG cars are taxed and high-MPG cars subsidized, with the exact tax and subsidy rates being selected so that the system generates no net revenue gain or loss for the government.

[4]The gasoline shortages and gas station queues of the 1970s were of this nature (look back at Box 3.3). OPEC reduced our oil supplies, but the U.S. government imposed price controls on U.S. refineries and service stations.

[5]Actually, the government can count on some of the coupons going unused and so can issue somewhat more coupons than there is production.

[6]Think about the three possible allocations: so many gallons per week (1) to each car, (2) to each licensed driver, or (3) to each legal resident. I like the third allocation, and not just on fairness grounds; do you (Q18.1)?

[7]Indeed, a smoothly working ration coupon market would end up being *exactly* like a Pigovian tax (which reduced gasoline consumption by exactly as much as the ration system) with the tax revenues distributed equally to all U.S. legal residents—exactly the same for every single legal resident, whether he or she consumes a lot of gas or very little gas. Make sure you see this equivalence (Q18.2).

[8]Or maybe Doug Adams was right when he said, "Anyone who is capable of getting themselves made President should on no account be allowed to do the job" (Adams, 1980).

Answers to Text Questions

"There is always a well-known solution
to every . . . problem—
neat, plausible, and wrong."

H. L. Mencken

CHAPTER 1 APPENDIX

Q1A.1 If the takeoff or landing required the same amount of traffic control effort regardless of the size of the plane, then the tax should be per plane, not per passenger. A tax per passenger that generated the same total revenue would, in effect, be too high a tax on big commercial planes and too low a tax on small private planes.

Q1A.2 Victims of highway accidents *are* already being taxed, not in money but in loss of life, limbs, and health. This probability that victims will be killed is enough to get them to take enough care to avoid being hit. The Pigovian tax is only needed on the hitter, who might otherwise not take enough care to avoid the externality. (More on this in Chapter 10.)

Q1A.3 Subsidizing nonkilling drivers by so much per mile is not a good idea. It might induce drivers to be more careful, but it would also induce drivers to drive more and nondrivers to become drivers. It could conceivably even increase highway deaths, if the greater mileage more than offset the fewer deaths per mile.

Q1A.4 The deposit paid when a car is bought is essentially a prepaid tax on auto litter—littering is the negative externality, because other people have to endure its unsightliness and the state has to hire people to tow it away. The return of the deposit at the end of the car's life is essentially a subsidy for picking up auto litter and disposing of it properly—a positive externality since it removes a negative externality.

CHAPTER 2

Q2.1 To save $200 by driving, you have to "spend" 10 extra hours. That is an implicit wage of $20 per hour.

Q2.2 What matters here is the average fixed cost. It consists chiefly of the average depreciation cost per mile over the entire time you plan to keep your new car. If you plan to keep your new $20,000 car for 5 years, the average depreciation cost will be about $2700 per year; but if you plan to keep it for 10 years, the average depreciation cost will be only about $1800 per year. The formulas are

$$\text{Depreciation per year} = (1 - 0.8^N)(20{,}000)/N \qquad [\text{Q2.2}-1]$$

$$\text{Depreciation per mile} = (\text{Depreciation per year})/VMT \qquad [\text{Q2.2}-2]$$

where VMT is your vehicle-miles traveled per year and N is the number of years you plan to keep the car (and it is assumed to depreciate in value by 20% per year). So, the more miles you drive per year (VMT) and the longer you keep the car (N), the lower the average depreciation cost per mile.

Q2.3 Higher-income people prefer to drive newer cars—the demand for car quality is income-elastic. So, when rich people buy new cars, they typically plan to replace them in a few years. But they will then run into the "lemons" problem: even if the car is a peach, potential used-car buyers will assume it to be a lemon, and the resale price will accordingly suffer (see Box 2.2). Leasing solves this problem. This may also help to explain why the implicit buy-back price of leased cars is above the Blue Book values on equivalent used-car sales—if all leased cars are returned after their initial lease period, then there is no adverse selection problem, so the average returned lease car *is* worth more than the average (i.e., lemony) car of the same age, model, and mileage being sold on the used-car market. Notice that once lessees are given the opportunity to buy the car after the lease period expires, the lemons problem creeps back in.

Q2.4 This is a problem of moral hazard. Recall that "moral hazard" means that a person can successfully avoid some of the consequences of some activity and therefore undertakes too much of that activity from a social viewpoint. It is difficult for the lessor to know whether a car has been well maintained during the lease period, and so maintenance that is not imminently necessary may be neglected on leased cars. The detailed and careful maintenance requirements in lease contracts are an attempt to overcome this temptation for the lessee to be negligent in maintenance. (We shall return to moral hazard when we think about insurance, legal liability, and "taking care" in Chapter 10.)

Q2.5 Such people are willing to trade life expectancy for dollars. This does not mean they are suicidally inclined, simply that they act as if they put finite value on their lives. If they valued their lives "infinitely," then no finite money payment would induce them to take additional life-threatening risk. Since almost everyone does trade off risk for money, this means we all place finite value on our lives.

CHAPTER 3

Q3.1 No math needed, just common sense. If the gasoline price went up by 10%, the marginal private cost of driving would go up by less than 5% since the time and risk part of the driving costs have not changed. So a price elasticity of one with respect to the marginal private cost of driving would become an elasticity of less than one-half with respect to the gasoline price.

Q3.2 It is always tempting for a government to keep things cheap and plentiful at home, and the temptation is greater if the product is an export since it is foreigners who seem to be deprived by the policy. But when oil prices are kept low, it means that a lot of gasoline is burned up on frivolous low-valued auto, bus, and truck trips. Each gallon so frittered has an opportunity cost—the dollars worth of imports that the export would have paid for. When exports are reduced, imports will be reduced too, since they have to be paid for, and imports will become more expensive in the local currency. Rich car owners and poor bus travelers gain, but everyone who consumes imported goods will end up consuming fewer of them and paying more for them.

Q3.3 Basically, the *economic* difference between gasoline and automobiles is that gasoline is a flow variable and automobiles a stock variable. We use up gasoline; we invest in automobiles. When the price of gasoline goes up, we buy less, but not much less because our driving habits change slowly. If the price stays up, however, we will increasingly find ways to further cut our gasoline consumption—by shopping less often, buying more fuel-efficient cars, moving closer to our workplace, etc. The opposite holds for cars. When price rises, we initially buy fewer, hoping the price will come back down or simply postponing the inevitable replacement of our current car(s). As time passes, however, cars wear out and must be replaced. Demand for automobiles is less price-elastic in the long run than the short run. When income changes, slowly changing habits mean that gasoline consumption is more responsive in the long run than the short run. But with automobiles, the reverse is true. Suppose your income rises 10%, and as a result you want to own an automobile stock that is 10% larger (in quantity or quality). To adjust to your new desired stock, you will buy a lot of car in the short run—a very high income elasticity—though you will eventually settle down to just periodically replacing your new larger stock of cars.

Q3.4 Except for a small interest cost, whatever I pay in gas taxes I get back, penny for penny. A refunded tax is no tax, and it will have no effect on consumption (except for a very, very small income effect because of the interest cost). "Refunding" the gasoline taxes to the poor can be achieved by cutting the income tax rates for the lowest income-tax brackets. On *average*, the poor will then get the taxes back, but on the *margin*, the price of gasoline is up by the amount of the new tax.

Q3.5 All of these gimmicks are replacing higher money costs with higher time costs. Both money and time are costs to individuals, and an increase in either will reduce consumption. But there is a difference. When you pay with an hour, you lose that hour and no one else gains; but when you pay with a dollar, your loss is someone else's gain. When we ration by time rather than by tax, the poor gain, the rich lose, *and* the government (that is all of us, collectively) loses the tax revenue we would have collected. On net, we are worse off because of the squandered time.

CHAPTER 4

Q4.1 This is not easy. If you use straight-line supply and demand functions and calculate arc elasticity, you will get an answer that is *approximately* two. To be accurate, you must use constant (at one-half) price elasticity of demand and supply curves. These can be written as

$$Q_D = aP^{-0.5} \qquad\qquad [Q4.1-1]$$

$$Q_S = bP^{+0.5}, \qquad\qquad [Q4.1-2]$$

where Q_D and Q_S are U. S. quantities demanded and supplied, P is U.S. price, and a and b are parameters of the functions. Initially, since half our oil is imported,

$$Q_D = 2Q_S. \qquad\qquad [Q4.1-3]$$

These three equations can be solved for the initial value of P, namely,

$$P = a/(2b). \qquad\qquad [Q4.1-4]$$

Once imports are cut off, you replace Equation [Q4.1−3] with $Q_D = Q_S$ and again solve the three equations for P, which is now

$$P = a/b. \qquad\qquad [Q4.1-5]$$

The import cutoff exactly doubles the price, from $a/(2b)$ to a/b.

Q4.2 Let us take a simple example (see Figure A). The demand curve for ocean shipping in the United States is a downward-sloped line. Assume all shipping is competitive. The average cost of operating U.S.-flag ships is P_{usa}, which is higher than the average cost of operating foreign-flag ships, P_{row} (where the subscript, row, stands for "rest of world"). If there are no government restrictions, Americans will choose foreign-flag ships at the lower price of P_{row}, and they will transport Q_{row} units of freight (where P_{row} meets the demand curve). But the U.S. government wants U.S.-flag ships, presumably for possible wartime use, to be able to ship Q_{usa} units of freight—with Q_{usa} at the intersection of P_{usa} and the demand curve. If the U.S. government now requires that American demanders use U.S. shipping, the volume of shipping will decline to Q_{usa} at a price of P_{usa}. In this simple example, all U.S. shipping is now done on U.S.-flag ships. The dead-weight loss of this policy, paid in higher prices for the goods shipped, is the loss of

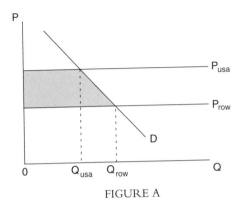

FIGURE A

consumer surplus, represented by the entire (shaded) area to the left of the demand curve between P_{row} and P_{usa}. Suppose, on the other hand, that the U.S.
government simply built enough ships to handle Q_{usa} units of freight, leased them
out to U.S. companies, and subsidized their losses. The losses would be ($P_{usa}-$
P_{row}) on each unit shipped, and Q_{usa} units would be shipped. The losses are represented by the rectangular area to the left of Q_{usa} between P_{row} and P_{usa}, a smaller
area than before.

Q4.3 The expected profit of A is

$$\text{Exp. Profit A} = 3ab + a(1-b) + 4(1-a)b + 2(1-a)(1-b), \quad [Q4.3-1]$$

which simplifies to

$$\text{Exp. Profit A} = 2 + 2b - a. \quad [Q4.3-2]$$

Player A's profit is lower if $a>0$, no matter what Player B does. So A should choose
$a=0$, that is, A should never cooperate. The game is symmetrical, so B should do
the same, that is, B should also never cooperate.

Q4.4 The problem with maintaining discipline in a cartel is that it always pays
to cheat, no matter what strategy others follow. But that assumes that others
choose their strategy independently of your strategy. Suppose you have learned
from playing the game over and over that your rival plays tit for tat with you. That
is, if you cheat, the rival cheats in the next period and continues to cheat every
period after that until you begin again to cooperate, at which point the rival re-
sumes cooperating. Look at the payoff matrix (repeated in the box on the next
page). Start at 3,3. You are Player A, and you consider cheating. If you do, you
will get a profit of 4 in the next period—an improvement over 3. But you know
that in the following period that your rival will also cheat and you will get only 2.
Over the two periods, you have totaled a profit of 6, no better than if you had
stayed at 3,3. Actually, you will do worse because now you have a tough choice to
make: either continue cheating and continue getting a profit of only 2, or go back

to cooperation, taking a further cut in profit to 1 on the way back to 3,3 (because you know from experience that B will resume cooperating in the period after you do). In short, if the game is going to continue for a long time and if you know your rival will play tit for tat, you find it in your best interest not to cheat.

	Strategies for B	
Strategies for A	Cooperate	Cheat
Cooperate	3,3	1,4
Cheat	4,1	2,2

Q4.5 The two cars will average only 24 MPG. Assume they each travel the same number of miles—as the government does assume in making CAFE calculations. Suppose they each go x miles. One car will use $x/20$ gallons of gasoline, and the other $x/30$ gallons. Between them, they will go $2x$ miles and use $(x/20 + x/30)$ gallons of gasoline. The average MPG is therefore

$$\frac{2x}{x/20 + x/30}, \qquad\qquad\qquad [Q4.5-1]$$

which is 24. Essentially, this is the same puzzle your high school math teacher probably gave you: if a hiker goes up the mountain at 2 MPH and back down at 6 MPH, what is the average speed of the whole hike? It is 3, not 4, MPH.

Q4.6 No. Once they own their luxury or gas-guzzling cars, the price of driving is the same as if the cars were not taxed, so there is no reason to think the amount of driving will be affected by the taxes. Well, maybe driving will be cut by a small amount. The taxes take some income away and, being slightly poorer, the drivers will have to cut back a little on all their purchases, including gasoline. But that would be true if we taxed small, cheap or fuel-efficient cars—or indeed, anything.

Q4.7 Why not cut back the quantity of gasoline and let price do the rationing? Cutting back the volume of civilian gasoline by one-third would probably have meant a near doubling of the price in the short run. Policymakers felt that this would have been too harsh to the poor, the elderly, and the handicapped, and too generous to the oil well owners and gasoline refiners. Why not simply set a price ceiling and let queuing determine the allocation of the limited supplies? Because this would have meant huge amounts of time wasted in queues, time that policymakers wanted people to spend working in labor-short war-goods factories. Why not allocate ration coupons per *person* (rather than per car)? Because people who did not drive or did not own cars had no use for the nonmarketable coupons. Why were the coupons nonmarketable? Because it was wartime, the idea was that no unnecessary driving would be done, and marketable coupons would have permitted people to buy gasoline for frivolity. If ration coupons were marketable, then they probably should be distributed per person, and nondrivers could sell their coupons as a reward for finding less gasoline-intensive means of transport.

Why not try gasoline rationing again? With marketable coupons, rationing would end up just like a tax, with the price of the coupons being the tax, but with a big difference—the "tax" revenues are distributed back as subsidies to those who use less gasoline than the ration allocation. For more on all this, wait for Chapter 18.

Q4.8 To see this quickly, assume there are only two barrels of oil left, one that will cost $10 to extract and a second that will cost $25, and one barrel is to be extracted now, with the other extracted next year. The present value of the cost of extracting the cheaper barrel first (PV_1) is

$$PV_1 = 10 + 25/(1+i), \qquad [Q4.8-1]$$

where i is the relevant interest rate. The present value of the cost of extracting the costlier barrel first (PV_2) is

$$PV_2 = 25 + 10/(1+i). \qquad [Q4.8-2]$$

PV_1 is less than PV_2.

Q4.9 Consider, for simplicity, a world of just two countries, each initially in oil equilibrium at a single world price. Suddenly world supply decreases and world price rises. The price elasticities of demand for oil are probably not the same in the two countries, and so the percentage decline in oil consumption would probably not be the same in each. If the governments tried to equate the percentage decline in consumption, price differentials would emerge between the countries, providing a field day for petroleum traders and speculators.

CHAPTER 5

Q5.1 It depends on how fast the relative stock of vehicles moves to the less strictly regulated light trucks. Assume all vehicles are driven the same number of miles. Let the current annual new-car pollution rate be k; with the new regulation, the rate will be $k/2$ (i.e., going from 98% emissions-free to 99% means halving the current rate of emissions). Light trucks will be permitted to continue to emit at a rate of $3k$. Since cars now make up 60% of the vehicle fleet, the overall average annual rate of emissions (call it P_0) is now

$$P_0 = 0.60k + 0.40(3k) = 1.80k. \qquad [Q5.1-1]$$

With the new regulations, and light truck sales being a fraction, x, of all family vehicles, the pollution rate will become P_1, where

$$P_1 = (1-x)(k/2) + x(3k) = 0.50k + 2.50kx. \qquad [Q5.1-2]$$

P_1 will be at least as big as P_0 if x rises from 0.40 to above 0.52. This is not at all unlikely. Sales of new light trucks have already passed sales of new cars, and this relative price change should accelerate the trend.

Q5.2 Such a registration tax is a tax on car ownership. The registration tax is the same regardless of how many miles the car is driven. It is, however, not the ownership of an old polluting car that causes external damages, but the operation of an old polluting car.

Q5.3 Remember, the money the government pays out is just a transfer from the government to the clunker owner. There is no *real* cost involved there. The real cost of the program is that new cars must be produced now rather than, say, 5 years from now (when the old cars would have been scrapped if there had been no program). Suppose these new cars cost $20,000 today. The present value of that $20,000 cost 5 years from now is $15,671 (at a 5% discount rate). The difference, $20,000-$15,671, is the cost of the program. Of course, the former clunker owners are driving a nicer car, and we should also count that as a benefit of the program. Don't feel bad if you missed Q5.3; you are in good company—the Office of Technology Assessment's benefit–cost study also missed it (OTA, 1992). Indeed, the OTA study counted the new-car sales as a benefit because "jobs were created." You should by now realize that the jobs argument is pernicious. Almost anything "creates" jobs—going to war requires increased armies and war-material production, serial killers force the hiring of additional police, etc. And anything that creates jobs in one place probably requires an increased budget there and hence less spending and fewer jobs somewhere else. Correctly, increased jobs are a cost—a new job in one place involves an opportunity cost, namely, the foregone output that the person would have produced elsewhere. Only if you are sure that the new jobs will just reduce unemployment is there no opportunity cost.

Q5.4 Agricultural products are heavily produced in a few states, so policies to benefit them have a bloc of very interested legislators supporting them. Ethanol subsidies raise the prices of all three: the price of corn, because it increases the demand for corn (to be used in ethanol); the price of production substitutes for corn, because the higher price of corn induces farmers to switch to corn from these production substitutes; and the price of consumption substitutes for corn, because the higher price of corn induces consumers to switch from corn to these consumption substitutes.

Q5.5 Since the older cars could use either fuel, their owners would always choose the cheaper. So leaded fuel could not be more expensive than unleaded fuel, or none at all would be demanded. In fact in the 1980s, unleaded fuel was generally priced several cents higher per gallon, though not due to cost considerations. Apparently, local gas stations sensed that new-car owners, with their higher incomes, would value their time more highly and would therefore search less for cheaper stations. The gas stations took advantage of this location-monopoly power by price discriminating.

Q5.6 In a tradable permit system, the *net* amount of money the firms turn over to the government is zero—permits and money are shuffled between the firms themselves. But with taxes, the government collects for every unit of un-abated pollution. All firms lose.

CHAPTER 6

Q6.1 Just because Activity X is the biggest source of some pollution, it does not follow that Activity X should be the first to be reduced. For cost effective-ness, we want to start by reducing the polluting activity that has the lowest mar-ginal abatement cost. That might be some other, smaller Activity Y. If, however, we want *big* reductions in the pollution, we will soon exhaust opportunities to reduce these smaller activities (like Y), and we will "probably" have to reduce Activity X as well.

Q6.2 Suppose there are two farmers. The profit from grazing sheep on the commons is 6 if only one farmer does it, but the total profit is only 4 (i.e., 2 apiece) if they both do it. Each considers two strategies: (1) graze sheep every other year, leaving the commons for the other farmer in alternate years; and (2) graze sheep every year regardless of what the other farmer does. The payoff ma-trix is shown in the box below; the two farmers are called A and B, with A's an-nual average profit given first and B's second. If they both alternate years, then each gets a profit of 6 half the time, for an annual average of 3. If they both graze always, they split a profit of 4 each year, for an annual average of 2. If A alternates and B grazes always, then A gets 2 every other year, for an annual average of 1, and B gets 6 half the time and 2 half the time for an annual average of 4.

	Strategies for B	
Strategies for A	Alternate	Always
Alternate	3,3	1,4
Always	4,1	2,2

Notice that this is the same payoff matrix as in Box 4.2. This is the "Prisoner's Dilemma" game. "Always" graze is the dominant strategy for each farmer.

Q6.3 As of 1997, greenhouse gas emissions were growing at 1.3% per annum. So

$$X_{2012} = (1.013)^{22}X_{1990},$$

where X_t indicates the quantity of emissions in year t (and the 22 is 2012 − 1990). The Kyoto target for emissions is

$$X^\star_{2012} = (0.93)X_{1990},$$

where $X^\star$ indicates the treaty target. Use these two equations to eliminate X_{1990} and find that the target $X^\star_{2012}$ is 30% less than the forecast X_{2012}.

Q6.4 This is a tricky question, and your answer depends upon how much economics you have already taken. First, think of a one-period vertical supply curve model and ask what an excise tax does to the price consumers pay. When the supply curve is vertical, it is effectively unchanged by being moved up by the amount of the tax. The suppliers have so much stuff and have nothing better to do than sell it (provided the tax is not so big that it makes them want to throw it away instead). So they sell the same amount whether it is taxed or not. As a result, the price consumers pay is not affected by the tax. The supplier pays the tax and keeps whatever is left over. If that was easy to do, now think of a two-period model, where the total supply to be sold over two periods is partly sold in the first period and partly in the second, and ask whether the excise tax increases or decreases the amount sold in the first period. For the sellers to be happy selling in each period, the after-tax price in the second period must be equal to $(1+i)$ times the after-tax price in the first period (where i is the relevant interest rate). If P_2 were smaller than $(1+i)P_1$, owners would sell it all in the first period and simply bank what they needed for the second-period consumption, earning interest rate i on their deposits. Symmetrically, if P_2 were greater than $(1+i)P_1$, they would borrow for their first-period consumption, sell it all in the second period, pay back the loan, and come out ahead. So, for sales to occur in both periods, when there is no tax, it must be that

$$P_2 = (1+i)P_1. \qquad [Q6.3-1]$$

If there is a tax of t per unit sold in each period, then Equation [6.3-1] becomes

$$P_2 - t = (1+i)(P_1 - t), \qquad [Q6.3-2]$$

or, rearranging terms,

$$P_2 = (1+i)P_1 - ti. \qquad [Q6.3-3]$$

If P_1 were lower with the tax, then P_2 would be lower too, and with prices lower in both periods than in the no-tax case, more would be demanded than exists. So P_1 must rise and P_2 must fall as a result of the tax. Less is sold in the first period and more sold in the second period than in the no-tax case. The total amount sold is still the same. The only good reason for the tax is to mop up the windfall gains of holders of Freon stockpiles.

Q6.5 First, replace the price elasticity of 0.5 with 1.0 in the arc price elasticity Equation [6.1]:

$$1.0 = \frac{(100 - Q)}{(100+Q)/2} \left| \frac{t}{(2.40+t)/2} \right. , \qquad [Q6.4-1]$$

Now proceed exactly as in the text, calculating the net social cost (i.e., lost consumer surplus minus gained tax revenue) and the CO_2 reduction, and you will again find a total social cost of $(50t + 25)$ dollars per ton of CO_2 removed. Notice that this is exactly the same cost per ton as we got in the text, with a price elasticity of 0.5. The higher price elasticity raises the total social cost and the CO_2 reduction by the same percentage.

CHAPTER 7

Q7.1 The calculation is as follows. The probability of dying on the highway this year is about 0.00015 (i.e., 40,000 deaths divided by 260 million people). The probability of not so dying is therefore 0.99985. Over an 80-year expected lifetime, the probability of not so dying is $(0.99985)^{80}$, or 0.98807. The probability of dying is 1 minus the probability of not dying, or 0.01193—slightly above 1 chance in 100.

CHAPTER 7 APPENDIX

Q7A.1 In a survey of over 1000 people, approximately half chose Town B and half Town C, so whatever you chose, you have a lot of company (Jones-Lee *et al.*, 1985). Nevertheless, half of those people chose badly. The move to Town B reduces your risk of death by 5 in 100,000, while the move to Town C reduces it by only 1 in 100,000. You should prefer to move to Town B. Congratulate yourself (and me) if you saw this more clearly the second time.

Q7A.2 Let your answer to the *i*th question be A_i; then your implicit value of life is V_i. The relevant equations equate the increase (or decrease) in the expected value of your life and the money you will pay (or must receive) to achieve (or accept) that change. The equations are

1. $(0.000010-0.000001)V_1=A_1/2$ (divided by 2 because two flights are involved, one going and one coming)
2. $0.001V_2=A_2$
3. $(\frac{1}{2})(7,000/280,000,000)V_3=A_3/5$ (with 280 million being roughly the total U.S. population, and A_3 is divided by 5 to roughly annualize the cost)

When I offer these choices to students, V_3 is almost always far and away the lowest of the three valuations. Why? Because they already know that smoke detectors are dirt cheap, and they tend to answer the actual price of smoke detectors rather than the maximum they would pay for one. Another way of putting this is that smoke detectors are a *very* low-cost way to save lives.

CHAPTER 8

Q8.1 Declaration as a "black spot" occurs when a road has an unusually bad accident year. On average, it will return to an average death toll the following year. We cannot easily tell whether the reduction was due to the special repairs or simply to the fact that an extreme outcome is usually followed by a less-extreme outcome. Say we rolled a die and whenever a 6 appeared, we declared it to be a jinxed die. If we then said some magic words, rolled it again, got a 4, and declared that the magic words had reduced the number by 2 (from 6 to 4), it would be similar to a claim that the repairs had improved the "black spot."

Q8.2 Once production of single-engine planes ceased in the early 1980s, the prices of the dwindling supply of 1970s aircraft rose steadily. The prices got so high that potential buyers began turning to "kit" planes, which were cheaper but required assembly by the buyer. Are they safe? They may not be legally operated over densely populated areas—does that answer the question?

Q8.3 Consider a two-vehicle crash, with one vehicle coming from the left and the other from the right, with f being the fraction of vehicles that are light trucks. The probability that the left vehicle was a light truck and the right a car is f times $(1-f)$; the probability that the right vehicle was a light truck and the left a car is also f times $(1-f)$; and the probability of one or the other case is therefore 2 times f times $(1-f)$. Now for something a little harder—a challenge for those with basic calculus in their tool kits. The death rate in two-truck crashes is some number, call it k; the death rate in two-car crashes is $2k$, twice as high; and the death rate in car-truck crashes is $4k$, four times as high (NRC, 1992). The expected number of deaths per two-vehicle collision is therefore equal to

$$kf^2 + 2k(1-f)^2 + 8kf(1-f)$$

since a fraction, f^2, of the accidents involve two trucks and cause, on average, k deaths; a fraction, $(1-f)^2$, of the accidents involve two cars and cause, on average, $2k$ deaths; and a fraction, $2f(1-f)$, of the accidents involve a car and a truck and cause, on average, $4k$ deaths. Now, take the derivative of the preceding expression with respect to f and find that the expected number of deaths is maximized at $f = 0.40$—coincidentally, and tragically, almost exactly the actual fraction of the U.S. vehicle fleet that is currently made up of light trucks.

CHAPTER 9

Q9.1 First, let us calculate the net benefit (i.e., benefit minus cost) of each of the three options, compared to doing nothing:

1. The net benefit of the seat belt only, from Equation [9.2], is

$$(B-C)_{belt} = 0.000045 V_L - 3 - 5.07P_t$$

2. The net benefit of an air bag only, from Equation [9.3], is

$$(B-C)_{abag} = 0.000015 V_L - 15$$

3. The net benefit of seat belt and air bag together, from Table 9.1 and the costs in the two previous equations, is

$$(B-C)_{both} = 0.000050 V_L - 3 - 5.07P_t - 15$$

Set each of these $(B-C)$ equations equal to zero, plot those three lines, and you have separated the areas where each of these choices is better than doing nothing. To separate the area where the seat belt is better than the air bag from the area where the air bag is better than the seat belt, set $(B-C)_{\text{belt}} = (B-C)_{\text{abag}}$ and plot that equation. Do the same for $(B-C)_{\text{belt}} = (B-C)_{\text{both}}$ and for $(B-C)_{\text{abag}} = (B-C)_{\text{both}}$. Now look at the six lines you have plotted, and you will see the area in which each of these options is superior to all the other options. These areas are shown in Figure 9.1.

Q9.2 The purchase of auto child-restraint seats is presumably income-elastic—one's own child's safety is certainly not an inferior good. So we should expect higher-income families to purchase more of them. But the use of the seats takes time, just like using adult seat belts, and higher-income families value their time more highly. Like use or nonuse of seat belts (in Figure 9.1), it is a matter of the relation between V_L (of the child by the parents of the child) and P_t (of the parents). Moreover, the poor drive older, less-safe cars, and risk compensation may induce their greater care in using child-restraint seats. All in all, it is plausible, though not certain, that the frequency of child-restraint use falls with higher income. A similar explanation may underlie, for example, facts like the following: bicycle ownership has doubled in Great Britain since 1975, but bicycling mileage per capita has halved (Lumsden, 1997).

Q9.3 In states without helmet laws, where fewer motorcyclists wear helmets, risk compensation suggests that they drive more carefully, so there would be fewer accidents per motorcycle. But when they do have an accident, they are more often without helmet, so the fatality rate per accident would be higher. The product of accidents/motorcycle and fatalities/accident equals fatalities/motorcycle. If fatalities/motorcycle are lower in states without helmet laws, it must mean that accidents/motorcycle come down by more than fatalities/accident go up.

CHAPTER 10

Q10.1 The first is adverse selection. The second is moral hazard (or what is sometimes called "induced demand"). The third goes by many names, but it is basically fraud.

Q10.2 Insurance companies base their premiums—the price they charge for the insurance—on *past* accident experience and their expenses depend on *current* accident experience. If accident rates go down steadily, they will steadily earn larger profit as they adjust their premiums downward, but always belatedly.

Q10.3 We cannot be sure from theory alone. Low-income drivers are better off if they did not drive at all before pay-at-the-pump coverage because the cost of insurance was so high; they are probably worse off if they drove before anyway, but without insurance. I add "probably" in the last sentence because pay-at-the-pump insurance lets previously uninsured motorists drive without fear of judicial punishment, and they presumably are better off on this score.

Q10.4 Again, we cannot be sure. They will tend to drive fewer miles because the price of gasoline is higher, and that will mean fewer accidents; but they may drive more miles or more recklessly because there is no longer a need to avoid notice by the law.

Q10.5 This is a good question. I do not have a clue why. There probably is not an *economic* answer to this one.

Q10.6 Certainly not as a Pigovian answer to externalities! The state fears that very high "high-risk pool" insurance rates will induce too many of these drivers to drive entirely without insurance.

CHAPTER 11

Q11.1 Recall what the externality is. Drunk drivers raise the probability that they will injure or kill someone else. The proper tax, therefore, depends on the social value we put on those endangered lives. The tax should be dollars per something, not time in jail per something. The fine should be a money fine. Once again, there is a clash between equity and efficiency.

Q11.2 Limiting the number of establishments that can serve alcohol has three important effects on lives. One, it gives the existing establishments protection from competition and hence lets them increase their prices, which reduces the amount of bar drinking. Two, in order to continue to enjoy this profit, they must avoid alcohol-related infractions that could lead to suspensions of their liquor licenses; they may, accordingly, be more concerned for the lives of their drinking or drunken customers—the same sort of incentive that "dramshop" laws provide, except that profit is a carrot and liability is a stick. And three, it means that potential customers must go further to get home after drinking, with the same effects discussed in the text concerning "dry" versus "wet" counties.

CHAPTER 12

Q12.1 It might be insurance company ignorance, but I never like to explain anything by assuming that businesses do *not* maximize profit. My guess is the following. In every state or county, there is a distribution of teenage driving "responsibility." The responsible drivers have fewer accidents, but it is hard for the insurance companies to know who they are. If responsible drivers tend to take drivers ed, the companies can use this as a signaling device for responsibility. This means that in areas where no drivers ed course is offered or all drivers are required to take it, a uniform insurance rate is set, but in areas where drivers ed is offered but is optional, the rate is lower for those with drivers ed and higher for those without. It is the same idea as employers or graduate schools favoring students who have checked the box on their letters of recommendation indicating that "I hereby waive my right of access to the contents of this letter"—they know that good students tend to check this waiver box and bad students tend not to.

Q12.2 Assume Player A chooses to swerve a random fraction, a, of the time, and Player B a random fraction, b, of the time. Then the expected "profit" to A is as follows:

$$\text{Exp. Profit A} = 3ab + 2a(1-b) + 4(1-a)b + 1(1-a)(1-b).$$

If $b=1$, this expected profit is $(4-a)$, which is smaller the bigger is a, so A should choose $a=0$ if $b=1$: A should not swerve if B swerves. If $b=0$, this expected profit is $(1+a)$, which is bigger the bigger is a, so A should choose $a=1$ if $b=0$: A should swerve if B does not swerve. But suppose b is neither 0 nor 1, but something in between. Then A maximizes expected profit by choosing $a=0$ if $b>\frac{1}{2}$ and by $a=1$ if $b<\frac{1}{2}$; but if $b=\frac{1}{2}$, then a does not matter to A's expected profit. Since it is all symmetrical for A and B, $a=b=\frac{1}{2}$ is a Nash equilibrium, in that neither player has an incentive to change strategy. But here, the expected profit of each player is 2.5, while the profit is either 2 or 4 with a pure strategy equilibrium.

CHAPTER 13

Q13.1 Assume Player A chooses to speed a random fraction, a, of the time, and Player B a random fraction, b, of the time. Then the expected "profit" to A is as follows:

$$\text{Exp. Profit A} = 4ab + 2a(1-b) + 1(1-a)b + 3(1-a)(1-b)$$

If $b=1$, this expected profit is $(3a+1)$, which is bigger the bigger is a, so A should choose $a=1$ if $b=1$: both speed. If $b=0$, this expected profit is $(3-a)$, which is smaller the bigger is a, so A should choose $a=0$ if $b=0$: both do not speed. But suppose b is neither 0 nor 1, but something in between. Then A maximizes expected profit by choosing $a=0$ if $b<\frac{1}{4}$ and by $a=1$ if $b>\frac{1}{4}$; but if $b=\frac{1}{4}$, then a does not matter to A's expected profit. Since it is all symmetrical for A and B, $a=b=\frac{1}{4}$ is a Nash equilibrium, in that neither player has an incentive to change strategy. But there, the expected profit of each player is only 2.5, while the profit is 3 or 4 with a pure strategy equilibrium.

Q13.2 The principal benefits and costs of right turns on red laws are as follows:

	Benefits	Costs
Private	Own time and gas saved	More own bent fenders
External	Others' time saved and less air pollution	More pedestrians hurt and killed

Recall that social cost equals the sum of private cost and external cost. If private benefit exceeds private cost, drivers will want right-turn-on-red laws. But only if social benefit exceeds social cost should "we" want them, where "we" includes not only drivers but also pedestrians and asthmatics.

CHAPTER 14

Q14.1 Think of constructing a special lane for just a few of the cars. The cost of the new lane is obvious—its construction and maintenance and the time and gas of the cars that use it. What would be the social benefit of this new lane? It would speed up traffic on the old lanes and thereby reduce time and gas costs there. For each car that moves from the old to the new lane, the saving in time and gas on the old lane is the marginal cost (MC) there. So the higher the MC on the old lanes, the greater the benefit of a new lane. When congestion rations lanes, the MC ends up higher (i.e., more use and more congestion) than when tolls ration use to optimal levels (see the appendix to this chapter). So the benefit of a new lane is higher when congestion rules, and the lane is more likely to prove socially beneficial. Optimally, there will be fewer lanes, not more, once optimal tolls are introduced.

Q14.2 To answer these questions, keep one thing in mind: the congestion is caused by cars, and the correct Pigovian tax is therefore so much per car (how much tax depends upon the degree of congestion). The answers then flow quickly. The toll should not be lower on old cars—or purple cars, electric cars, or whatever cars—because a car is a car is a car, as far as congestion is concerned. The toll per car should not be affected by the number of passengers in the car. The car itself is what causes the congestion, and a car causes the same amount of congestion regardless of the number of passengers. Carpooling is encouraged because the resulting toll per *passenger* is lower in multi-occupant cars. Do you still have that nagging intuition that says we should further encourage carpooling? Try the following numerical example. Suppose it costs Mr. A and Ms. B $3 extra each day in time, gas, and inconvenience to carpool, so, when there are no tolls, they do not carpool. The marginal time, gas, and inconvenience cost to *others* of one extra car is discovered to be $2, and the correct Pigovian toll of $2 is charged. If A and B carpool, they will save $2 in tolls but incur $3 in additional costs; they will *correctly* make the decision *not* to carpool. If, however, cars with multiple riders are exempted from tolls, carpooling will save them $4 in tolls and only cost them $3 in additional costs; now, they will *incorrectly* make the decision to carpool—incorrectly because it costs them $3 but only saves other commuters $2.

Q14.3 My guess is that we would not vote to tax ourselves $45 per person per year to continue subsidizing our downtown parking structures. We put up with the subsidies because we do not realize how big they are. As long as gasoline is dirt cheap, we do not really need to go downtown much, and we do not need centrally located and densely packed stores. Expensive gasoline would probably do more to revitalize downtown Ann Arbor than subsidies to the downtown parking structures.

Q14.4 With a free market, off-street parking fees would have to cover the cost of the land, labor, and capital needed to provide the parking spaces, or else private providers could not break even. Because of this fee, people who parked would have to be willing to pay the real cost of their parking or they would not park— exactly the rationing system we want from free markets. Parking would cost more—obviously, it is no longer subsidized—and there would be less demanded and supplied of it. Overall, however, we would be better off because we would not be paying for costly parking spaces that people really were not willing to pay for but paid for anyway by having the costs buried in their retail prices and their apartment and office rents.

CHAPTER 14 APPENDIX

Q14A.1 Notice in Figure 14A.2 that once congestion appears, there is a trade-off between speed and flow, all the way out to the maximum flow (F_{max}). Drivers value greater speed, which means reduced time to destination, and usually the actual or optimal outcome will involve greater speed and smaller flow than at F_{max}.

Q14A.2 Since a fraction Y/N of the people drive at a speed of $(a-bY/3)$, and the other $(1-Y/N)$ of the people drive at a speed of $(a-b(N-Y))$, we can find the overall average speed (AS_{HOV}):

$$AS_{HOV} = (Y/N)(a-bY/3) + (1-Y/N)(a-b(N-Y))$$

Take the derivative of that with respect to Y, set this derivative equal to zero—notice that you are getting a maximum and not a minimum—and solve for Y, which equals $3N/4$. There are $N/4$ cars in each lane. But as long as Y is greater than about $N/3$, the average speed on the highway is improved by the HOV lane. To show that, just set $AS_{HOV} = a - bN/2$ and solve for the Y that equates the average speeds with and without an HOV lane.

CHAPTER 15

Q15.1 The lost profits are not a *real* damage of the oil spill, but just a transfer, since tourists presumably just vacation elsewhere and boost the profits of the tour operators in some other area. If, however, these tourists are very disappointed and do not enjoy their alternative vacation as much, or they have to pay higher travel costs to get to an equivalent alternative vacation, then these losses of well-being *are* real costs of the oil spill. But the tour operators' profit losses are not a good measure of the tourists' welfare losses.

Q15.2 This is an impossible question, and your answer is just as good, and maybe better, than mine. It is one of many second-best questions. If the first-best response to a negative externality—the Pigovian tax—is not feasible, politically or administratively, is a second-best response better than doing nothing? For example, if higher gasoline taxes are not possible, should we encourage a stronger OPEC or recreate the Standard Oil monopoly (that we broke up in 1911) so that it would restrict output and raise gasoline prices? How about resource-wasting third-best solutions? Should we insist that every worker in a refinery have an idle backup worker standing beside him or her, which would raise gasoline costs and ultimately gasoline prices?

CHAPTER 16

Q16.1 If the federal government paid, for example, one-half of all bridge repair, and bridge corrosion were the only damage from using salt, then the states would see salt only doing one-half of the money damage it really does. Switching to CMA would only abate one-half of the salt damage, from the state's viewpoint, so the benefit of this high-cost alternative to salt is reduced by half by this government policy. One easy solution would be for the federal government to make lump-sum highway transfers to the states and stop paying for one-half of bridge repair costs.

Q16.2 Consider two roads. Road 1 costs $1 and needs replacing every year; road 2 costs $2 and needs replacing every third year. Using a discount rate of i, we calculate the present values of their costs (PV_1 and PV_2):

$$PV_1 = 1 + (1+i)^{-1} + (1+i)^{-2} + \cdots = 1/(1-[1+i]^{-1})$$
$$PV_2 = 2 + 2(1+i)^{-3} + 2(1+i)^{-6} + \cdots = 2/(1-[1+i]^{-3}).$$

Set PV_1 equal to PV_2 and solve for i. PV_2 is less than PV_1 for any i less than 62% per annum (formally, the condition is $i^2+i<1$).

CHAPTER 17

Q17.1 Remember how we calculate lost consumer surplus when a price goes up. $1 in new taxation per gallon would raise the gasoline price from about $1.20 per gallon to about $2.20 per gallon. On the assumption that the long-run price elasticity is one, this new tax would eventually lower American consumption by nearly half, from 100 billion gallons to 55 billion gallons per year. The exact formula is

$$1 = \frac{100-Q}{(100+Q)/2} \left| \frac{1.00}{3.40/2} \right.$$

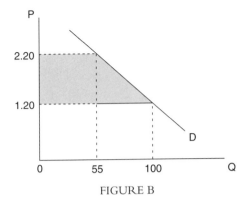

FIGURE B

which solves for Q = 55 billion gallons (see Figure B). Of the current 100 billion gallons purchased each year, 55 billion gallons would continue to be bought, but at a $1.00 per gallon higher price. That is a loss on the gallons consumers continue to purchase of $55 billion per year (i.e., $1.00 per gallon times 55 billion gallons). And for the 45 billion gallons that are no longer purchased because of the higher price, consumers would have been willing to pay an average of $1.70 per gallon (i.e., the average of $1.20, which all discouraged buyers would have paid, and $2.20, which no discouraged buyer is willing to pay). Their lost consumer surplus is $23 billion (i.e., the difference between $1.70 and $1.20, all times 45 billion gallons). The total lost consumer surplus is the sum of $55 billion and $23 billion, or $78 billion—the shaded area in Figure B. Divided by our 260 million population, that is about $300 per person. But government taxes rise by $43 billion (net of the lost taxes on the gas no longer bought). That is about $165 per person of transfers, leaving about $130 per person of deadweight loss—though this $130 per year is offset by a lot of reduced external costs.

CHAPTER 18

Q18.1 Think of the incentives each scheme creates. Giving out so many coupons per car encourages the purchase of new cars. The only reason this allocation worked in World War II was that no new civilian vehicles were being produced at the time. Giving out so many coupons per licensed driver encourages people who do not drive to waste time getting licensed in order to take advantage of the subsidy when they sell their coupons. I will let you decide if giving out so many coupons per person encourages people to have babies—if so, the allocation should be so many coupons per adult.

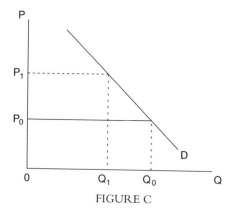

FIGURE C

Q18.2 Look at Figure C. Initially, gas consumption is Q_0 at price P_0. The marketable ration coupon system now allocates coupons good for Q_1/N gallons to each of the N legal residents. This reduces the number of gallons consumed to Q_1. At price P_0, excess demand arises. The price of gasoline does not rise—it is not gasoline that is scarce, it is the coupons. The price of coupons goes to (P_1-P_0); the total price of gasoline becomes P_1, the sum of P_0 at the gas station and (P_1-P_0) for the coupon. (Even those who "just" use their own coupons should recognize that the cost of their gas is also P_1, because of the foregone opportunity to sell the coupon.) Those unwilling to buy gas at a total price of P_1 sell coupons, and those anxious to buy gas at a price of P1 buy coupons. Now consider the Pigovian tax of (P_1-P_0). This also reduces gas consumption to Q_1 and raises $(P_1-P_0)Q_1$ in tax revenue, which is returned to the legal residents in equal shares. To see that each resident is exactly as well (or badly) off under either system, consider three people. One, someone who uses no gas sells his coupons for $(P_1-P_0)Q_1/N$ or gets a gas tax rebate of $(P_1-P_0)Q_1/N$. Two, someone who consumes Q_1/N gallons (and hence neither buys nor sells coupons) pays $(P_1-P_0)Q_1/N$ in gas tax and gets exactly that rebate. And three, someone who consumes $2Q_1/N$ gallons needs to buy Q_1/N coupons and pays $(P_1-P_0)Q_1/N$ for them; with a tax, this person pays $2(P_1-P_0)Q_1/N$ in gas tax but gets $(P_1-P_0)Q_1/N$ of it back as a rebate.

References

*"Economics is extremely useful
as a form of employment for economists."*

John Kenneth Galbraith

Aaron, P., and D. Musto. 1981. "Temperance and Prohibition in America: A Historical Overview." In M. H. Moore and D. R. Gerstein (Eds.). *Alcohol and Public Policy: Beyond the Shadow of Prohibition.* National Academy Press, Washington DC.

Adams, D. 1980. *The Hitchhiker's Guide to the Galaxy.* Harmony Books, New York NY.

Adams, J. G. U. 1985. *Risk and Freedom: The Record of Road Safety Regulation.* Transport Publishing Projects, London.

Adams, J. G. U. 1995. *Risk.* UCL Press, London.

Adams, S. 1996. *The Dilbert Principle.* HarperCollins, New York NY.

Adelman, M. A. 1980. "The Clumsy Cartel." *Energy Journal,* Jan.

Adelson, A. 1996. "Pushing Lemons over State Lines." *New York Times,* 27 Aug.

Akerlof, G. A. 1970. "The Market for 'Lemons': Qualitative Uncertainty and the Market Mechanism." *Quarterly Journal of Economics,* Aug.

Alberini, A., D. Edelstein, W. Harrington, and V. McConnell. 1994. "Reducing Emissions from Old Cars: The Economics of the Delaware Vehicle Retirement Program." Discussion Paper 94-27, Resources for the Future, Washington DC.

Alberini, A., W. Harrington, and V. McConnell. 1996. "Estimating an Emissions Supply Function from Accelerated Vehicle Retirement Programs." *Review of Economics and Statistics,* May.

American Automobile Association (AAA). Undated. *Balancing the Budget at the Ga$ Pump.* Government Affairs Department, Falls Church VA.

Ann Arbor Observer. 1996a. "Parking Crunch." Nov.

Ann Arbor Observer. 1996b. "Parking Tax?" Dec.

Asch, P., and D. T. Levy. 1987. "Does the Minimum Drinking Age Affect Traffic Fatalities?" *Journal of Policy Analysis and Management,* Winter.

229

Asch, P., and D. T. Levy. 1990. "Young Driver Fatalities: The Roles of Drinking Age and Drinking Experience." *Southern Economic Journal*, Oct.

Aschenbrenner, M., and B. Biehl. 1994. "Improved Safety through Improved Technical Measures? Empirical Studies Regarding Risk Compensation Processes in Relation to Anti-Lock Braking Systems." In R. M. Trimpo and G. J. S. Wilde (Eds.). *Challenges to Accident Prevention: The Issue of Risk Compensation Behavior*. Styx Publications, Groningen.

Augustyniak, C. M. 1998. "Asbestos Case Study." In Morgenstern, 1998.

Baltagi, B. H., and J. M. Griffin. 1984. "U.S. Gasoline Demand: What Next?" *Energy Journal*, 1.

Barbier, E. B., J. C. Burgess, and D. W. Pierce. 1991. "Technological Substitution Options for Controlling Greenhouse Gas Emissions." In Dornbusch and Poterba, 1991.

Barron, J. 1997. "Lease or Buy? It's More Than a Matter of Money." *New York Times*, 16 Oct.

Baum, H. M., J. K. Wells, and A. K. Lund. 1990. "Motor Vehicle Crash Fatalities in the Second Year of 65 MPH Speed Limits." *Journal of Safety Research*, Spring.

Baum, H. M., J. K. Wells, and A. K. Lund. 1991. "The Fatality Consequences of the 65 MPH Speed Limits, 1989." *Journal of Safety Research*, Winter.

Becker, G. S. 1968. "Crime and Punishment: An Economic Approach." *Journal of Political Economy*, Mar./Apr.

Bedard, P. 1994. "What If Airbags Don't Work on Smart People?" *Car and Driver*, Nov.

Behbehani, R., V. S. Pendakur, and A. T. Armstrong-Wright. 1984. *Singapore Area Licensing Scheme: A Review of the Impact*. Water Supply and Urban Development Department. World Bank, Washington DC.

Bennet, J. 1995. "Auto Makers Begin to Rethink Prices." *New York Times*, 23 Jan.

Bigness, J. 1995. "As Auto Companies Put More Plastic in Their Cars, Recyclers Can Recycle Less." *Wall Street Journal*, 10 July.

Birnbaum, J. 1994. "A Poor Credit Rating May Affect Auto Policy." *New York Times*, 27 Aug.

Blincoe, L. J. 1996. *The Economic Cost of Motor Vehicle Crashes, 1994*. Department of Transportation. NHTSA Technical Report HS-808-425, July.

Blomquist, G. 1979. "Value of Life Saving: Implications of Consumption Activity." *Journal of Political Economy*, May/June.

Blomquist, G. 1984. "The 55 MPH Speed Limit and Gasoline Consumption." *Resources and Energy*, Mar.

Blum, V. 1998. "High-Polluting SUVs May Be Taken Down A Notch By EPA." *Chicago Tribune*, 21 Oct.

Blumberg, L. J. 1992. *Second-Best Alcohol Taxation: Balancing Appropriate Incentives with Deadweight Loss*. Ph.D. dissertation. Department of Economics, The University of Michigan, Ann Arbor MI.

Blumenauer, E. 1998. "Stop Drunk Drivers by Taking Their Cars." *Wall Street Journal*. 3 Feb., Letter.

Blumenstein, R. 1997. "Giant Potholes Waylay Michigan Drivers." *Wall Street Journal*, 8 May.

Blumenstein, R. 1998. "Auto Industry Reaches Surprising Consensus: It Needs New Engines." *Wall Street Journal*, 5 Jan.

Blumstein, C., and P. Komor. 1996. "Another Look at the Strategic Petroleum Reserve: Should Its Oil Holdings Be Privatized?" *Journal of Policy Analysis and Management*, Spring.

Bohi, D. R., and M. A. Toman. 1993. "Energy Security: Externalities and Policies." *Energy Policy*, Nov.

Bohm, P. 1981. *Deposit-Refund Systems: Theory and Applications to Environmental, Conservation, and Consumer Policy.* Resources for the Future. Washington DC.

Borenstein, S. 1991. "Selling Costs and Switching Costs: Explaining Retail Gasoline Margins." *Rand Journal of Economics,* Autumn.

Borenstein, S. 1993. "Price Incentives for Fuel Switching: Did Price Differences Slow the Phase-Out of Leaded Gasoline?" Department of Economics Working Paper, University of Michigan, Jan.

Bowles, S. 1998. "Sharing a Ride a Luxury to Some." *USA Today,* 29 Jan.

Box, P. C. 1970. *Traffic Control and Roadway Elements: Their Relationship to Highway Safety.* Highway Users Federation for Safety and Mobility. Washington DC.

Boyd, J., and H. Kunreuther. 1995. "Retroactive Liability and Future Risk: The Optimal Regulation of Underground Storage Tanks." Discussion Paper 96-02. Resources for the Future, Washington DC.

Bradsher, K. 1997a. "Ford to Raise Output Sharply of Vehicles That Use Ethanol." *New York Times,* 4 June.

Bradsher, K. 1997b. "Government Studies New Risk on Road." *New York Times,* 11 June.

Bradsher, K. 1997c. "Start Expanding That Garage for Detroit's Next Generation." *New York Times,* 17 June.

Bradsher, K. 1997d. "A Deadly Highway Mismatch Ignored." *New York Times,* 24 Sept.

Bradsher, K. 1997e. "Big Insurers Plan to Increase Rates on Large Vehicles." *New York Times,* 17 Oct.

Bradsher, K. 1997f. "Trucks, Darlings of the Drivers, Are Favored by the Law, Too." *New York Times,* 30 Nov.

Bradsher, K. 1997g. "Light Trucks Have Passed Cars on the Retail Sales Road." *New York Times,* 4 Dec.

Bradsher, K. 1997h. "Plan Allows Big Vehicles to Skirt Rules on Pollutants." *New York Times,* 19 Dec.

Brannigan, M. 1997. "ValuJet Finds Comeback Takes Longer Than Expected." *Wall Street Journal,* 1 May.

Broadman, H. J. 1986. "The Social Cost of Imported Oil." *Energy Policy,* June.

Brodsky, H. 1993. "Retreading Industry Rolling Right Along." *New York Times,* 9 Nov., Letter.

Brown, D. B., S. Maghsoodloo, and M. E. McArdle. 1990. "The Safety Impact of the 65 MPH Speed Limit: A Case Study Using Alabama Accident Records." *Journal of Safety Research,* Winter.

Brown, R. W., R. T. Jewell, and J. Richer. 1996. "Endogenous Alcohol Prohibition and Drunk Driving." *Southern Economic Journal,* Apr.

Brown, W. 1998. "How Dangerous Are Light Trucks?" *Washington Post,* 10 Feb.

Brulle, R. J. 1982. "An Assessment of the Pollution Prevention Activities of the U.S. Coast Guard." Masters thesis, The University of Michigan, Ann Arbor MI.

Bunde, J. 1997. "The BikeBus'ters from Aarhus, Denmark." In R. Tolley (Ed.). *The Greening of Urban Transport,* ed. II. Wiley, New York NY.

Bureau of the Census. Various years. Statistical Abstract of the United States. U.S. Department of Commerce. Washington DC.

Cameron, M. W. 1991. *Transportation Efficiency: Tackling Southern California's Air Pollution and Congestion.* Environmental Defense Fund, New York NY.

Cameron, M. W. 1994. *Efficiency and Fairness on the Road: Strategies for Unsnarling Traffic in Southern California.* Environmental Defense Fund, New York NY.

Canterbury, J. L. 1997. "Pay-As-You-Throw: Offering Residents a Recycling and Source Reduction Incentive." *MSW Management,* Nov./Dec.

Carrington-Crouch, R. 1996. "The Remediation of Leaking Underground Storage Tanks." *Remediation Management,* Mar./Apr.

Carson, I. 1996. "Living with the Car." *The Economist,* 22 June.

Casey, S. M., and A. K. Lund. 1992. "Changes in Speed and Speed Adaptation Following Increase in National Maximum Speed Limit." *Journal of Safety Research,* Fall.

Caswell, M. F. 1993. "Balancing Energy and the Environment." In Gilbert, 1993.

Chaloupka, F. J., H. Saffer, and M. Grossman. 1993. "Alcohol-Control Policies and Motor-Vehicle Fatalities." *Journal of Legal Studies,* Jan.

Charles River Associates. 1991. *Policy Alternatives for Reducing Petroleum Use and Greenhouse Gas Emissions.* Motor Vehicle Manufacturers Association, Detroit MI.

Chelimsky, E. 1991. *Automobile Weight and Safety.* General Accounting Office GAO/T-PEMD-91-2, Apr. Washington DC.

Child, C. 1995. "Makers Give Buyers What They Want: More Power." *Automotive News,* 12 June.

Child, C., and D. L. Harris. 1996. "GM Shifts Gears, Begins to Reduce Leasing Subsidies." *Automotive News,* 28 Oct.

Christian, N. M. 1997. "Next, Maybe GM Will Hand Out a Bicycle to Each of Its Employees." *Wall Street Journal,* 9 June.

Cline, W. R. 1992. *The Economics of Global Warming.* Institute for International Economics. Washington DC.

Clinton, W. J. 1997. *Remarks on Global Climate Change.* Speech to the National Geographic Society, 22 Oct.

Clotfelter, C. T., and J. C. Hahn. 1980. "Assessing the National 55 MPH Speed Limit." In D. Nachmias (Ed.). *The Practice of Policy Evaluation.* St. Martin's, New York NY.

Coase, R. 1960. "The Problem of Social Cost." *Journal of Law and Economics,* Oct.

Coate, D., and M. Grossman. 1988. "Effects of Alcoholic Beverage Prices and Legal Drinking Ages on Youth Alcohol Use." *Journal of Law and Economics,* Apr.

Collins, C. 1998. "For Older Drivers, a Choice Between Freedom and Safety." *New York Times,* 21 Oct.

Collins, G. 1997. "New York Is Hot Again, but Its Traffic Is Frozen." *New York Times,* 22 Dec.

Connelly, M. 1996. "Lincoln-Mercury May Alter Position on Lease Purchases." *Automotive News,* 28 Oct.

Connelly, M. 1997. "Ford Backs Off Aggressive Leasing Strategy." *Automotive News,* 22 Dec.

Cook, P. J., and G. Tauchen. 1984. "The Effect of Minimum Drinking Age Legislation on Youthful Auto Fatalities, 1970-1977." *Journal of Legal Studies,* Jan.

Corrales, M., M. Grant, and E. Chan. 1996. *Indicators of the Environmental Impacts of Transportation.* Apogee Research Inc. Prepared for EPA, Office of Policy, Planning, and Evaluation, Washington DC.

Council on Environmental Quality (CEQ). 1984. *Fifteenth Annual Environmental Quality Report.* U.S. Government Printing Office, Washington DC.

Crandall, R. W. 1992. "Policy Watch: Corporate Average Fuel Economy Standards." *Journal of Economic Perspectives,* Spring.

Crandall, R. W., H. K. Gruenspecht, T. E. Keeler, and L. B. Lave. 1986. *Regulating the Automobile.* Brookings Institution. Washington DC.

Crandall, R. W., and J. D. Graham. 1989. "The Effects of Fuel Economy Standards on Automobile Safety." *Journal of Law and Economics,* Apr.

Culotta, E. 1995. "Will Plants Profit from High CO2?" *Science,* 5 May.

Cushman, J. H. 1998a. "Makers of Diesel Truck Engines Are under Pollution Inquiry." *New York Times,* 11 Feb.

Cushman, J. H. 1998b. "Why Scary Highways Can Be the Safer Choice." *New York Times,* 21 Oct.

Cushman, J. H. 1998c. "Record Pollution Fines Planned Against Makers of Diesel Engines." *New York Times,* 22 Oct.

Dahl, C. A. 1986. "Gasoline Demand Survey." *Energy Journal,* 1.

Dahl, C. A. 1995. "Demand for Transportation Fuels: A Survey of Demand Elasticities and Their Components." *Journal of Energy Literature,* Fall.

Dahl, C. A., and T. Sterner. 1991. "Analyzing Gasoline Demand Elasticities: A Survey." *Energy Economics,* July.

Dahl, J., and L. Miller. 1996. "Which Is the Safest Airline? It All Depends. . . ." *Wall Street Journal,* 24 July.

Daly, M., and M. Wilson. 1983. *Sex, Evolution, and Behavior.* Willard Grant Press. Boston MA.

Dance, B. 1991. "Why American Roads All Go to Pot." *Washington Monthly,* Nov.

Dao, J. 1996. "Pataki Signs Bill to Combat Drinking by Young Drivers." *New York Times,* 26 June.

Dao, J. 1997. "A Ruling Gives a Big Push to Electric Cars in New York State." *New York Times,* 6 Aug.

Dardis, R. 1980. "The Value of Life: New Evidence from the Marketplace." *American Economic Review,* Dec.

Davis, S. C., and D. N. McFarlin. 1996. *Transportation Energy Data Book.* Oak Ridge National Laboratory, Oak Ridge TN.

Department of Energy (DOE). 1998. *Comprehensive National Energy Strategy.* DOE, Washington DC.

Department of Transportation (DOT). 1996. *Transportation Statistics Annual Report, 1996.* Bureau of Transport Statistics, Washington DC.

Devlin, R-A. 1997. *No-Fault Automobile Insurance and Accident Severity: Lessons Still to Be Learned.* Paper 9707. Department of Economics, University of Ottawa, Ontario.

De Wolf, V. A. 1986. *The Effect of Helmet Law Repeal on Motorcycle Fatalities.* NHTSA Technical Report HS-807-065. Department of Transportation, Washington DC.

Dillingham, A. E. 1985. "The Influence of Risk-Variable Definition on Value-of-Life Estimates." *Economic Inquiry,* Apr.

Dixit, A. K., and B. J. Nalebuff. 1991. *Thinking Strategically: The Competitive Edge in Business, Politics, and Everyday Life.* Norton, New York NY.

Dornbusch, R., and J. M. Poterba (Eds.). 1991. *Global Warming: Economic Policy Responses.* The MIT Press, Cambridge MA.

Downs, A. 1992. *Stuck in Traffic: Coping with Peak-Hour Traffic Congestion.* Brookings Institution, Washington DC.

DuMouchel, W., A. F. Williams, and P. Z. Zador. 1987. "Raising the Alcohol Purchase Age: Its Effects on Fatal Motor Vehicle Crashes in 26 States." *Journal of Legal Studies,* Jan.

Eads, G. C. 1995. "How Much More Efficient Will 'More Efficient' Motor Vehicles Actually Be? Putting the Potential for New Vehicle Fuel Economy Improvement in Perspective." *Resolve, 1995.* Appendix D.

Economist. 1993. "Sitting Comfortably?" 6 Dec.

Economist. 1994. "Electronic Road-Pricing: Healthy Regime." 11 June.

Economist. 1996a. "America's Airlines: A DeValued Service." 22 June.

Economist. 1996b. "Green Taxes Are Good Taxes." 16 Nov.

Economist. 1996c. "Still Sparring." 20 July.

Economist. 1996d. "The American Way of Death." 27 July.

Economist. 1997a. "A Cooling Off Period." 29 Nov.

Economist. 1997b. "Living with the Car." 6 Dec.

Eisinger, J. 1996. "Sweet Poison." *Natural History,* July.

Elving, R. D. 1990. "Budget Talks Reawaken Oil-Import Fee Debate." *Economics & Finance.* 7 July.

Environmental Protection Agency (EPA). Various years. *National Air Quality, Monitoring, and Emissions Trends Report.* EPA, Washington DC.

Environmental Protection Agency (EPA). 1988. *Regulatory Impact Analysis of Technical Standards for Underground Storage Tanks.* EPA, Washington DC.

Environmental Protection Agency (EPA). 1989. *Analysis of Air Toxics Emissions, Exposures, Cancer Risks and Controllability in Five Urban Areas.* EPA, Washington DC.

Environmental Protection Agency (EPA). 1993a. *State Scrap Tire Programs.* EPA, Washington DC.

Environmental Protection Agency (EPA). 1993b. *Understanding Oil Spills and Oil Spill Response.* EPA, Washington DC.

Environmental Protection Agency (EPA). 1995a. *National Air Pollutant Emission Trends, 1900-1994.* EPA, Washington DC.

Environmental Protection Agency (EPA). 1995b. *Inventory of U.S. Greenhouse Gas Emissions and Sinks: 1990-1994.* EPA, Washington DC.

Environmental Protection Agency (EPA). 1995c. *UST Program Facts: Implementing Federal Requirements for Underground Storage Tanks.* EPA, Washington DC.

Environmental Protection Agency (EPA). 1996a. *Air Quality Criteria for Particulate Matter.* EPA, Washington DC.

Environmental Protection Agency (EPA). 1996b. *Air Quality Criteria for Ozone and Related Photochemical Oxidants.* EPA, Washington DC.

Environmental Protection Agency (EPA). 1997. *The Benefits and Costs of the Clean Air Act, 1970 to 1990.* EPA, Washington DC.

Environmental Protection Agency (EPA). 1998. *Tier 2 Study.* EPA, Washington DC.

Evans, L. 1985. "Driver Behavior Revealed in Relations Involving Car Mass." In L. Evans and R. C. Schwing (Eds.). *Human Behavior and Traffic Safety.* Plenum Press, New York NY.

Evans, L. 1986. "The Effectiveness of Safety Belts in Preventing Fatalities." *Accident Analysis and Prevention,* June.

Evans, L. 1990. "Motorized Two-Point Safety Belt Effectiveness in Preventing Fatalities." 34th Annual Proceedings, Association for the Advancement of Automotive Medicine, 1-3 Oct.

Evans, L. 1991. *Traffic Safety and the Driver.* Van Nostrand-Reinhold, New York NY.

Evans, L. 1997. "Air Bags: Even the Smartest Technology Is a Dumb, Dangerous Mandate." *Detroit Free Press*, 16 June.

Evans, L., M. C. Frick, and R. C. Schwing. 1990. "Is It Safer to Fly or Drive?" *Risk Analysis*, May.

Evans, W. N., and J. D. Graham. 1991. "Risk Reduction or Risk Compensation? The Case of Mandatory Safety-Belt Use Laws." *Journal of Risk and Uncertainty*, Jan.

Falkowski, C. L. 1986. "The Impact of 2-Day Jail Sentences for Drunk Drivers in Hennepin County, Minnesota." *Journal of Safety Research*, Spring.

Federal Highway Administration (FHA). Various years. *Highway Statistics*. Department of Transportation, Washington DC.

Federal Highway Administration (FHA). 1982. *Final Report on the Federal Highway Cost Allocation Study*. Department of Transportation. Washington DC.

Fialka, J. J. 1997. "Clear Skies Are Goal As Pollution Is Turned into a Commodity." *Wall Street Journal*, 3 Oct.

Fialka, J. J. 1998. "Auto and Oil Companies Disagree on How to Curb Sulfur Pollution." *Wall Street Journal*, 13 May.

Fisher, A., L. G. Chestnut, and D. M. Violette. 1989. "The Value of Reducing Risks of Death: A Note on New Evidence." *Journal of Policy Analysis and Management*, Winter.

Flanigan, G., J. Johnson, D. Winkler, and W. Ferguson. 1989. "Experience from Early Tort Reforms: Comparative Negligence since 1974." *Journal of Risk and Insurance,* June.

Forester, T. H., R. F. McNown, and L. D. Singell. 1984. "A Cost-Benefit Analysis of the 55 MPH Speed Limit." *Southern Economic Journal*, Jan.

Foster, M. S., J. A. Tarpley, and S. Dearn. 1990. "To Clean or Not to Clean: The Rationale, Methods, and Consequences of Removing Oil from Temperate Shores." *Northwest Environmental Journal*, Nov.

Frame, P. 1996a. "U.S. Says Rollover Rule Too Costly." *Automotive News*, 10 June.

Frame, P. 1996b. "ABS Fares Poorly in New Study of Fatal Crashes." *Automotive News*, 16 Dec.

Frech, H. E., and W. C. Lee. 1987. "The Welfare Cost of Rationing-by-Queueing across Markets: Theory and Estimates from the U.S. Gasoline Crises." *Quarterly Journal of Economics*, Feb.

Freeman, A. M. 1982. *Air and Water Pollution Control: A Benefit-Cost Assessment*. Wiley, New York NY.

French, M. 1987. *Economic Analysis of Gasoline Tax Increases*. Report to the American Automobile Association by Wharton Econometric Forecasting Associates, 22 May.

Friedland, M., M. Trebilcock, and K. Roach. 1990. *Regulating Traffic Safety*. University of Toronto Press, Toronto.

Fuller, G. E., and I. O. Lesser. 1997. "Persian Gulf Myths." *Foreign Affairs*, May/June.

Gaudry, M. 1991. "Measuring the Effects of the No-Fault Quebec Automobile Act with the DRAG Model." In G. Dionne (Ed.). *Contributions to Insurance Economics*. Kluwer Academic, Dordrecht/Norwell MA.

General Accounting Office (GAO). 1989. *Traffic Congestion: Trends, Measures, and Effects*. GAO/PEMD-90-1, U.S. Congress.

General Accounting Office (GAO). 1990. *Gasoline Marketing: Uncertainties Surround Reformulated Gasoline as a Motor Fuel*. U.S. Congress.

General Accounting Office (GAO). 1993. *Reducing Vehicle Emissions with Transportation Control Measures*. GAO/RCED-93-169. U.S. Congress.

Gilbert, R. J. (Ed.). 1993. *The Environment of Oil*. Kluwer Academic, Dordrecht/Norwell MA.

Giuliano, G., K. Hwang, and M. Wachs. 1993. "Employee Trip Reduction in Southern California: First Year Results." Transportation Research A. Mar.

Goodstein, E. 1992. "Saturday Effects in Tanker Oil Spills." *Journal of Environmental Economics and Management*, Nov.

Goodwin, P. B. 1992. "A Review of New Demand Elasticities with Special Reference to Short and Long Run Effects of Price Changes." *Journal of Transport Economics and Policy*, May.

Gordon, D. 1991. *Steering a New Course: Transportation, Energy, and the Environment*. Union of Concerned Scientists. Island Press. Washington DC.

Gordon, P., and H. W. Richardson. 1993. *Trends in Congestion in Metropolitan Areas*. Symposium for the Study on Urban Transportation Congestion Pricing. National Research Council. June.

Grace, M. 1998. "Court Voids Non-Polluting Car Rule." *Albany Times-Union*, 12 Aug.

Green, K. 1995. *Defending Automobility: A Critical Examination of the Environmental and Social Costs of Auto Use*. Policy Study 198. Reason Foundation. Los Angeles CA.

Greene, D. L. 1990. "CAFE or Price? An Analysis of the Effects of Federal Fuel Economy Regulation and Gasoline Price on New Car MPG, 1978-89." *Energy Journal* 3.

Greene, D. L. 1992. "Vehicle Use and Fuel Economy: How Big Is the 'Rebound' Effect?" *Energy Journal* 1.

Greene, D. L., and P. N. Leiby. 1993. *The Social Costs to the United States of Monopolization of the World Oil Market, 1972-1991*. Report 6744. Oak Ridge National Laboratory, Oak Ridge TN.

Griffin, J. M. 1985. "OPEC Behavior: A Test of Alternative Hypotheses." *American Economic Review*, Dec.

Grigalunas, T. A., and J. J. Opaluch. 1990. "The Environment." In R. S. Farrow (Ed.). *Managing the Outer Continental Shelf Lands: Oceans of Controversy*. Taylor & Francis, London.

Grossman, M., and H. Saffer. 1987. "Beer Taxes, the Legal Drinking Age, and Youth Motor Vehicle Fatalities." *Journal of Legal Studies*, June.

Grossman, M., F. J. Chaloupka, H. Saffer, and A. Laixuthai. 1993. *Effects of Alcohol Price Policy on Youth*. Working Paper 4385. National Bureau of Economic Research, Cambridge MA.

Grossman, M., J. L. Sindelar, J. Mullahy, and R. Anderson. 1993. "Alcohol and Cigarette Taxes." *Journal of Economic Perspectives*, Fall.

Guha, R., and M. Waldman. 1997. *Leasing Solves the Lemons Problem*. Working Paper. Department of Economics, Cornell University, Ithaca NY.

Gupta, S., and W. Mahler. 1995. "Taxation of Petroleum Products: Theory and Empirical Evidence." *Energy Economics*, Apr.

Hahn, R. W. 1995. "An Economic Analysis of Scrappage." *Rand Journal of Economics*, Summer.

Halpert, J. E. 1993. "Scarcity of Car Coolant Could Prove Costly." *New York Times*, 26 Dec.

Hammitt, J. K. 1998. "Regulatory Impact Analysis and Stratospheric-Ozone Depletion: U.S. Policy and the Montreal Protocol." In Morgenstern, 1998.

Hansson, L. 1990. *The Swedish Approach to Multi-Modal Transportation Planning*. Association of American Railroads 1990 Intermodal Policy Conference, 6 Apr.

Harrington, W. 1997. "Fuel Economy and Motor Vehicle Emissions." Discussion Paper 96-28REV. Resources for the Future, Washington DC.

Harrington, W., M. A. Walls, and V. D. McConnell. 1994-95. "Using Economic Incentives to Reduce Auto Pollution." *Issues in Science and Technology*, Winter.

Hart, S. 1986. "Huge City Subsidies for Autos, Trucks." *California Transit*, Sept.

Hau, T. D. 1992. *Economic Fundamentals of Road Pricing: A Diagrammatic Analysis*. World Bank Working Paper 1070. Washington DC.

Hemenway, D. 1993. "Nervous Nellies and Dangerous Dans." *Journal of Policy Analysis and Management*, Spring.

Henry, J. 1997. "Leasing." *Automotive News*, 22 Sept.

Henry, J. 1998. "Value Subtracted." *Automotive News*, 23 Mar.

Hinrichs, R. A. 1996. *Energy: Its Use and the Environment*. Saunders College, Philadelphia PA.

Hird, J. A. 1994. *Superfund: The Political Economy of Environmental Risk*. Johns Hopkins Press, Baltimore MD.

Hopkins, T. D. 1992. "Oil Spill Reduction and Costs of Ship Design Regulation." *Contemporary Policy Issues*, July.

Horwich, G., and D. L. Weiner. 1984. *Oil Price Shocks, Market Response, and Contingency Planning*. American Enterprise Institute, Washington DC.

Houghton, J. J., L. G. Meiro Filho, B. A. Callander, N. Harris, A. Kattenberg, and K. Maskell (Eds.). 1996. *Climate Change 1995: The Science of Climate Change*. Contribution of Working Group I to the Second Assessment Report of the Intergovernmental Panel on Climate Change. United Nations Environmental Program.

Hubbard, H. M. 1991. "The Real Cost of Energy." *Scientific American*, Apr.

Hymans, S. H. 1971. "Consumer Durable Spending: Explanation and Prediction." Brookings Papers on Economic Activity 2.

Ingersoll, B. 1998. "Old GM Analysis of Fiery Car Deaths May Haunt Firm over Fatalities Since." *Wall Street Journal*, 18 Feb.

Insurance Institute for Highway Safety (IIHS). 1997. *Facts: 1996 Fatalities*. IIHS, Washington DC.

Jacobs, J. B. 1989. *Drunk Driving: An American Dilemma*. University of Chicago Press, Chicago IL.

Jensen, C. 1993. "Could Car Safety Design Increase Women's Risk?" *Ann Arbor News*, 23 July.

Job, A., and T. Lankard. 1998. "GM Gets Credit in Flex-Fuel Change." *Detroit News*, 31 May.

Johnston, J. D. 1997. *Driving America: Your Car, Your Government, Your Choice*. The AEI Press, Washington DC.

Jondrow, J., M. Bowes, and R. Levy. 1983. "The Optimal Speed Limit." *Economic Inquiry*, July.

Jones, B. 1987. "Oregon's Habitual Traffic Offender Program: An Evaluation of the Effectiveness of License Revocation." *Journal of Safety Research*, Spring.

Jones-Lee, M. W., M. Hammerton, and P. R. Philips. 1985. "The Value of Safety: Results of a National Sample Survey." *Economic Journal*, Mar.

Kahane, C. J. 1994. *Preliminary Evaluation of the Effectiveness of Antilock Brake Systems for Passenger Cars*. NHTSA Technical Report HS-808-206. Department of Transportation. Washington DC.

Kahane, C. J. 1996. *Fatality Reduction by Air Bags: Analyses of Accident Data through Early 1996*. NHTSA Technical Report HS-808-470. Department of Transportation, Washington DC.

Kamerud, D. B. 1988. "Benefits and Costs of the 55 MPH Speed Limit: New Estimates and Their Implications." *Journal of Policy Analysis and Management*, Winter.

Keeble, J. 1991. *Out of the Channel: The Exxon Valdez Oil Spill in Prince William Sound*. HarperCollins, New York NY.

Keeney, R. L. 1990. "Mortality Risks Induced by Economic Expenditures." *Risk Analysis*, Mar.

Keeney, R. L. 1997. "Estimating Fatalities Induced by the Economic Costs of Regulations." *Journal of Risk and Uncertainty*, Jan.

Kenkel, D. S. 1993a. "Drinking, Driving, and Deterrence: The Effectiveness and Social Costs of Alternative Policies." *Journal of Law and Economics*, Oct.

Kenkel, D. S. 1993b. "Prohibition Versus Taxation: Reconsidering the Legal Drinking Age." *Contemporary Policy Issues*, July.

Kenkel, D. S. 1996. "New Estimates of the Optimal Tax on Alcohol." *Economic Inquiry*, Apr.

Keoleian, G. A., M. Manion, J. W. Bulkley, and K. Kar. 1996. "Industrial Ecology of the Automobile." White Paper. National Pollution Prevention Center, Ann Arbor MI.

Kerr, R. A. 1997. "Greenhouse Forecasting Still Cloudy." *Science*, 16 May.

Kessler, J., and W. Schroeer. 1995. "Meeting Mobility and Air Quality Goals: Strategies That Work." *Transportation*, Aug.

Ketkar, K. W. 1995. "Protection of Marine Resources: The U.S. Oil Pollution Act of 1990 and the Future of the Maritime Industry." *Marine Policy*, Sept.

Khazzoom, J. D. 1988. "Gasoline Conservation versus Pollution Control: Unintended Consequences, Continued." *Journal of Policy Analysis and Management*, Fall.

Khazzoom, J. D. 1991. "The Impact of a Gasoline Tax on Auto Exhaust Emissions." *Journal of Policy Analysis and Management*, Summer.

Khazzoom, J. D. 1995. "An Econometric Model of the Regulated Emissions for Fuel-Efficient New Vehicles." *Journal of Environmental Economics and Management*, Mar.

Khazzoom, J. D. 1997. "Impact of Pay-at-the-Pump on Safety through Enhanced Vehicle Fuel Efficiency." *Energy Journal*, July.

Kim, J. J. 1996. "Surge of 'Off-Lease' Vehicles Changes the Way Consumers Look at Used Cars." *Wall Street Journal*, 29 Nov.

Kleit, A. N. 1990. "The Effect of Annual Changes in Automobile Fuel Economy Standards." *Journal of Regulatory Economics*, June.

Kling, C. L. 1994. "Emission Trading vs. Rigid Regulations in the Control of Vehicle Emissions." *Land Economics*, May.

Kohn, R. E. 1993. "Pigouvian Penalty for Oil Spills." *Energy Economics*, July.

Kolstad, C. D., T. S. Ulen, and G. V. Johnson. 1990. "Ex Post Liability for Harm vs. Ex Ante Safety Regulation: Substitutes or Complements?" *American Economic Review*, Sept.

Kolstad, J. L. 1989. "Require Safety Seats for Little Travelers." *USA Today*, 24 May.

Korb, L. J. 1996. "Holding the Bag in the Gulf." *New York Times*, 18 Sept.

Krebs, M. 1997. "Two Rivals Teaming Up to Build Electric Car." *New York Times*, 28 Feb.

Krupnick, A. J. 1993. "Vehicle Emissions, Urban Smog, and Clean Air Policy." In Gilbert, 1993.

Krupnick, A. J., and R. J. Kopp. 1988. *The Health and Agricultural Benefits of Reductions in Ambient Ozone in the United States*. Resources for the Future. Washington DC.

Krupnick, A. J., and M. A. Walls. 1992. "The Cost-Effectiveness of Methanol for Reducing Motor Vehicle Emissions and Urban Ozone Levels." *Journal of Policy Analysis and Management*, Summer.

Krupnick, A. J., M. A. Walls, and H. C. Hood. 1993. "The Distributional and Environmental Implications of an Increase in the Federal Gasoline Tax." Discussion Paper ENR 93-24. Resources for the Future, Washington DC.

Kwoka, J. E. 1983. "The Limits of Market-Oriented Regulatory Techniques: The Case of Automotive Fuel Economy." *Quarterly Journal of Economics*, Nov.

Laixuthai, A., and F. J. Chaloupka. 1993. "Youth Alcohol Use and Public Policy." *Contemporary Policy Issues*, Oct.

Lave, C. A. 1985. "Speeding, Coordination, and the 55-MPH Limit." *American Economic Review*, Dec.

Lave, C. A., and W. E. Weber. 1970. "A Benefit-Cost Analysis of Auto Safety Features." *Applied Economics*, Oct.

Lave, L. B. 1981. "Conflicting Objectives in Regulating the Automobile." *Science*, 22 May.

Lave, L. B. 1988. "The Greenhouse Effect: What Government Actions Are Needed?" *Journal of Policy Analysis and Management*, Spring.

Lavin, D. 1994. "Stiff Showroom Prices Drive More Americans to Purchase Used Cars." *Wall Street Journal*, 1 Nov.

Lawson, J. 1991. "Assessment of Potential Cost-Effectiveness of a Regulation Requiring Air Bags in Passenger Cars." Evaluation and Data Systems Division. Road Safety and Motor Vehicle Regulation. Transport Canada. Ottawa.

Lee, D. B. 1993. *Full Cost Pricing of Highways*. Department of Transportation, Washington DC.

Lee, D. R., P. E. Graves, and R. L. Sexton. 1992. "Controlling the Abandonment of Automobiles: Mandatory Deposits versus Fines." *Journal of Urban Economics*, Jan.

Lee, L. W. 1984. "The Economics of Carpools." *Economic Inquiry*, Jan.

Leman, C. K., P. L. Schiller, and K. Pauly. 1997. *Re-Thinking HOV—High Occupancy Vehicle Facilities and the Public Interest*. Chesapeake Bay Foundation, Annapolis MD.

Leone, R. A., and T. W. Parkinson. 1990. *Conserving Energy: Is There a Better Way? A Study of CAFE Regulation*. Association of International Automobile Manufacturers. Washington DC.

Lerner, P. 1993. "Road Kill." *Washington Monthly*, Dec.

Lesser, J. A., and J. A. Weber. 1989. "The 65 MPH Speed Limit and the Demand for Gasoline: A Case Study for the State of Washington." *Energy Systems and Policy* 3.

Levy, D. T. 1990. "Youth and Traffic Safety: The Effects of Driving Age, Experience, and Education." *Accident Analysis and Prevention*, Aug.

Levy, D. T., and P. Asch. 1989. "Speeding, Coordination, and the 55-MPH Limit: Comment." *American Economic Review*, Sept.

Litman, T. 1995. *Transportation Cost Analysis: Techniques, Estimates, and Implications*. Victoria Transportation Policy Institute, Vancouver.

Lovins, A. B., and L. H. Lovins. 1995. "Reinventing the Wheels." *The Atlantic Monthly*, Jan.

Lucchetti, A., and G. Stern. 1996. "Freon's Price Gives Motorists the Chills." *Wall Street Journal*, 11 July.

Lumsden, L. 1997. "Recreational Cycling." In R. Tolley (Ed.). *The Greening of Urban Transport*. Wiley, New York NY.

Lund, A. K., and A. F. Williams. 1985. "A Review of the Literature Evaluating the Defensive Driving Course." *Accident Analysis and Prevention*, Dec.

Lund, A. K., A. F. Williams, and P. Zador. 1986. "High School Driver Education: Further Evaluation of the DeKalb County Study." *Accident Analysis and Prevention*, Aug.

MacKenzie, J. J. 1994. *The Keys to the Car: Electric and Hydrogen Vehicles for the 21st Century.* World Resources Institute. Washington DC.

MacKenzie, J. J., R. C. Dower, and D. T. Chen. 1992. *The Going Rate: What It Really Costs to Drive.* World Resources Institute, Washington DC.

Males, M. A. 1986. "The Minimum Purchase Age for Alcohol and Young-Driver Fatal Crashes: A Long-Term View." *Journal of Legal Studies,* Jan.

Mannering, F., and C. Winston. 1987. "Recent Automobile Occupant Safety Proposals." In C. Winston (Ed.). *Blind Intersection? Policy and the Automobile Industry.* Brookings Institution, Washington DC.

Mannering, F., and C. Winston. 1995. "Automobile Air Bags in the 1990s: Market Failure or Market Efficiency?" *Journal of Law and Economics,* Oct.

Manning, W. G., E. B. Keeler, J. P. Newhouse, E. M. Sloss, and J. Wasserman. 1989. "The Taxes of Sin: Do Smokers and Drinkers Pay Their Way?" *Journal of the American Medical Association,* 17 Mar.

Marcus, A. A. 1992. *Controversial Issues in Energy Policy.* Sage Publications, Thousand Oaks CA.

Marsh, S. L. 1996. "Petroleum Cleanup Standards May Be Eased." *Environmental Protection,* Oct.

Martin, D. 1998. "New York Set To Toughen Emission Tests." *New York Times,* 15 Oct.

Mashaw, J. L., and D. L. Harfst. 1990. *The Struggle for Auto Safety.* Harvard University Press, Cambridge MA.

Mathews, A. W. 1998. "Auto Makers Will Fight New Air-Bag Proposal." *Wall Street Journal,* 15 Sept.

Mathis, J. C. 1996. "Crash Raises Concern about Safety of Older Drivers." *Ann Arbor News,* 9 June.

May, A. D. 1990. *Traffic Flow Fundamentals.* Prentice-Hall, New York NY.

McAdams, C. L. 1993. "Tire Shredding: An Old Tune with New Lyrics." *Waste Age,* Oct.

McAllister, W. 1998. "That Burning Sensation." *Washington Post,* 15 Jan.

McCarthy, P. S. 1991. "Highway Safety and the 65 MPH Speed Limit." *Contemporary Policy Issues,* Oct.

McConnell, M., D. P. Moynihan, and J. L. Lieberman. 1997. "Auto Insurance: A Better Way." *Wall Street Journal,* 22 Sept.

McConnell, V. D., M. A. Walls, and W. Harrington. 1995. "Evaluating the Costs of Compliance with Mobile Source Emission Control Requirements: Retrospective Analysis." Discussion Paper 95-36. Resources for the Future, Washington DC.

McKenzie, R. B., and D. R. Lee. 1990. "Ending the Free Airplane Rides of Infants: A Myopic Way of Saving Lives." Briefing Paper 11. Cato Institute, Washington DC.

McPhee, J. 1993. "Duty of Care." *New Yorker,* 28 June.

Merrill, L. 1996. "Used Oil Collection Programs." *MSW Management,* Sept./Oct.

Miller, J. 1998. "GM Pickups Become '99s for CAFE." *Automotive News.* 4 May.

Miller, P., and J. Moffet. 1993. *The Price of Mobility: Uncovering the Hidden Costs of Transportation.* Natural Resources Defense Council, New York NY.

Mills, E. S., and L. J. White. 1978. "Government Policies toward Automotive Emissions Control." In A. F. Friedlaender (Ed.). *Approaches to Controlling Air Pollution.* MIT Press, Cambridge MA.

Miron, J. A., and J. Zwiebel. 1991. "Alcohol Consumption during Prohibition." *American Economic Review,* May.

Missoulian. 1996. "Customs Reports Surge in Seizures of Illegal Freon." 13 Aug.

Moffet, J. 1991. *The Price of Mobility.* Natural Resources Defense Council, New York NY.

Morgenstern, R. D. (Ed.). 1998. *Economic Analysis and Environmental Decision-Making.* Resources for the Future, Washington DC.

Muller, A. 1980. "Evaluation of the Costs and Benefits of Motorcycle Helmet Laws." *American Journal of Public Health,* June.

Nader, R. 1965. *Unsafe at Any Speed: The Designed-In Dangers of the American Automobile.* Grossman, New York NY.

Nadis, S., and J. J. MacKenzie. 1993. *Car Trouble.* Beacon Press, Boston MA.

National Academy of Science (NAS). 1989. *A Continuing Road Hazard: Drunken Pedestrians.* News Report. NAS, Washington DC.

National Highway Traffic Safety Administration (NHTSA). 1980. *The Effect of Motorcycle Helmet Use Law Repeal—A Case for Helmet Use.* Report to the Congress HS-805-312. Department of Transportation, Washington DC.

National Highway Traffic Safety Administration (NHTSA). 1983. *Final Regulatory Analysis: Center High-Mounted Stoplamps.* Federal Motor Vehicle Safety Standard 108. Department of Transportation, Washington DC.

National Highway Traffic Safety Administration (NHTSA). 1985. *An Evaluation of Child Passenger Safety: The Effectiveness and Benefits of Safety Seats.* HS-806-890. Department of Transportation, Washington DC.

National Highway Traffic Safety Administration (NHTSA). *Traffic Safety Facts: 1993.* Department of Transportation, Washington DC.

National Research Council (NRC). 1984. *55: A Decade of Experience.* Special Report 204. Transportation Research Board, Washington DC.

National Research Council (NRC). 1992. *Automotive Fuel Economy: How Far Should We Go?* National Academy Press, Washington DC.

New York Times (NYT). 1994. "Predicting Bad Driving." 7 Dec.

Nichols, A. L. 1998. "Case Study: The RIA for the 1985 Lead-in-Gasoline Phasedown." In Morgenstern, 1998.

Niskanen, W. A., and S. H. Hanke. 1977. "Land Prices Substantially Underestimate the Value of Environmental Quality." *Review of Economics and Statistics,* Aug.

Nivola, P. S., and R. W. Crandall. 1995. *The Extra Mile: Rethinking Energy Policy for Automotive Transportation.* Brookings Institution, Washington DC.

Noah, T. 1995. "Administration Considers Wider Ethanol Subsidies." *Wall Street Journal,* 15 June.

Nomani, A. Q. 1997. "How Aggressive Tactics Are Getting Drivers to Buckle Up." *Wall Street Journal,* 11 Dec.

Nomani, A. Q., and J. Taylor. 1997. "Shaky Statistics Are Driving the Air-Bag Debate." *Wall Street Journal,* 22 Jan.

Nordhaus, W. D. 1991. "Economic Approaches to Greenhouse Warming." In Dornbusch and Poterba, 1991.

Nordhaus, W. D. 1994. *Managing the Global Commons: The Economics of Climate Change.* MIT Press, Cambridge MA.

Nordheimer, J. 1996. "Gender Gap Not Worth Closing." *New York Times,* 10 Aug.

Norwood, J. 1990. "Distinguished Lecture on Economics in Government: Data Quality and Public Policy." *Journal of Economic Perspectives,* Spring.

Nussbaum, B. D. 1992. "Phasing Down Lead in Gasoline in the United States: Mandates, Incentives, Trading and Banking." In T. Jones and J. Corfee-Morlot (Eds.). *Climate Change: Designing a Tradeable Permit System*. Organization for Economic Cooperation and Development (OECD), Paris.

O'Connor, K. 1998. "Renovations To Cost $30 Million." *Michigan Daily*, 6 Nov.

Office of Technology Assessment (OTA). 1989. *Catching Our Breath: Next Steps for Reducing Urban Ozone*. OTA-O-412. U.S. Congress, Washington DC.

Office of Technology Assessment (OTA). 1990. *Replacing Gasoline: Alternative Fuels for Light-Duty Vehicles*. OTA-E-364. U.S. Congress, Washington DC.

Office of Technology Assessment (OTA). 1991a. *Changing by Degrees: Steps to Reduce Greenhouse Gases*. OTA-O-482. U.S. Congress, Washington DC.

Office of Technology Assessment (OTA). 1991b. *Improving Automobile Fuel Economy: New Standards, New Approaches*. OTA-E-504. U.S. Congress, Washington DC.

Office of Technology Assessment (OTA). 1992. *Retiring Old Cars: Programs to Save Gasoline and Reduce Emissions*. OTA-E-536. U.S. Congress, Washington DC.

Office of Technology Assessment (OTA). 1994. *Saving Energy in U.S. Transportation*. OTA-ETI-589. U.S. Congress, Washington DC.

Office of Technology Assessment (OTA). 1995. *Advanced Automotive Technology: Visions of a Super-Efficient Family Car*. OTA-ETI-638. U.S. Congress, Washington DC.

Okie, S. 1997. "Drinking a Risk for Cyclists." *Washington Post*, 4 Feb.

Peckham, H. H., M. L. Steneck, and N. H. Steneck. 1992. *The Making of the University of Michigan, 1817-1992*. University of Michigan Press, Ann Arbor MI.

Peltzman, S. 1975. "The Effects of Automobile Safety Regulation." *Journal of Political Economy*, Aug.-Dec.

Peterson, S., G. Hoffer, and E. Millner. 1995. "Are Drivers of Air-Bag-Equipped Cars More Aggressive? A Test of the Offsetting Behavior Hypothesis." *Journal of Law and Economics*, Oct.

Pigou, A. C. 1920. *The Economics of Welfare*. Macmillan, New York NY.

Pindyck, R. S. 1979. *The Structure of World Energy Demand*. MIT Press, Cambridge MA.

Pisarski, A. E. 1992. *Travel Behavior Issues in the 90s*. Department of Transportation. Federal Highway Administration, Washington DC.

Policy Dialogue Advisory Committee. 1996. *Majority Report to the President to Recommend Options for Reducing Greenhouse Gas Emissions from Personal Motor Vehicles*. Available at http://www.citizen.org/orgs/public_citizen/CMEP/transportation/cartalk.html

Polinsky, A. M. 1983. *An Introduction to Law and Economics*. Little, Brown and Company, New York NY.

Polinsky, A. M., and S. Shavell. 1994. "A Note on Optimal Cleanup and Liability after Environmentally Harmful Discharges." *Research in Law and Economics* 16.

Porter, R. C. 1974. "The Long-Run Asymmetry of Subsidies and Taxes as Anti-Pollution Policies." *Water Resources Research*, June.

Porter, R. C. 1978. "A Social Benefit-Cost Analysis of Mandatory Deposits on Beverage Containers." *Journal of Environmental Economics and Management*, Dec.

Porter, R. C. 1983. "Michigan's Experience with Mandatory Deposits on Beverage Containers." *Land Economics*, May.

Porter, R. C. 1996. *The Economics of Water and Waste: A Case Study of Jakarta, Indonesia*. Avebury Press, Aldershot.

Poterba, J. M. 1991. "Is the Gasoline Tax Regressive?" In D. Bradford (Ed.). *Tax Policy and the Economy 5*. MIT Press, Cambridge MA.

Prager, J. H. 1998. "Would-Be Truckers Take Easy Road to Licenses." *Wall Street Journal*, 5 Feb.

Preston, J. 1998. "Battling Sprawl, States Buy Land for Open Space." *New York Times*, 9 June.

Preusser, D. F., A. F. Williams, and P. L. Zador. 1984. "The Effect of Curfew Laws on Motor Vehicle Crashes." *Law and Policy*, Jan.

Rae, J. B. 1965. *The American Automobile: A Brief History*. University of Chicago Press, Chicago IL.

Rechtin, M. 1997. "California Wants Smog Limits on Trucks to Match Cars." *Automotive News*, 15 Dec.

Reitman, V., and N. M. Christian. 1997. "Chrysler Plans on Minivans Using Ethanol." *Wall Street Journal*, 10 June.

Renner, M. 1988. "Rethinking the Role of the Automobile." Worldwatch Paper 84. Worldwatch Institute, Washington DC.

Resolve, Inc. 1995. *Draft Final Report to the Policy Dialogue Advisory Committee* ("Car Talk"). 28 Aug. Washington DC.

Rhyner, C. R., L. J. Schwartz, R. B. Wenger, and M. G. Kohrell. 1995. *Waste Management and Resource Recovery*. CRC Press, Boca Raton FL.

Rigdon, J. E. 1993. "Older Drivers Pose Growing Risk on Roads As Their Numbers Rise." *Wall Street Journal*, 29 Oct.

Rodgers, G. B. 1993. "All-Terrain Vehicles: Market Reaction to Risk Information." *Economic Inquiry*, Jan.

Rodgers, G. B. 1996. "Revisiting All-Terrain Vehicle Injury Risks: Response to Critique." *Journal of Regulatory Economics*, Sept.

Rosenthal, A. J. 1975. "Noise Pollution Control of the Automobile." In F. P. Grad (Ed.). *The Automobile and the Regulation of Its Impact on the Environment*. University of Oklahoma Press, Norman OK.

Ross, H. L. 1982. *Deterring the Drinking Driver: Legal Policy and Social Control*. Lexington Books, Lanham MD.

Rossetti, M. A., and B. S. Eversole. 1993. *Journey to Work Trends in the United States and Its Major Metropolitan Areas, 1960-1990*. Department of Transportation. Federal Highway Administration, Washington DC.

Ruhm, C. J. 1995. "Alcohol Policies and Highway Vehicle Fatalities." Working Paper 5195. National Bureau of Economic Research, Cambridge MA.

Russell, C. S. 1990. "Monitoring and Enforcement." In P. R. Portney (Ed.). *Public Policies for Environmental Protection*. Resources for the Future, Washington DC.

Rutledge, G. L., and C. R. Vogan. 1995. "Pollution Abatement and Control Expenditures." *Survey of Current Business*, May.

Saffer, H. 1994. "Alcohol Advertising and Motor Vehicle Fatalities." Working Paper 4708. National Bureau of Economic Research, Cambridge MA.

Saffer, H., and M. Grossman. 1987. "Drinking Age Laws and Highway Mortality Rates: Cause and Effect." *Economic Inquiry*, July.

Salant, S. W. 1984. "The Design of a Self-Enforcing Multilateral Agreement among Oil-Importing Countries." *Contemporary Policy Issues*, Mar.

Samuel P. 1995. "Highway Aggravation: The Case for Privatizing the Highways." *Policy Analysis* 231. Cato Institute, Washington DC.

Sawyers, A. 1996. "Freon Price Skyrockets in 'Feeding Frenzy.'" *Automotive News*, 24 June.

Schelling, T. C. 1968. "The Life You Save May Be Your Own." In S. B. Chase (Ed.). *Problems in Public Expenditure Analysis*. Brookings Institution, Washington DC.

Schelling, T. C. 1978. "Hockey Helmets, Daylight Saving, and Other Binary Choices." *Micromotives and Macrobehavior*. Norton, New York NY.

Schelling, T. C. 1991. "Economic Responses to Global Warming: Prospects for Cooperative Approaches." In Dornbusch and Poterba, 1991.

Schemo, D. J. 1996. "Where Gas Guzzlers Live On, Kings of the Road." *New York Times*, 31 Oct.

Schwing, R. C., and D. B. Kamerud. 1988. "The Distribution of Risks: Vehicle Occupant Fatalities and Time of Week." *Risk Analysis*, Mar.

Scism, L. 1995. "A Bad Credit Record Can Get You Rejected for Auto Insurance." *Wall Street Journal*, 6 Nov.

Segal, D. 1993. "Crash Cow." *Washington Monthly*, Dec.

Serumgard, J. R., and M. H. Blumenthal. 1993. "A Practical Approach to Managing Scrap Tires." *MSW Management*, Sept./Oct.

Shoup, D. C. 1995. "An Opportunity to Reduce Minimum Parking Requirements." *Journal of the American Planning Association*, Winter.

Shoup, D. C. 1997. "The High Cost of Free Parking." *Journal of Planning Education and Research*, Fall.

Shoup, D. C., and D. H. Pickrell. 1978. "Problems with Parking Requirements in Zoning Ordinances." *Traffic Quarterly*, Oct.

Shoup, D. C., and R. W. Willson. 1992. "Employer-Paid Parking: The Problem and Proposed Solutions." *Transportation Quarterly*, Apr.

Shprentz, D. S. 1996. *Breathtaking: Premature Mortality Due to Particulate Air Pollution in 239 American Cities*. Natural Resources Defense Council, New York NY.

Sloan, F. A., B. A. Reilly, and C. M. Schenzler. 1994. "Tort Liability versus Other Approaches for Deterring Careless Driving." *International Review of Law and Economics*, Sept.

Small, K. A. 1983. "The Incidence of Congestion Tolls on Urban Highways." *Journal of Urban Economics*, Jan.

Small, K. A., C. Winston, and C. A. Evans. 1989. *Road Work: A New Highway Pricing and Investment Policy*. The Brookings Institution, Washington DC.

Smeed, R. J. 1949. "Some Statistical Aspects of Road Safety Research." *Journal of the Royal Statistical Society*, Ser. A, Part I.

Smith, E., and R. Wright. 1992. "Why Is Automobile Insurance in Philadelphia So Damn Expensive?" *American Economic Review*, Sept.

Smith, R. T. 1988. "International Energy Cooperation: The Mismatch between IEA Policy Actions and Policy Goals." In G. Horwich and D. L. Weimer (Eds.). *Responding to International Oil Crises*. American Enterprise Institute for Public Policy Research, Washington DC.

Sperling, D., and M. A. DeLuchi. 1993. "Alternative Transportation Energy." In Gilbert, 1993.

Sperling, D. 1995. *Future Drive: Electric Vehicles and Sustainable Transportation*. Island Press, New York NY.

Spolander, K. 1968. "One Year with Right-Hand Traffic." Report 11. National Swedish Road Safety Board. Drivers License and Research Departments, Stockholm.

Stevens, W. K. 1995. "Price of Global Warming? Debate Weighs Dollars and Cents." *New York Times*, 10 Oct.

Stevens, W. K. 1996. "A Skeptic Asks, Is It Getting Hotter, or Is It Just the Computer Model?" *New York Times*, 18 June.

Stoffer, H. 1997. "Higher Tax or CAFE Needed to Meet Treaty." *Automotive News*, 22 Dec.

Stoffer, H. 1998a. "Clinton Tax Proposal Stirs a Class Conflict." *Automotive News*, 9 Mar.

Stoffer, H. 1998b. "EPA Says Mack Engines Pass Tests but Pollute; Truckmaker Sues." *Automotive News*, 22 June.

Sugarman, S. D. 1994. "'Pay at the Pump' Auto Insurance: The Vehicle Injury Plan (VIP) for Better Compensation, Fairer Funding, and Greater Safety." *Journal of Policy Analysis and Management*, Spring.

Sullivan, A. 1990. "Oil Firms, Shippers Seek to Circumvent Laws Setting No Liability Limit for Spills." *Wall Street Journal*, 26 July.

Tarpgaard, P. T. 1986. "U.S. Shipping Subsidies and Ocean Shipping of Petroleum: Policy Choices." *Contemporary Policy Issues*, Oct.

Teresi, D. 1995. "The Case for No Helmets." *New York Times*, 17 Jan.

Tolley, R. S., and B. J. Turton. 1995. *Transport Systems, Policy and Planning: A Geographic Approach*. Longman Scientific and Technical, New York NY.

Van Houtven, G., and M. L. Cropper. 1996. "When Is a Life Too Costly to Save? The Evidence from U.S. Environmental Regulations." *Journal of Environmental Economics and Management*, May.

Verde, T. 1996. "A Dump with Tires by the Acre Becomes a Thorn for Rhode Island." *New York Times*, 2 Dec.

Viano, D. C. 1991. "Effectiveness of Safety Belts and Air Bags in Preventing Fatal Injury." *Frontal Crash Safety Technology for the Nineties*. Society of Automotive Engineers International Congress, Warrendale MI.

Vickrey, W. 1969. "Current Issues in Transportation." In N. W. Chamberlain (Ed.). *Contemporary Economic Issues*. R. D. Irwin Homewood IL.

Viscusi, W. K. 1993. "The Value of Risks to Life and Health." *Journal of Economic Literature*, Dec.

Viscusi, W. K. 1996. "The Dangers of Unbounded Commitments to Regulated Risk." In R. W. Hahn (Ed.). *Risks, Costs, and Lives Saved: Getting Better Results from Regulation*. Oxford University Press, London.

Viscusi, W. K., W. A. Magat, A. Carlin, and M. K. Dreyfus. 1994. "Environmentally Responsible Energy Pricing." *Energy Journal* 15(2).

Vise, D. A. 1998. "D.C. Begins to Overhaul Meters Ravaged by Vandals." *Washington Post*, 19 Feb.

Vitaliano, D. F. 1992. "An Economic Assessment of the Social Costs of Highway Salting and the Efficiency of Substituting a New Deicing Material." *Journal of Policy Analysis and Management*, Summer.

Votey, H. L. 1988. "The Economic Perspective on Controlling the Drunken Driver." In M. D. Laurence, J. R. Snortum, and F. E. Zimring (Eds.). *Social Control of the Drinking Driver*. University of Chicago Press, Chicago IL.

Wagenaar, A. C. 1983. *Alcohol, Young Drivers, and Traffic Accidents*. Lexington Books, Lanham MD.

Wagenaar, A. C. 1985. "Mandatory Child Restraint Laws: Impact on Childhood Injuries Due to Traffic Crashes." *Journal of Safety Research*, Spring.

Wagenaar, A. C., R. G. Maybee, and K. P. Sullivan. 1988. "Mandatory Seat Belt Laws in Eight States: A Time-Series Evaluation." *Journal of Safety Research*, Summer.

Wagenaar, A. C., F. M. Streff, and R. H. Schultz. 1990. "Effects of the 65 MPH Speed Limit on Injury Morbidity and Mortality." *Accident Analysis and Prevention*, Dec.

Wald, M. L. 1995. "F.A.A. Calls Baby Safety Seats a Bad Idea." *New York Times*, 8 June.

Wald, M. L. 1996. "Concern about the Safety of Children in Automobiles." *New York Times*, 18 Sept.

Wald, M. L. 1997a. "On-Off Switches for Car Air Bags Will Be Allowed." *New York Times*, 18 Nov.

Wald, M. L. 1997b. "Preaching Caution, Officials Allow Cutoff Switch for Air Bags." *New York Times*, 19 Nov.

Wald, M. L. 1997c. "Tough Action on Drunken Driving Pays Off." *New York Times*, 26 Nov.

Wald, M. L. 1998a. "Auto's Converters Increase Warming As They Cut Smog." *New York Times*, 29 May.

Wald, M. L. 1998b. "Honda and Ford Are Fined Millions." *New York Times*, 9 June.

Wald, M. L. 1998c. "Death Rate on U.S. Roads at a Reported Low." *New York Times*, 27 Oct.

Walker, K., and J. B. Wiener. 1995. "Recycling Lead." In J. D. Graham and J. B. Wiener (Eds.). *Risk versus Risk: Tradeoffs in Protecting Health and the Environment*. Harvard University Press, Cambridge MA.

Wall Street Journal (WSJ). 1993. "Air Bags Inflate Personal-Injury Claims." 10 Nov.

Wall Street Journal (WSJ). 1997a. "Big U.S. Industries Launch Attack on Warming Treaty." 12 Dec.

Wall Street Journal (WSJ). 1997b. "Top 4 Auto Makers in U.S. Back Standard for Low Emissions." 19 Dec.

Waller, P. F. 1995. "Michigan Should Retain Motorcycle Helmet Law." *Ann Arbor News*, 11 June, Letter.

Walls, M. A. 1990. "Welfare Cost of an Oil Import Fee." *Contemporary Policy Issues*, Apr.

Walls, M. A., A. J. Krupnick, and H. C. Hood. 1993. "Estimating the Demand for Vehicle-Miles-Traveled Using Household Survey Data: Results from the 1990 Nationwide Personal Transportation Survey." Discussion Paper ENR 93-25. Resources for the Future, Washington DC.

Walls, M. A., and J. Hanson. 1996. "Distributional Impacts of an Environmental Tax Shift: The Case of Motor Vehicle Emissions Taxes." Discussion Paper 96-11. Resources for the Future, Washington DC.

Wang, Q., D. Sperling, and C. Kling. 1993. "Light Duty Vehicle Exhaust Emission Control Cost Estimates Using a Part-Pricing Approach." *Journal of the Air and Waste Management Association*, Nov.

Warrick, J. 1997. "15 Arrested, 3 Firms Charged with Smuggling of Ozone-Damaging CFCs." *Washington Post*, 10 Jan.

Weimer, D., and A. R. Vining. 1989. *Policy Analysis: Concepts and Practice*. Prentice-Hall, New York NY.

Weitzman, M. L. 1977. "Is the Price System or Rationing More Effective in Getting a Commodity to Those Who Need It Most?" *Bell Journal of Economics*, Autumn.

Wells, K., D. Machalaba, and C. Solomon. 1993. "Unsafe Oil Tankers and Ill-Trained Crews Threaten Further Spills." *Wall Street Journal*, 12 Feb.

Wenzel, T. 1995. "Pay-As-You-Drive Auto Insurance As a Means of Reducing Greenhouse Gas Emissions." In M. D. Levine (Ed.). *1994 Annual Report of the Energy Analysis Program.* Lawrence Berkeley National Laboratory, Berkeley CA.

Wernle, B. 1998. "No Boom, No Doom, Just Cycling Back to Normal." *Automotive News*, 9 Mar.

White, L. J. 1982. *The Regulation of Air Pollutant Emissions from Motor Vehicles.* American Enterprise Institute, Washington DC.

Wildavsky, A. 1979. "No Risk Is the Highest Risk of All." *American Scientist*, Jan.-Feb.

Wilde, G. J. S. 1982. "The Theory of Risk Homeostasis: Implications for Safety and Health." *Risk Analysis*, Dec.

Wilkinson, J. T. 1987. "Reducing Drunken Driving: Which Policies Are Most Effective?" *Southern Economic Journal*, Oct.

Williams, A. F., R. S. Karpf, and P. L. Zador. 1983. "Variations in Minimum Licensing Age and Fatal Motor Vehicle Crashes." *American Journal of Public Health*, Dec.

Williams, A. F. 1987. "Effective and Ineffective Policies for Reducing Injuries Associated with Youthful Drivers." *Alcohol, Drugs, and Driving*, July-Dec.

Williams, A. F. 1994. "Youthful Drivers and Motor Vehicle Crash Risk." *Alcohol, Drugs, and Driving*, Jan.-Mar.

Williams, R. H. 1994. "Fuel-Cell Vehicles: The Clean Machine." *Technology Review*, Apr.

Young, H. P. 1996. "The Economics of Convention." *Journal of Economic Perspectives*, Spring.

Zador, P., J. Moshman, and L. Marcus. 1982. "Adoption of Right Turn on Red: Effects on Crashes at Signalized Intersections." *Accident Analysis and Prevention*, June.

Zaidel, D. M., and I. Hocherman. 1986. "License Renewal for Older Drivers: The Effects of Medical and Vision Tests." *Journal of Safety Research,* Fall.

Zuckermann, W. 1991. *End of the Road: From World Car Crisis to Sustainable Transportation.* Chelsea Green, New York NY.

Index